ADVANCE PRAISE FOR

Research as Praxis

"In *Research as Praxis: Democratizing Education Epistemologies*, Myriam N. Torres and Loui V. Reyes offer a beautifully written and intellectually well-grounded challenge to researchers: to critically examine how power relations permeate our research, who benefits from our work, and ultimately whose voice matters. Rooted in a clear vision of freedom and participatory democracy, *Research as Praxis* lucidly articulates an alternative to positivism. This book should be required reading in all education doctoral programs."

—*Christine Sleeter, Professor Emerita,*
California State University Monterey Bay

"This is at once a cutting critique of scientific research in education and a constructive exposition of one of its alternatives, namely research as praxis through which the possibility of radical participatory democracy comes alive. This text exemplifies the conceptual and rhetorical unmasking of the scientific orthodoxies that perpetuate de-humanizing, neo-liberal, and self-serving, market-based approaches to educational reform. Kudos to Myriam N. Torres and Loui V. Reyes."

—*Angela Valenzuela, Author,* Subtractive Schooling
and Leaving Children Behind

Research as Praxis

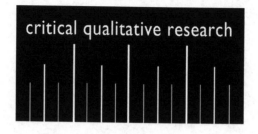

critical qualitative research

Shirley R. Steinberg & Gaile S. Cannella
General Editors

Vol. 4

The Critical Qualitative Research series is part
of the Peter Lang Education list.
Every volume is peer reviewed and meets
the highest quality standards for content and production.

PETER LANG
New York • Washington, D.C./Baltimore • Bern
Frankfurt • Berlin • Brussels • Vienna • Oxford

Myriam N. Torres & Loui V. Reyes

Research as Praxis

Democratizing Education Epistemologies

PETER LANG
New York • Washington, D.C./Baltimore • Bern
Frankfurt • Berlin • Brussels • Vienna • Oxford

Library of Congress Cataloging-in-Publication Data

Torres, Myriam.
Research as praxis: democratizing education
epistemologies / Myriam N. Torres, Loui V. Reyes.
p. cm. — (Critical qualitative research; v. 4)
Includes bibliographical references and index.
1. Action research in education. 2. Critical pedagogy.
3. Democracy and education. 4. Qualitative research.
I. Reyes, Loui V. II. Title.
LB1028.24.T67   370.72—dc22   2010050806
ISBN 978-1-4331-1129-7 (paperback)
ISBN 978-1-4331-1130-3 (hardcover)
ISSN 1947-5993

Bibliographic information published by **Die Deutsche Nationalbibliothek**.
Die Deutsche Nationalbibliothek lists this publication in the "Deutsche
Nationalbibliografie"; detailed bibliographic data are available
on the Internet at http://dnb.d-nb.de/.

The paper in this book meets the guidelines for permanence and durability
of the Committee on Production Guidelines for Book Longevity
of the Council of Library Resources.

© 2011 Peter Lang Publishing, Inc., New York
29 Broadway, 18th floor, New York, NY 10006
www.peterlang.com

Printed in the United States of America

This book is dedicated to the memory of
Paulo Freire
and Orlando Fals-Borda
Pioneers and Masters in Democratizing Research

Contents

**5 Decolonizing Family Literacy in a Culture
    Circle: Reinventing the Family Literacy
    Educator's Role 189**
Loui V. Reyes & Myriam N. Torres

Foreword

The societal crisis faced by the United States at the beginning of this twenty-first century is expressed in multiple ways: by an increase of poverty, particularly among single mothers and their children; by inequality and the lack of access to fundamental amenities—for example, adequate universal health care; by an overwhelming number of people in prison; and by disproportionate military expenditures. Above all, it is manifested in the failure of the educational system to allow each child to develop to his or her fullest capacity and to instill in each a social consciousness that will contribute toward creating a world of equality, justice, and lasting peace, a world that seems more elusive than ever.

Public school education for everyone is one of the fundamental values of this nation; it is believed to be essential to achieving true democracy. Democracy has been touted as a core justification for the existence of this nation. Paradoxically, though, it has been used to justify wars, invasions, and the uprooting of truly democratic experiments in other countries. Furthermore, the promise of equal opportunity and the value of democracy supposedly inherent in public education have disappeared as the schools have become less democratic and more segregated but less equal with each passing year.

We have the privilege of knowing some extraordinary educators and have heard of others who work consistently with great commitment to bring about a liberating form of education that will indeed be true to democratic principles. At the same time, there are schools in this country where educators are abysmally lacking in any notion of respect for the youth they hold in their buildings... schools that fail to promote any form of positive growth and instead are breeding grounds for adult lives of despair and societal dysfunction.

How can it be possible that this most powerful nation should drastically fail to provide opportunities for access to the highest quality education for its youth? The question, asked with naive sincerity, is unanswerable, yet it leads to a much more troublesome question: Is it possible that this failure is a response to interests that are not aligned with the legitimate rights and aspirations of the people?

The authors of this book have focused their reflection on the significance of what has been labeled "scientific educational research" and its impact on education. After a careful analysis of the conditions that led to the hegemony of this "scientific" form of research—positivism—, which controls almost exclusively all funds for educational research, they propose a new paradigm known as "Participatory Action Research," inspired by the work of Paulo Freire, Orlando Fals-Borda, and others as a way of supporting a liberatory form of true democratic education. They rebaptized this type of inquiry as Research as Praxis.

The authors include an example of a Participatory Action Research project aimed at decolonizing family literacy practices rooted in the deficit thinking model and the imposition of middle-class European American values on non-mainstream families.

This well-researched book, supported by the luminous thinking of dedicated educators,—who are not afraid of questioning their own processes as well as the status quo and the forces that support it, is indeed a work of hope.

We can only add our own hope that many educators will be inspired to engage in Participatory Action Research and in Family Literacy with the same spirit that informs these authors.

In their words, "It is a social responsibility to work as educators *with* people in order to understand and shape a world that is more just, democratic, sustainable, and peaceful."

Alma Flor Ada and F. Isabel Campoy

Acknowledgments

We thank Donaldo Macedo, who enthused us to engage in writing this book and provided us with kernel ideas.

A sabbatical semester at New Mexico State University allowed deep sustained concentration for developing highly theoretical sections of the book.

Doctoral students, participants in the Research as Praxis seminar, and colleagues in the Department of Curriculum and Instruction provided comments and challenges to be substantive in our reasoning and grounded in our theories and proposals.

We express special gratitude to Shirley Steinberg for validating our work and speeding up the review process.

Grateful acknowledgment is hereby made to Sage Publications for permission to use the following publication as Chapter 5:

Reyes, L. V., & Torres, M. N. (2007). Decolonizing family literacy in a culture circle: Reinventing the family literacy educator's role. *Journal of Early Childhood Literacy, 7*(1), 73–94.

Daniel Petersen provided patient assistance in proofreading our numerous drafts.

Dr. Jennifer Villa was very helpful in the laborious formatting process.

Introduction

Toward Democratic and Socially Responsive Research in Education

Myriam N. Torres, Cristina Gonzalez, & Loui V. Reyes

"The philosophers have only interpreted the world, in various ways; the point is to change it." XI Theses on Feuerbach by Marx and Engels.

In society in general and education in particular we are suffering from a "democratic deficit," which is at the center of all crises (Chomsky, 2009). In education research, such a deficit manifests itself as its "repositivization" by overemphasizing the *unity of science* through universal principles "underlying all scientific inquiry" (National Research Council, 2002, p. 2) and the adoption of standards for reporting (American Educational Research Association, 2006, 2009). Under the rhetoric of rigor and the drive to make education research a science, diversity in research approaches—democratic ways for seeking knowledge and understanding—is increasingly restricted to following those principles and standards. The problem is that these standards are based on exclusively positivist criteria of research quality.

Another factor that is eroding democracy in education research—diversity of equally valued epistemological paradigms—is the alleged neutrality of value-free research. Many researchers know that this is a myth, but what is not a myth is how neutrality is used as a cover-up to advance political agendas. Indeed, O'Connor (2007) documents how "neutrality" is a smokescreen to advance the right-wing agenda of dismantling research in the public interest and public education altogether. Meanwhile, the corporate takeover of the educational system (the latest in a series of social services takeovers) is in process. This scenario goes under the canopy of neoliberalism by bashing our public schools (Emery & Ohanian, 2004), rendering colleges of education irrelevant (Darling-Hammond & Youngs, 2002), and making higher education an academic capitalism (Giroux, 2002; Slaughter & Rhoades, 2004; Washburn, 2005). The free market has become the infallible dogma for success and prosperity (Giroux, 2002, 2004; Hursh, 2008). Not surprisingly, private interests and priorities are better served while public interest is set aside. The state is increasingly abdicating its responsibility to fund research in the public interest and public education as well. Thus, democracy as academic freedom in research and other educational practices is highly constrained.

In these circumstances, research in the public interest actually goes against the grain. It is difficult to get funding for research projects on segregation, inequality, inequity, top-down curricula and pedagogy, and lack of resources. As researchers abandon their concerns for the social responsiveness of their projects, what prevail are segregationist, dehumanizing, and antidemocratic educational practices (Bracey, 2003; Kozol, 2005; Meier & Wood, 2004; Olfman, 2003; Valenzuela, 2005).

Social responsiveness of research also gets minimized because, traditionally, research and social action are separated into two different activities carried out by different persons and/or specialists. This schism is not only peculiar to positivist researchers but also is common in qualitative, postmodern, and critical researchers. For example, postmodernist/poststructuralist researchers overemphasize the politics of difference which has been taken to the extreme of absolute contingency or relativism by some strands of these movements. Absolute contingency or relativism weakens the urgency of organizing for social change, fragments organizations, and holds back the political vision of liberation and emancipation by considering them as impossible and illusive (Beck, 1993; Cole, 1994; Darder, Baltodano, & Torres, 2009; Kelly, Cole, & Hill, 1999). With few exceptions, the *de facto* idea of social relevance of research is exhausted by describing, documenting, and denouncing the conditions in education. Researchers hope that their research will be of use for improving education or society at large when practitioners, policy makers, or activists take that knowledge and act on it. Nader (Nader & Goodman, 2009) calls our attention to the abundance of documentation and denunciation, but few significant transformative actions are coming from that existing knowledge.

Research as Praxis (RAP), although not a panacea for solving all social and educational problems, may be a vehicle for addressing the democratic deficit and lack of social responsiveness of research through collective inquiry and social action. Research as Praxis (RAP) is a re-appropriation and expansion of what has been known, mostly in the so-called Third World, as Participatory Action Research (PAR) and some strands of Action Research, especially the emancipatory strands that keep the goal of social transformation and liberation at their core. RAP is considered not only a research paradigm, but a philosophy of life and work in which there is a dialectical interplay of research, education, and activism. Hence, RAP constitutes a human praxis *par excellence,* as it is deeply rooted in the 11th Thesis on Feuerbach by Marx and Engelsf: "The philosophers have only interpreted the world, in various ways; the point is to change it" (Marx & Engels, 1970/1845, p. 123). Actually, this is a call to all concerned educators and researchers to go beyond just interpreting the world, but to change it. RAP goes beyond the contemplative character of most conventional research, to work *with* the people according to their own identification of the issues that concern and interest them, through their engagement in collective inquiry, and action as a dynamic interplay.

RAP is also grounded on radical participatory democracy, which implies a epistemological break (Fals-Borda, 1985, 1991); that is, the human subjects move from being passive participants as merely providers of information or performing according to a protocol given to them, to become co-researchers and decision makers in every step in the process of collective inquiry and action. The ultimate goal is transformation toward a better world (e.g., more humane, equitable, peaceful, and sustainable) in terms of the well-being of research participants and their communities. This complex process is carried out through dialogical encounters, in which popular knowledge and academic knowledge meet and become mutually enhanced.

Doing RAP type of work in the education field requires social consciousness and a strong commitment to work on the side of people with fewer opportunities in life, and who are suffering the impact of bad policies, marketization of education, and the decline of teaching and learning practices. One of the major responsibilities of RAP inquirers is to devise the conditions for radical participatory democracy to take place when people get together to study their reality, plan, and engage in action for improving their own situations.

Some researchers have the social consciousness and commitment for making a research project responsive to the interests, needs, and dreams of the people they are working with. However, they can be caught up in the formalities of the many conventional approaches to research. The following is a testimony of Cristina's and Loui's initial perception of research as something like RAP. However, when they engaged in their dissertation work, the formalities of conventional research pulled them in other directions, not without their stubborn resistance and feelings of disappointment. They had not been exposed to RAP or any other type of research different from quantitative and qualitative approaches.

Testimonial of Two Doctoral Students

What is research? Why do it? What purposes does it serve? Whose interests are addressed? Who benefits from research projects? These are questions we (Loui and Cristina) struggled with during our doctoral program as we deconstructed the idea of "doing" research. How would we develop a research project? We learned that the purpose of research is to construct meaning about a phenomenon that includes humans, a complex and rich intersection of life experiences. In the doctoral coursework, we wrote a myriad of research papers, none leading to what would become a research project. Initially, in working with two professors, we were introduced to qualitative research and theoretical frameworks that appealed to us based on our professional backgrounds working with social service agencies and schools. We experimented with interviewing, observing, and analyzing data during short excursions in one of our courses. That was the extent of our experience with qualitative research. In addition, we were reading everything we could find on this "type" of research.

Statistics courses introduced us to the realm of positivism. We had entered the sanctity of the academic world with much trepidation. Positivism was puzzling. We actually did conduct short research projects and learned how to master the various tools needed in this type of research. The process seemed sterile and perfunctory. The idea of absolute, objective, and generalizable truths did not fit in our thinking. The process of learning this research was painful. It was then that we were introduced to Guba and Lincoln (1989) that led the way out of this quandary.

On positivism, Donaldo Macedo later noted in our conversations (personal communication, 1995), "what benefit is there for the third graders who are failing at reading, given an intervention by the researcher but are still failing at reading after the research project is completed? What does this prove? Ultimately, the research project must be positioned within a political project that informs our practice about the ultimately ethical dilemmas in this work."

Shortly after our foray into positivism, it became clear to us that we must denounce and renounce this paradigm [or this ideological construct] and that another research process was in order. While we denounced the positivism inherent in educational research, we also were not enamored with qualitative research. What direction should we take? This journey for understanding led us in a quest that took many turns.

We had encountered into the language of criticism in Dr. Garcia's courses at New Mexico State University through the reading of Giroux, McLaren, Macedo, feminist researchers, and critical theorists. We began in earnest to study research practices and their implications in the communities where this work would take place. We re-discovered Paulo Freire through our work with Donaldo Macedo. His work spoke to us. Freire speaks vehemently about the importance of ethics in the conduct of research; that we work with the people and for the people we "research." There really was no clear pathway to do research this way at the time, none that was documented and theorized to our knowledge. For this reason, we were ushered into the qualitative strand of research and were at times cautioned not to tread into uncharted waters in our research process. In other words, how close does one get to the "subjects"? Is going to their baptisms and family reunions too close? In one of our meetings with Donaldo, he was reading one of my data entries, and he stopped and asked, "So what is in it for this family to work with you? What are they getting out of this? You are getting your doctorate, but what do they get?" I (Cristina) was puzzled and confused. Can we do something for the family such as providing them information about the politics of public schools and how to navigate these politics? Do I go with the parents to their children's conferences at school?

We attempted to reconcile what we perceived as a disconnect between wanting to be part of the family and the community in the co-construction of meaning and the theoretical constructs that cautioned us against this. How does one co-construct? How do we know that the process of co-construction is equal, fair? In wanting to become coherent in this endeavor, we created a group of doctoral students to study this phenomenon further. We refined the process we would take in our research. We attempted to co-opt qualitative research in order to announce and embrace praxis for our work. This was much more challenging than when we first imagined it. There was not much in the literature about this type of research in academia. Evidence of this work was present in the Action Research vogue in the social sciences, but yet not tied to rigorous academic training in doctorate programs, at least not in colleges of education in the mid–1990s.

It is no accident that we did not move toward RAP. The dissertations in the end were in fact written in third-person style, albeit with participant voices, but third person nonetheless, and it is not clear how our work affected the people with whom we collaborated in our research projects. We wanted participatory and transformative research projects for our participants. However, we stayed in the balcony contemplating them instead.

Overview of the Book

This book consists of five chapters that go from denouncing the socio-political and economic forces that have put profit before people in every dimension of human activity, with no regard to the social responsiveness of research, to announcing a counter-hegemonic approach to research grounded in radical participatory democracy and social transformation toward a better world of human well-being, justice, peace, and environmental sustainability. Chapter 1 is a *denunciation* of the myths of conventional research associated with the U.S. No Child Left Behind education policy that has enthroned positivist epistemologies under the mantra of scientifically based research. This phenomenon is connected to globalized neoliberal capitalism that has transformed democratic ideals, such as academic freedom in teaching and research, into a 'corporatocratic' academic capitalism. In addition to this conservative revamping of research, social justice educators and researchers have to face the debilitating discourse of a strand we call 'paralyzing postmodernism'. The chapter ends by describing the social and educational impact of these oppressing systems. By and large, this first chapter sets the rationale for embracing research as praxis.

Chapter 2 concerns the origins, philosophical underpinnings, methodological strategies of RAP as a counter-hegemonic force of possibilities for social change in the public interest. RAP is considered a new paradigm of research, with a distinctive philosophy of life and work, and the interplay of research, education (teaching), and activism. As a social praxis, RAP is grounded in three distinctive principles:

1. radical participatory democracy;
2. collective action for transformation toward a better world; and
3. commitment to work for social justice in solidarity with the popular classes as core values of researchers' roles.

The central thesis in chapter 3 is that the criteria for assessing quality of research are paradigmatic. RAP, as a distinctive paradigm of research, has its own criteria of quality, based on its principles, which in turn demand the engagement of research participants in the definition of specific criteria and the evaluation of research processes and results. Thus, as RAP inquirers, we need to develop three sets of "goodness and relevance" criteria with the people participating in each research project. Each set corresponds to each principle: open-endedness criteria (principle: radical participatory democracy), social responsiveness criteria (principle: collective action for social transformation), and commitment criteria (principle: commitment to radical democracy, ethical, and socially responsive work).

The epistemological relevance of action is the thesis of chapter 4. Action is not merely "application" of the research results to education practice, to solve problems, and to support policy. In RAP work, action can be a source of knowledge and community building, and it could be the beginning of a research project. At any rate, there is a wide range of voices calling in unison for organized action despite a generalized passivity, especially in educators, not necessarily in support of the status quo, but because of fear or hopelessness, given their deteriorated work conditions. RAP work has been and should be connected with larger social movements.

Lastly, chapter 5 is an example of a RAP project concerning the decolonization of family literacy in a culture circle. The study reported here is a co-optation of a top-down family literacy relative care training program while re-inventing the family literacy educator. The relational pedagogy used in the culture circle opened the possibility for participants to resist the top-down curriculum and bring to bear their experiential knowledge, cultural values, and popular wisdom in order to rethink their training in ways that were socially, culturally, and linguistically responsive. The role of outside researchers is deeply examined and re-invented by pointing to the vulnerabilities, pitfalls, and successes encountered.

References

American Educational Research Association. (2006). Standards for reporting empirical social science research in AERA Publications. *Educational Researcher, 35*(6), 33–40.

American Educational Research Association. (2009). Standards for reporting on humanities-oriented research in AERA publications. *Educational Researcher, 38*(6), 48–486.

Beck, C. (1993). Postmodernism, pedagogy, and philosphy of education. In EPS/PES (Ed.), *Philosophy of Education Society: Yearbook–1993.*

Bracey, G. (2003). *On the death of childhood and the destruction of public schools.* Portsmouth, NH: Heinemann.

Chomsky, N. (2009, October). Coups, UNASUR, and the US. *Z Magazine, 22,* 21–26.

Cole, S. E. (1994). Evading the subject: The poverty of contingency theory. In H. W. Simons & M. Billig (Eds.), *After postmodernism: Reconstructing ideology critique* (pp. 38–57). Thousand Oaks, CA: Sage Publications.

Darder, A., Baltodano, M., & Torres, R. (2009). Critical pedagogy: An introduction. In A. Darder, M. P. Baltodano, & R. D. Torres (Eds.), *The critical pedagogy reader* (2nd ed.) (pp. 1–20). New York, NY: Routledge/Taylor & Francis.

Darling-Hammond, L., & Youngs, P. (2002). Defining "highly qualified teachers": What does "scientifically-based research" actually tell us? *Educational Researcher, 31*(9), 13–25.

Emery, K., & Ohanian, S. (2004). *Why is corporate America bashing our public schools?* Portsmouth, NH: Heinemann.

Fals-Borda, O. (1985). *Knowledge and people's power: Lessons with peasants in Nicaragua, Mexico, and Colombia* (B. Maller, Trans.). New Delhi, India: Indian Social Institute.

Fals-Borda, O. (1991). Some basic ingredients. In O. Fals-Borda & M. A. Rahman (Eds.), *Action and knowledge: Breaking the monopoly with participatory action research* (pp. 3–12). New York, NY: The Apex Press.

Giroux, H. (2002). Neoliberalism, corporate culture, and the promise of higher education. The university as a democratic public sphere. *Harvard Educational Review, 74*(2), 425–463.

Giroux, H. (2004). Neoliberalism and the demise of democracy: Resurrecting hope in dark times. *Dissident Voice.* Retrieved from www.dissidentvoice.org/Aug04/Giroux0807.htm.

Guba, E., & Lincoln, Y. (1989). *Fourth generation evaluation.* Newbury Park, CA: Sage Publications.

Hursh, D. (2008). *High-stakes testing and the decline of teaching and learning: The real crisis of education.* Lanham, MD: Rowman & Littlefield.

Kelly, J., Cole, M., & Hill, D. (1999). *Resistance postmodernism and the ordeal of the undecidable: A Marxist critique.* Paper presented at the British Educational Research Association Annual Conference.

Kozol, J. (2005). *The shame of the nation: The restoration of apartheid schooling in America.* New York, NY: Crown Publishers.

Marx, K., & Engels, F. (1970/1845). *The German ideology.* New York, NY: International Publishers.

Meier, D., & Wood, G. (Eds.). (2004). *Many children left behind: How the No Child Left Behind Act is damaging our children and our schools.* Boston, MA: Beacon Press.

Nader, R., & Goodman, A. (2009). Ralph Nader on the G-20, healthcare reform, Mideast talks and his first work of fiction, *Only the Super-rich Can Save Us! Democracy Now Radio TV.*

National Research Council. (2002). *Scientific research in education.* Washington, DC: National Academic Press.

O'Connor, A. (2007). *Social science for what? Philanthropy and the social question in a world turned rightside up.* New York, NY: Russell Sage Foundations.

Olfman, S. (Ed.). (2003). *All work and no play... How educational reforms are harming our preschoolers.* Westport, CT: Praeger.

Slaughter, S., & Rhoades, G. (2004). *Academic capitalism and the new economy: Market, state, and higher education.* Baltimore, MD: Johns Hopkins University Press.

Valenzuela, A. (Ed.). (2005). *Leaving children behind: How "Texas-style" accountability fails Latino youth.* New York, NY: SUNY Press.

Washburn, J. (2005). *University, Inc.: The corporate corruption of higher education.* New York, NY: Basic Books.

Chapter 1

Denouncing the Myths and Pitfalls of Research Practices: From Corporatocracy to Paralyzing Postmodernism

Myriam N. Torres & Loui V. Reyes

Freire (2005) challenges all of us to denounce oppressing systems and announce how a better world is possible. Within this frame, Research as Praxis is presented as an alternative paradigm to conventional research practices that at best do not challenge and at worst support the status quo.

The neoliberal turn of education converts public schools and universities, including research activities, into business-like institutions, subservient to corporations. Consequently, market values override the education values of human fulfillment and democratic strengthening.

Mystification of Education Research: "Scientifically Based Research" (NCLB)

The current state of affairs of educational research is frozen in time, if not regressing to the past when we needed to justify any approach that deviated from the positivist paradigm. Mystification of educational research as promoted in the NCLB Act (2002) is the culprit of reductionism that closes people's thinking and feelings when studying social and human phenomena, including, of course, education. Educators and researchers have fallen into 'stupidification' (Macedo's term, 2006) as a result of this reductionism. One of the authors, speaking to a school administrator was told that children could not learn Spanish well because they had not been tested on their Spanish. Even though it was suggested to her that there are many other factors such as the low social status of Spanish, which works to diminish the importance of learning Spanish, she insisted that the problem was the lack of testing of the students' learning of Spanish. This incident is an example of colonization and "stupidification" of school personnel, who have been bombarded with discourses of accountability, standards, curricula, pedagogy, and assessment based on "scientifically based research."

Concerning the education research establishment at the national level, Feuer et al. (2002) commenting on the National Research Council (2002) report on Scientific Research in Education go back and forth between endorsing the premises of the positivist research played out in the National Research Council report and making an effort to appear to be critiquing it. Their use of notions of culture and research community, and of context-responsive research, somewhat softens the narrow definition of education research under the promise of improving its quality, and hence its relevance to policy and practice. Feuer et al. make some statements that are obviously rhetorical given the positivist frame, postulates, and principles of the whole article. For example, they contend that there is "no attempt to minimize other 'non-scientific' ways of research" and that "there are legitimate research frameworks." The real situation created by this regulation is that any epistemology and research methodology that does not meet the standards and guidelines is 'non-scientific,' which carries a wagon load of negative implications: not disseminated, not valued, not funded, under-rated for tenure and promotion, not used for educational policy and practice, and so on. While the authors admit the influence of politics, values, and conceptual frames on the research process and results, they consider it a function of OERI (Office of Educational Research and Improvement), now the IES (Institute of Education Sciences) to shield research from political influence. The question to ask would be: whose politics is kept away and whose politics is unexamined? In addition, the insistence on objectivity, based on the premises and guidelines of the positivist approach to research described in the document, preclude questioning the actual agendas underlying that "objectivity."

According to the National Research Council (2002) report on SRE, OERI has the mission of nurturing a scientific community culture, protecting the scientific process from political maneuvers, attracting a cadre of intellectuals to build a network of researchers, and in partnership with organizations developing guidelines and standards for reporting research. For Elizabeth St. Pierre (2002), the NRC's agenda set seems a totalitarian system of thought, science, and government that privileges one methodology (quantitative experimental) and co-opts qualitative, subordinating it to the criteria and ideology of the quantitative experimental approach. She considers that we cannot afford to take this research mandate lightly. In the same vein, Horn (2004) refers to a 2004 AERA symposium concerning the NRC report *Advancing Scientific Research in Education,* whose proponents and defenders actually self-validate their own setup by assuring that randomized experiments have raised the quality and quantity of research proposal granted funding.

While most of us as educators/researchers, who do not follow the positivist mold, are working hard with the minimal opportunities we find to get our projects going, the research establishment continues pursuing their agenda: *Standards for Reporting on Empirical Social Science Research in AERA Publications* (2006) and *Standards for Reporting on Humanities–Oriented Research in AERA Publications* (2009). Howe (2009) demonstrates that the trumpeted education sciences, specifically the scientific research in education (SRE) is a tacit form of positivism, hence constitutes a 'new orthodoxy.' Its proponents (NRC) embrace three dogmas:

1. qualitative vs. quantitative;
2. fact different from value; and
3. empirical social science vs. humanities-oriented research.

They set six principles of scientific research: empirical test of a question, theoretical framework of the research question, use of appropriate methods to address the question, showing a chain of reasoning, replication and generalization, and making research available for revision and criticism. If researchers are not in accord with these principles, their research is not considered scientific or cognitively significant. Furthermore, promoters of SRE, or the return to the hegemony of positivist research, proclaim the unity of science; that is, scientific research is similar in all fields, and empirical verification is its key defining characteristic.

Concerning the implications of this new orthodoxy of education research represented by SRE, Howe (2009) spells out several:

1. omitting values, because they aren't verifiable nor cognitively significant, creates a cover-up, given that values are implicitly incorporated into the descriptive vocabulary of research, in the policy-making, program designs, research methods, design, collection of data, and interpretation. These values are inevitably political and cannot be explained within the SRE frame;
2. experimental methodology is privileged and assigned a higher epistemological status;
3. intentionality and volition of research participants are considered a problem of control of variables;
4. the difference between causal inferences in physics experiments and human subject experiments is the degree of precision or error;
5. SRE makes visible the dichotomy between empirical social sciences and humanities-oriented research, which leads to separation between research and other scholarly activities, ignoring the fact that humanities research can be also empirical;
6. research that is not "scientific" in accordance with the SRE definition, will not influence policy or practice, and will not be funded, disseminated, or valued.

In this state of affairs where epistemology and research methodology are practically mandated by excluding research paradigms and approaches that do not fit into the positivist mold, RAP type of work is by definition thrown into the 'humanities-oriented research' which is not empirical and therefore not scientific. For us, this approach would not be a major problem, except for the implications for seeking funding, publishing, influencing policy and practice, and academic promotions in many cases. This reality is another reason for embracing RAP as a venue for democratizing research, not only among investigators but also concerning research participants.

We now know that the trumpeted "scientifically based research" underlying the NCLB's rhetoric, especially the "Reading First Initiative," is actually a scam carried out by people with commercial and political interests. This initiative was based on the report of the National Reading Panel (NRP). In turn, this panel was made up of participants mostly from the National Institute of Child and Health Development (NICHD), and only one teacher of reading was included. There were many maneuvers to exclude people who were not like-minded as the majority of the panel who were already inclined to phonics as the "scientifically based approach" to reading instruction (Yatvin, 2002; Coles, 2003). The NRP report was slanted to support phonics with unsubstantiated evidence; on the contrary, blatant lies were delivered about the supporting studies. For example, the U.S. Secretary of Education (Ron Paige) told reading teachers that the panel had studied 100,000 articles and concluded that the best strategy for teaching literacy was phonics. Let's do the math and unmask the reality of this scam. Could the panel of 15 members possibly have read this enormous number of articles in a period of 18 months (April 1998 to October 1999). As Yatvin (2002) alleges, by October 1999 only 428 studies were reviewed for the report. In addition, "thousands of studies were rejected without analysis, because their titles, publishing circumstances, or abstracts revealed that they did not meet the panel's criteria" (p. 368). She also points out that there was no research staff support despite the money available. As we know, this was just propaganda with no real basis (Yatvin, 2002; Coles, 2003; Metcalf, 2002). At the end, the results of the NRP were used as the basis for Bush's education council's Reading First Initiative and became an important component of the NCLB Act.

Another scam was unveiled about the origins of the Reading First Initiative and its bias toward phonics: A member of McGraw–Hill Publishers was asked to organize a task force of "reading experts" by President Bush, with the support of Congress, in order to help eliminate the nation's "reading deficit." McGraw–Hill Publishers already had a phonics-based reading program. Not surprisingly, the task force consistently slanted their views in favor of a phonics approach to literacy under the stamp of "scientifically based research" (Coles, 2003; Yatvin, 2002). The phonics approach has been dressed in many different outfits that help promoters co-opt the language (e.g., readers and writers workshop) of other approaches such as whole language. Bakhtin (1986) helps us to frame the teaching and learning of language using phonics as teaching *dead language.* He and Voloshinov (1973) strongly criticized the study of language focused on the system and not in the real life language use. Expanding this perspective into the domain of education, Torres and Reyes (2005) frame the NCLB's Reading First initiative as the policy that institutionalizes the teaching of language as dead and dreary. In contrast, the authors propose to embrace "living language" as the focus of the study of language, its philosophy, and pedagogy. In other words, the teaching of language should be based on meaningful language events of students themselves.

Concerning the use of research for policy and for improving practice, Lather's (2008) review of Hess' (2008) edited book *When Research Matters: How Scholarship Influences Education Policy* points to what she calls a "re-positivization" of the research use (for policy and for practice) issues. She refuses "to concede science to scientism" (p. 361). Nonetheless, she recognizes that the contributors to the volume are moving a step ahead from the orthodox positivist paradigm and its naïve idea of "rigor" as a guarantee for improvement of education. They also recognize the limits of the research/policy nexus as merely technical matter and move to the realm of relationships as part of democracy. Although the research-practice connection is a concern for both researchers and practitioners, across different paradigms of research, there are clear differences among them about how to make this connection. Lather's position is that this issue of use of research is more philosophical than instrumental. She characterizes it as "post-empiricist qualitative methodology," with critical edge, aimed at improving quality of practice. Lather argues that the Institute of Education Sciences (IES) has produced "policy entrepreneurs" rather than convergent, cumulative and replicable findings. Nor has the "rigor talk" prevented the 'Reading First' debacle. She asks: "what are the standards and evidence look like when exclusion and fixities of what's scientific are not precisely the debate?" Contestation of the results is at the very core of the scientific activity. This principle helps us to contest the intelligibility of policy within the NCLB re-positivization of educational research with the 'doctrine' of scientifically based research. Like Lather, we see the dangerous hegemonic understanding of evidence, objectivity, reason, measurement, responsible knowledge production, and use of research results.

As part of the "scientism" revamped by the cacophony of the NCLB Act and the SRE report, the boundaries of the thinkable and procedures of inquiry have been demarcated strongly. Specifically, the Institutional Review Boards at research institutions are reincarnating this scientism at the expense of multiple perspectives, paradigms, and methodologies for doing research. The most common issues they allege for not approving the latter proposals include the following: the "informed consent" forms should be written at a lower literacy level, which assumes that the participants' literacy levels are extremely low. The IRB members base their demands on their own assumptions and biases of Hispanic and/or immigrant participants. In addition, RAP language such as "liberation," "conscientization," and "countervailing power" are not understood by IRB members and consequently they demand that researchers elaborate these ideas further. Basing their demands on traditional models of research, they ask for stricter definition of the procedures with the participants (timelines, meeting dates, specific directions for each step of the procedure, and so on). This demand of having everything established *a priori* creates for RAP researchers a catch-22 situation. On the one hand, the researcher needs IRB approval to begin the research, but on the other hand, the RAP researcher cannot come into the community with a set agenda. Otherwise, it is difficult to talk about participatory democracy in the setting of the research agenda. Another problem with the IRB as it stands in academia is its strict reliance on the positivist model of research with humans based exclusively on the medical model. Their assumption is that human participants are non-responsive to their environment and interactions with the researcher as if they were non-human objects of research. We now know that this assumed inertia of the objects of study does not exist even in the physical subatomic world, which resulted in what is known as Heisenberg's indetermination principle.

The IRB process reflects the hegemony of the so-called 'scientific culture' and the institutional power to sanction and paralyze any initiative outside them. These 'scientific principles' are so entrenched in higher education that they stifle those who dare to challenge the establishment. We can speak from our own experiences and those of our students.

It has become clear that our strategic work inside the institution should be to open a dialogue with other like-minded colleagues about the reductionist view of research institutionalized by the IRB process, and move toward opening the IRB to include other research paradigms such as RAP. In the meantime, we continue our work with our students by having them enter their respective communities, not as researchers, but as educators or community workers. We base this decision on the unique characteristic of RAP: interplay of research, teaching, and community work. Once a student identifies the focus the community wants, the student will be able to prepare the proposal for the IRB, making official their role as RAP researcher.

Global Neoliberal Capitalism

The problem of educational research is not isolated but part of a global trend toward marketization of culture, politics, and education. We need to come to terms with NCLB as a policy, which results in the consolidation of market fundamentalism representing the 'New Alliance' between neo-conservatives and liberals (Apple, 2004). This alliance can be referred to as global neoliberal capitalism, in which the market is the organizing principle of economy, politics, social affairs, and social services, and is outside the control of the people (Giroux 2004a) thus maintaining white supremacy (Macedo & Gounari 2006). This leads to a post-welfarist state where the power of de-regulated corporations and privatized 'public' institutions is greater. In this way government functionaries abdicate their responsibility to the people who elected them. They may call themselves public servants, but in reality they are only serving the special interest groups that support their election and political agendas.

We have created a metaphor to describe these phenomena: Imagine a strange, yet very real creature we may want to call a "sucktopus," a distant relative of the octopus with an infinite number of pervasive tentacles invading every area of education (curriculum development, evaluation, teacher preparation, administration, tutoring, communications, and so on). This creature *sucks* the life of people and their humanness, their hope, their energy for counter-acting and also their commitment to social responsibility. Education then becomes a business where everything is for sale, and schools resemble, or are in fact, shopping malls. Democratic ideals in education become a distant historical affair. Business dictates the curriculum and administers its control through testing and taking over schools when they do not meet the unrealistic and punitive standards imposed top-down by the greedy, irresponsible, and abusive corporatocracy. Following our metaphor of the "sucktopus," its tentacles inject the poison of market values over all areas of education.

In the United States, the Business Roundtables (BRTs) are the engine of the 'sucktopus' that overtook public education. Emery and Ohanian (2004), in their extensive research on this subject identified institutes, research centers, and foundations that cover every specific educational area. Thus, in educational administration, the Institute of Educational Leadership trains administrators

with business models for education. This dynamic becomes evident
when one reads the mission statement of many schools across the
country. The Center for National Policy Institute is creating the
blueprint for educational policies wherever they can introduce
them. The "Public Agenda," a non-profit public relations company,
is promoting the BRT agenda and limiting the debate to its agendas. Opinion polls promoted by foundations, such as the Annen-
berg Institute on standards, manufacture public consent through
the guise of scientific and neutral statistical procedures. Meanwhile, researchers are finding little money to conduct their research and have to sell out to the foundations behind the
corporations of the BRT. By doing so, they find themselves engaged in promoting the market agenda under the aura of "scientific research."

Accountability continues to be the banner of the BRT's takeover of education. According to Molnar (1996) the business execu-
tives call upon educational institutions to address their needs
under the claim that America needs to have the competitive
advantage in the global market, "soon, it seems no area of school
life is beyond corporate scrutiny or without business involvement"
(p. 2). The corporatization of education promoted through so-called
school reform has been very systematic since the Reagan years,
specifically with the infamous "Nation at Risk" report (1983). This
takeover has clearly two lines of action. One is the discrediting of
public education which started officially with that document and
continues today.   Berliner and Biddle (1995) document the manufacture of crisis in education, which starts with a profusion of
myths including the one of public discontent with their schools and
the myth that private schools are better than public schools. These
authors document also the recklessness of the right-wing advocacy
for vouchers, standards, privatization, and so on. The other line of
action concerns the creation of the corporate blueprint of school
reform, which is no more than the selling of public schools to
entrepreneurs. Emery and Ohanian (2004) document the multiple
fronts by which the business community, represented among
others by Edward Rust, is becoming embedded into the education
domain.   This business entrepreneur, the CEO of State Farm

Insurance, leads or belongs to multiple committees and agencies created to advance such embeddings. For example, he is co-chair of the Business Coalition for Excellence of Education and chair of the Education Task Force of the Business Round Table, which has been creating BRTs in every state in partnership with the state department of education. He was also co-chair of a subcommittee on Educational Policy of the Committee for Economic Development, President Bush's transition Advisory Team Committee on Education (Emery & Ohanian, 2004). Rust's report in 1999, entitled "No Turning Back: A Progress Report on the Business Roundtable Education Initiative," clearly states the business agenda for education and its commitment to strangle schools under the guise of accountability, assessment of students' achievement, standards, rewards, and punishments. He declares: "It is said that large organizations such as schools don't change because they see the light; they change because they feel the heat." In March 2001, before the House Committee on Education, "Rust called for aligning assessment systems to standards, annual state testing, professional development in standards and assessment literacy; basing state accountability on increased student performance...and high quality research-based data supplied by the federal government" (Emery & Ohanian, 2004, p. 38). Rust goes on to recommend to the House Education Committee that the authorization of Elementary and Secondary Education Act should include a direct statement for increasing accountability of student achievement. He declares: "States should establish an accountability system with clear consequences for schools, principals and teachers who persistently fail over time to meet standards. Consequences may include replacing personnel, restructuring or closing schools, and providing options for students to enroll elsewhere."

There is no doubt about the immersion of the business ideology and accountability as the driving force and values in education reform. The NCLB, and its clone, the new policy "Race to the Top" (RTTT), are obsessive about raising scores in standardized testing and the subsequent steps of school 'labeling,' social scorn and punishments for not meeting the benchmarks, and the infamous AYP: "In probation," "in correction," and "restitution." The latter represents the complete takeover of the school by the state to be given to a private school management corporation (e.g., Edison Schools). This approach ends up being a disaster for schools, not only educational goals (no real accountability to the taxpayers), but also as a business, as Molnar (2005) and Saltman (2005) demonstrate. This taking over of the public education system by the business community in conjunction with or the tacit agreement of the federal and state governments did not happen gradually, but through a massive attack on various fronts. For example, evidence of these massive attacks on public education is seen in the proliferation of vouchers, testing, standards, penalties to schools that do not meet the AYP, attacks on teachers' unions or their co-optation, standardized curricula and pedagogy, and finally media that systematically discredit schools and educators.

The entrenchment of the power of market fundamentalism in the social institutions and the corporate media prevents a clear and definitive trial of the market principles (de-regulation, privatization, globalization), even under the alarming economic crisis we have fallen into. Broad and Cavanagh (2008) refer to a G-20 Summit hosted by the U.S. government as "Swear Off 'Market Fundamentalism." Shamelessly, President Bush affirmed that the economic crisis was not caused by de-regulation, but on the contrary, by too much government intervention. In other words, what is needed is more de-regulation of the markets. President Bush's outrageous statement went unexamined by the mainstream media. Torres and Mercado (2007) describe this resonance effect as the way an item becomes "news" nowadays in mainstream media and for the public. One of the outcomes that we can anticipate from this media and governmental complicity is that this type of market doctrine is pushing not only the country but the whole world toward the abyss. Of course, the most vulnerable people are those who fall first with no possibility of bailouts or any time of consideration. Naomi Klein (2008) considers that the irregularities with this bailout management involve not only corruption but criminal actions against most people of the country and with huge repercussions in the world, especially those people at the verge of losing everything, even their hope. Meanwhile the government has abdicated its responsibility for protecting public interest and has systematically sided with the major donors, corporations, and elites to protect and increase profits for the rich.

All this is congruent with the shock doctrine that Naomi Klein (2007) describes in her book of the same name. She began documenting the research on mental therapy using electroshocks by a psychiatrist with the name of Cameron at McGill University in the 1950s. She traces connections with Milton Friedman's economic theory of a 'free' market based on the same principles of shock therapy. The core of this theory is that the free market can regulate itself and cannot do anything bad. Conversely, government regulations cannot do anything good. Friedman and his fellow students, the infamous "Chicago Boys," tested this theory in Chile under the dictator Pinochet with American backing and continued through the world—Argentina, Indonesia, China, South Africa, Poland, Russia, Bolivia, Bangladesh, Iraq, Afghanistan, and also the United States. In the USA the market fundamentalism started openly under Reagan and continues today. This doctrine involves the creation of disasters at economic, social, and political levels, hence the name given by Klein "Disaster Capitalism." These disasters and the confusion that follow them are the perfect terrain to introduce the measures that promise to alleviate the crisis, but what they really do is open the country to the big international corporations, eliminate regulations, and take over natural resources. They rob the country with impunity as is happening with the infamous bailout in the United States. These 'sucktopuses' invade every dimension of society, including education. They exploit people by subjecting them to their goals, thus meeting corporate ends and profits while at the same time demanding from the schools an education of workers that increases the applicant pool of desperate people trying to gain any type of employment (usually at the bottom rung in our society). Individuals are made to believe that if they invest more money in their education, they will obtain a better–paying job. Emery and Ohanian (2004) indicate that the contrary is true. High school graduates have better chances to get a job than college graduates. Corporate agencies are creating submissive, fearful individuals whose imagination is repressed and suffocated, creating instead a new form of non-declared slavery.

With the phrase "Hi tech hucksters go to schools," Molnar (1996) refers to those who are profiting from school captive audiences. The Channel One "educational" newscast and advertising, Nike's branding and billboards, the Bill and Melinda Gates Foundation are courting and bribing school administrators to let them enter and make their profits. They sell their products, many of which are harmful for students. For example, school vending machines sell mostly junk food, including water which is sold for seven thousand times the price of tap water, even though it is simply bottled tap water. Commercialism in schools commodifies the very values of education. It strips away all non-monetary values. Thus, democracy, autonomy, curiosity, creativity, solidarity, happiness, children's well-being, and so on are redefined in market values, consequently dropped as important ideals of education. For example, democracy has been redefined as freedom to choose from the available choices of products for sale. Actually, the consumer is offered a very narrow range of choices. As Molnar (2005) argues, the real freedom is in the "sovereignty" of the consumers. They are active in the selection of the alternatives to choose from. Consumerism is a direct result of commercialism, where the different media play a definite role. Chomsky (1989) and Herman and Chomsky (1988) refer to this role as a conduit for the "manufacture of consent.". The impact of media in the minds of children and adolescents is captured magisterially by Ariel Dorfman (1983) when he describes the impact of industrially produced entertainment. He maintains that this is not only entertainment but what he calls a "secret education," which consists of models of violence, sex roles, fashions, but also ways of how to love, how to buy, how to conquer. Above all, they teach us "how to forget the past and suppress the future" (p. ix) and keep quiet and docile. As we can see, this is the best way to create and maintain an alienated society where the ones who dare to ask questions are labeled as persons with a "negative personality," "troublemakers," "radicals," "heretics," as "unpatriotic," or even as "terrorists."

The infiltration of the market ideology, or market fundamentalism as Giroux (2004a) refers to it, is multidimensional and multilayered. Following are some examples of its infiltration in the educational system. Boyles (2005) and his associates provide an acute analysis and evidence of this marketization using the lucrative school lunch market with fast food stuffing. Corporations have infiltrated teacher education programs (Porfilio & Yu, 2006) with the values and criteria of the market, obviously with very detrimental results: teachers are providers of goods and students are "consumers"; standardized curriculum and evaluation (competences), including teaching training often carried out by private-for-profit companies, and which becomes a direct assault on academic freedom, diversity, and education for the public interest; hiring and managing of personnel based on market values and needs; recruiting students not primarily for educating them, but for increasing the enrollment numbers and hence profits. Steinberg and Kincheloe (1997) and their associates document the corporate construction of childhood under the guise of candid entertainment (e.g., Disney) or even educational texts, fashion, and so forth. They point to the creation of the consumer mind isolated from significant adults, and this consumer mind epitomizes the postmodern childhood. They also highlight the "cultural pedagogies" administered by many vested self-service groups in contrast to education by parents and teachers whose primary interest is the child's well-being.

Academic Capitalism

The globalized neoliberal capitalism, as market fundamentalism, has also invaded higher education (Giroux, 2002, 2004a, 2004b). Commercialization of the university research discoveries results in a shift from an emphasis on public-interest to private-interest driven activities. Slaughter and Rhoades (2004) and Slaughter and Leslie (1997) have developed a theory referred to as "academic capitalism," by which they mean the process of marketization of institutional and professional functions and activities. This dynamic implies a certain permeability between the external market-driven forces and the internal core functions of universities: instruction, research, and service. These core activities become commodities when they are actually replaced and come to depend on seeking external funding and/or on generating supplemental revenues. At the same time, the proportion of state and federal funding of higher public education has steadily declined despite the steady increase of general expenses. Hanley (2005) illustrates this point indicating that by 1980 the average state funding for public higher education institutions was 44%, in 2002 it was 32%. In 2004 the state funding shrank 2% on average. In some states the shrinkage was higher, such as in California where it was 5.9%. We are witnessing a rapid decline of the proportion of state funding for public higher education, and such patterns do not happen by accident. Selingo (2003) points to "the disappearing state in higher education." Replacing the state, the market forces have become the driving authority within these institutions.

This self-created dependence on private donors consumes not only money but energy and time, and most significantly, it erodes academic freedom. This fundamental right of faculty is at the core of research, scholarship, and freedom of speech inside and outside the classroom, free from the administration's political and economic agendas. We need to remember that the core meaning of *university* is a multiplicy of perspectives and meanings created, brought in, recognized, cultivated, and projected to the community. This legacy has been the pride of academia, and the tenure policy, founded on academic freedom, is the mechanism to protect academia from the self-interested trends in the market and the political and economic powers of society. On the other hand, dependence on donors for funding research and other projects, especially in the public higher education institutions, sets the agenda in terms of donors' and/or adminstrators' interests, not the diverse interests of faculty, and even less the public interest. Thus, the faculty's enslavement to market pressures is further ensured, stripping away their autonomy and democratic participation in the direction (shared governance) of the university's major activities.

For Hanley (2005) these trends are the manifestation of the dynamics of the neoliberal ideology as it infiltrates into academia. This dynamic involves competition, commercialization, and casualties, Hanley points out.   According to this neoliberal ideology, institutions need to compete for "customers": students and entertainment fans (e.g., sports). Within the institution, academic units need to compete against one another for resources, with faculty and department "productivity" measured in student credit hours and external research funding brought to the university.   Meanwhile, student tuition has skyrocketed. During the 1993–2003 decade tuition increased 47% for four-year colleges and universities.

Indicators of commercialization of universities are patents, partnership with corporations, and corporate–sponsored professorships.   The following case described by Bok (2003) illustrates who benefits the most from these partnerships and patents, even though he is not completely against academic capitalism: "The Novartis Company agreed to give the Department of Plant and Microbial Biology at the University of California, Berkeley, the sum of $25 million over five years, a figure amounting to approximately 30 to 40 percent of the departments' entire research budget.   According to the agreement, Novartis gained the right to review in advance all proposed publications based on research supported by the company (or by the federal government) and to ask the university to apply for a patent on any findings contained in the research" (p. 151).

In 1980, the U.S.   Government (1980) passed the Bayh-Dole Act, facilitating universities to own and license patents from research paid with public funds.   Actually, the pattern of the latest educational policies at all academic levels is the transfer of money from public funds to private hands. The privatization and commercialization of academia are fundamentally transforming professional life in the American university, with serious consequences for each of the three activities traditionally assigned to faculty (Hanley, 2005).

This commercialization is also present in the administrative functions and services, giving rise to academic administrative capitalism. It is becoming more and more common for universities to outsource with private companies student services (e.g., campus bookstores and cafeterias, vending machines with exclusive contracts, janitorial labor, distance education courses / program offerings that fall outside the purview of faculty, for the purpose of generating profit (Slaughter & Rhoades, 2004). Even searches for candidates for high–ranking administrators are given to private companies under the guise of efficiency and impartiality.

The third most dramatic impact of the "neoliberalization" of academia, according to Hanley (2005), has to do with the casualties of the new labor practices. He illustrates this with some statistics coming from the American Association of University Professors (AAUP, 2003; Bok, 2003). At that time, 44.5% of all faculty were part time, and all types of non-tenure track faculty amounted to 60%, a percentage that continues to rise. The most dramatic casualty is the long-standing practice of tenure-track academic positions, the bastion that protects academic freedom of research and speech in the classroom and outside of it. Hanley (2005) even goes on to say that "American academics live in a post-tenure university" (p. 3) and indicates how "academic life in the United States mutates at an ever faster pace" (p. 3). Worst of all is that the real impacts of this academic capitalism have not been discussed or resisted by most faculty. The most dramatic impact of this process of weakening of tenure is the removal from faculty of decision making concerning programs, curricula, evaluation, curiosity-driven research, new faculty review for appointments, academic events, and regulations. Unfortunately, these decisions are in effect made from outside by donors or even contractors whose main interest is to make money and/or to foster good will to their benefit.

The other labor practice that is objectionable is the use of the casual labor of contingent faculty members. They serve at the will of administrators and are therefore subject to their political and economic agenda. They are, thus, academic employees with no de-facto academic freedom and stability. Their positions are flexible, cheaper, and have fewer benefits, if any, than tenured faculty. As Hanley (2005) puts it, these new labor practices have tremendously devastating consequences for the academic profession. It is resulting in nothing less than the de-professionalization of academia. Of course, as Hanley argues, some administrative personnel and upper faculty (depending on the field of expertise) benefit from these changes. They may be close to retirement from academia and are seeking connections for their post-retirement managerial positions in the industry.

Unfortunately, faculty professional organizations have been very slow in responding, and they seem more engrossed in "self-idealization" than in defending their own academic profession. Subverting the academic functions to market driven internal and external forces is not inexorable argue Slaughter and Rhoades (2005). The building of countervailing power should start with information and conscientization. Most faculty are unaware of the danger of the neo-liberalization of academia that is no less than de-professionalization, putting in jeopardy the future of higher education.

NCLB as an Example of Oppressive Education Policies

The deceitful message of NCLB and its clone "Race to the Top" in recent policy has incremented its oppressive power in that people who have been hurt by it still believe that the intentions are good but need more funding. However, when we examine its true intentions and implications, we discover painfully the market-driven values for privatization of public education (Emery & Ohanian, 2004; Giroux, 2002, 2004b). As a result, we witness the dehumanization of children and teachers who are seen more as commodities than as persons with agency (Meier & Wood, 2004; Valenzuela, 2005). Democratic education and solidarity have been assaulted and replaced by standards, testing, and accountability as if schools were businesses. Angela Valenzuela (2005) writes of the insidious nature of this movement as it plays out in Texas. "The state's version of accountability, which is at its core a business model, played into the hands of an emerging conservative political and economic elite, helping advance a privatization

agenda aimed at implementing their ultimate form of accountability—the market" (p. 263). This is the true intent of the NCLB policy
that has its origins in Texas. Furthermore, the NCLB policy has a
far-reaching agenda that dares to mandate the so-called "scientific-based research" as the only valid and fundable approach. There
are powerful interests that have propelled the passage of this law.
For instance, the Cato Institute, the Fordham Foundation, the
Heritage Foundation, the Hudson Institute, the Manhattan
Institute, and others receive money from such wealthy benefactors
as Joseph Coors, David Packard, John Walton, and Texas' own
James P. Leininger. These institutions' main focus is to "discredit
public education and open education as a new market for profit,
and consolidate a 'conservative world view'" (p. 267). In fact,
Leininger's public policy think tank the Texas Public Policy Foundation (TPPF), labors under the umbrella of the Children's Educational Opportunity Foundation, which promotes vouchers or, as
they call them, "scholarships" for families through the Horizon
Program (Valenzuela, 2005). These same groups promote education policy research as well.

The most conservative pundits, including those who promote
the scientifically based research, would have us believe that the
discussion about educational research approaches is over and
complete or, as Neuman (2002) proclaims, we now know that *only
scientifically based research* is demanded in the policy initiative of
NCLB. This requirement implies that education researchers must
emulate the medical model of randomized experiments, trials,
treatments /interventions, statistical analysis, and so forth.

This narrow conception of scientific research puts us back at
least five decades with respect to the debates about practice and
conceptualization of educational research. It forces us to begin
again with a justification of alternatives that are more responsive
to human nature, instead of emulating medical models or natural
sciences methods that objectify human beings and are irrelevant
for solving real social problems. In this way, conventional research continues to contemplate the world without transforming it.

Paralyzing Postmodernism/Poststructuralism

As if we did not have enough problems with the takeover of the educational systems by neoliberal capitalism in education, some trends of postmodernism and poststructuralism put conceptual strings on our collective struggles for social transformation, justice, and attempts to take back public education from the tentacles of the market sucktopus. They critique the metanarrative of transformation or liberation and consider it impossible to reach consensus for collective actions. Nonetheless, we consider that postmodernism and poststructuralism have many virtues, but also paralyzing characteristics. The positive sides of postmodernism (the virtues) have an enchanting effect on people that have been marginalized and/or are in disagreement with the establishment. Lyotard (1984) espoused postmodernism in reaction to commodification and technologization of education and knowledge which had been reduced to skills and competences susceptible to measurement. Lyotard questions the so called "metanarratives" by which the establishment—often the Eurocentric white male validates thinking, writing, and speaking, and relationships as well. These metanarratives refer to fundamental concepts such as truth, epistemological certitude, liberating and emancipatory projects, and critical understanding of reality. Postmodernists/post-structuralists (Lyotard, 1984; Lather, 1991, 1998) argue that these goals and principles are foundational, rationalist, essentialist, and therefore part of modernist thought which needs to be overcome.

In this new world order, the local, contextual, and personal become central; and at the same time, postmodernists unmasked the deep seated biases such as racism, sexism, classism, Eurocentrism, heterosexism, linguoracism, and so on. We like to use the metaphor of the mermaid, who in mythology would enchant her victims until they succumbed to her. In postmodernism the ideas are often very enchanting (as is the mermaid), which prevents the followers from realizing that this enchantment may lead to the abyss of absolute contingency, which necessarily results in nihilism, fatalism, cynicism, and ultimately brings about a paralyzing state. We argue that an awareness of the fine line between the enchanting qualities of some postmodernist theories and their moving to a paralyzing state is critical to RAP inquirers.

Postmodernism and poststructuralism are not monolithic systems of thought, but they are also employed in art, literature, architecture criticism, and so on; actually, there are multiple understandings of each. According to Beck (1993) there are progressive postmodernists and conservative ones who align with the respective political ideologies. He identifies another, "resistance" postmodernism. This idea refers to a "cultural and adversarial postmodernism" (Lather, 1991, p. 1) and is defined as dialogical, anti-hierarchical, non-dualistic, multivocal, and escapes definitions. It is a rebellion against the established dominant forms of oppression, including ways of knowing, perceiving, thinking, and feeling. For Lather (1998) the postmodernism of resistance is an opposition to the phallocentric dominance of western culture, in which man is the "one who knows." She replaces this idea with uncertainty or "not being sure" as the hallmark of "radical feminism." Unfortunately, by making this contrast, Lather falls into the essentializing of women's and men's nature. Kelly et al. (1999) critique Lather's essentialist framework and her overemphasis on identity and difference. They argue that this overemphasis creates an infinite differentiation among people and hence infinite divisiveness, which incapacitates people from talking and working with one another because, in addition, there is no certainty about anything. We consider this way a dangerous path for postmodern feminism.

Although we consider that postmodernism and poststructuralism have similar characteristics, we acknowledge that each has different origins. Postmodernist theories are centered on aesthetics and history and act as a reaction to modernity projects. On the other hand, the origins of poststructuralist theories are literary criticism and formalist theories of language (Brown & Jones, 2001; Peters & Burbules, 2004). Even though these two strains of thought have different origins, both converge in a similar critique of modernism/structuralist hegemonic issues.

Mainstream postmodern and poststructural critique goes against what constitutes the emancipatory goals and tenets of Research as Praxis (RAP). The following are the major critiques by postmodernists and poststructuralists of modernist theories and practices that directly or indirectly disarticulate the philosophical underpinning of RAP.

Against metaphysics / enlightenment and foundations

Postmodernism's common characteristic is the attack on the Enlightenment and the notion of the universal reason as well as the debunking of all foundational and totalizing theories considered as metanarratives (e.g., Marxism, humanism) that range from reactionary through critical emancipatory metanarrative. At the same time, postmodernists and post-structuralists validate ideas of fragmentation (no cohesiveness, no wholeness, no stability) of the reality and the self. This principle leads to uncertainty, ambiguity of truth, prediction, and knowledge, and therefore, of meaning. We cannot rely on external verities; consequently meaning is provisional. The emphasis is put on the diverse accounts, stories, and contingencies. Everything is local, context-bound. The truth is local, fragmented in little local stories with irreconcilable truths (Foucault, 1972, 1980; Derrida, 1981; Lyotard, 1984; Jameson, 1984; Lather, 1989; Rorty, 1989).

Postmodernists are also opposed to binaries: the logic of western thought traditionally attributes the bad characteristics of the binary to the so-called "weaker" features (e.g., rational vs. emotional, culturally rich vs. culturally deprived, male vs. female, or heterosexual vs. homosexual) (Derrida, 1981); they also critique the notion of boxing categories such as power, class, gender, race, ethnicity (Foucault, 1977).

Another distinctive characteristic of postmodernists is their declared anti-foundational stance. They argue for no origins or final destinations, and for an end to metaphysics because we live in fragmented and ever changing relationships in the world (Beck, 1993; Maclure, 1995). The anti-foundational perspective not only targets approaches to knowledge and morality, but also the very foundations of our institutions, which are referred to as cultural crises (Lankshear, Peters, & Knobel, 1996).

Linguistic Turn. Postmodernists and poststructuralists place language at the center of social relations, identity, and knowledge. Derrida (1981) argues that language is everything. In the same manner, Baudrillard (1988) assures us that language and images have no referent but to one another. There is no point in looking outside language because it does not reflect reality or express thought. There is no truth behind it, no origins, no first, last of deepest things, eternal verities, and no original meanings. For Foucault (1972) power is tied to language and knowledge. In this new context, language is not transparent or just a means to convey thoughts, expressions, and identities. Language constitutes them.

Inquiry/Knowledge/Epistemology. Postmodernist/ poststructuralist research is mostly a deconstruction process in order to destabilize oppositions, binaries, and closure of meaning and possibilities. Deconstruction is not neutral, and it is considered an intervention (Derrida, 1981, p. 93). Understandings are created in discourse; consequently, research is set of writing practices (Maclure, 1995). Knowledge is an interactive creation for understanding reality and life. This knowledge creation is actually a creation of text which is partly autobiographical narrative because it is context bound. Expert knowledge is therefore questioned.

Postmodernists and poststructuralists (e.g., Ellsworth, 1989, Ladson-Billings, 1997; Fine, 1997) contest the notion of emancipation, alleging that it relies on foundational ideas of rationality as the norm for thinking, the goal of dialogue as reaching consensus, and the meta-narratives of liberation. The action research movement in education has been criticized because it is transformative, consciousness raising, and emancipatory. These goals are considered modernist and impossible to achieve. Brown and Jones (2001) address directly the issue of emancipatory claims in the theory, practice, and writing of action/teacher research: "Any emancipatory perspective presupposes values which cannot be agreed upon universally or permanently" (p. 4). Whose interests are to be emancipated? They question the interests behind the emancipatory project and what counts as "improvement" of practice, "How can a researcher 'observe' reality and be part of it, and thus be implicated in its continual creation and recreation?" (p. 5). They also question the foundations upon which empowerment and enlightenment rest. Action research should move away "from a rationalist focus concerned with effecting productive change through a systematic process."

Brown and Jones (2001) as well as Peters & Burbules (2004) consider that the idea of the self (practitioner researcher) as knowable and perfectable is untenable. In like manner, the stressing of practice over theory and the value given to experience as authentic, relevant, and insightful for other educators, as opposed to top-down theories, are not really clearly defined alternatives as most action researchers claim. Brown (1994) points out the excessive relativism as he tries to reconstruct the ideology critique. He argues that relativism brought forward by postmodernists "does not entail a society without standards. Rather, the conjoining of deconstruction and epistemology helps us to recognize where and how the standards are to be established cooperatively, constantly renewed and periodically reshaped" (p. 28). He maintains that cognitive, moral, and civic truths are no longer seen as fixed entities according to a meta-theoretical blueprint, but they are invented in an ongoing self-reflective community. However, he critiques postmodernists because they eschew the moral and political realms. Lyotard (1984) and many other postmodernists reduce them to relativism.

Critique of Postmodernists'/Poststructuralists' Critiques

We ask: at what point do the gems of postmodernism become rubble? The response to this question is an intellectual duty for all critical educators and RAP practitioners before embracing postmodernist endeavors. The enchanting qualities of the gems may blind us to the paradoxes in their theoretical statements and their debilitating impact on social responsibility and political action. Rikowski and McLaren (2002) spell out a strong critique of post-modernism: "[I]n many parts of the capitalist world, postmodern-ist politics still attests to contemporary relevance...it claims to be the only politics available. [We] collectively discern a need to clear the decks of such junk theory and debilitating 'political' posturing because of the urgent tasks ahead...." In the same vein, Helen Raduntz (1998) refers to the problem of postmodernism as a "sterile theoretical cul-de-sac, lacking the social responsibility for transformative action" (p. 14).

Defining postmodernism goes against the same rhetoric that rejects attempts at definitions. Rikowski and McLaren (2002) critique Usher and Edwards (1994) in their "definition" of post-modernism as an "attitude toward life" or a certain "state of mind" that implies a superior theory of thinking and discourse. They posit the obvious flaw of postmodernism: "For us, a commitment to social justice that seeks to end social inequalities is a better 'attitude' to adopt" (p. 4). Rikowski and McLaren find the postmo-dernist work a "celebration of aimless anarchism" (p. 4).

Postmodernism/Post-Structuralism Anti-Metaphysical and Anti-Foundational Critique

First, we need to highlight the gem of postmodernism concerning its anti-metaphysical, anti-enlightenment, and anti-foundational stances. The main gem consists of a strong debunking of the established western thought, full of myths, biases, and exclusions. However, it becomes rubble when it falls into absolute contingen-cy/relativism which engenders solipsism, nihilism, fatalism, hopelessness, and, ultimately, paralysis. Maclure (1995) calls this an "insoluble paradox." The contingency makes it impossible to formulate a coherent discourse about the contingent subject, and to account for political and social interests (Cole, 1994). The lack of rational reflection leads us to give up the critical interrogation of ideologies (McLaren, 1997).

In the same vein as Maclure, Beck (1993), following Dewey, rejects this absolute contingency and points out the need for "enduring interests and ideals." He sees the need for stability and direction for our life projects; even though they may vary in different cultures, they are not eternal or universal. Without this relative stability, people are left without a basis for living. Understanding matters in relation to local context, to a person's experiences, to a historical moment, which is the cul-de-sac of postmodernism, does not necessarily mean lack of direction and principles. We need to ask: what kind of goals and principles? How do we come about them? Brown (1994), referring to these types of relative principles, claims that they can be "cooperatively developed and constantly renewed." He also asks important questions: How can we recover the central role of social theory in forming a democratic public space? Can we create a politically constructive movement for intellectually deconstructive critique?

Rikowski and McLaren (2002), following Cole, Hill, & Rikowski (1996) argue that postmodernism "attempts to negates the Enlightenment project, and with it reason and rationality, along with any attempts to secure 'knowledge'. Meta-narratives, ethics and value, and any appeals to 'truth' are also scuppered" (pp. 4–5). The results have been described, from relativism to paralysis, setting thus the path and the shield for the Radical Right to take over many of the functions of society, especially education, under the slogan of the "Third Way," the lurking conservative branch of postmodernism. In political action and social movement, the impact of this "postmodernist turn" on educational theory, policy, and perspectives, is more of degeneration than advancement. The educational institutions have fallen into a stronghold of postmodern discussions, while the corporatization of education is advancing in making these institutions work toward their interests of preparing a skilled labor force.

Self as fragmented, unstable, not in control. A gem in postmodern thought is its acknowledgment of the dangers of essentializing, normalizing, and marginalizing those who are different from the norms in power. Postmodernists and poststructuralists promote the characteristics of the self as multiple, diverse, fragmented, unstable, "not so sure", transient, not completely knowable, not perfectable, and not in control of the situation (Rorty, 1989; Lather, 1998). However, Beck (1993) responds to this type of postmodernist self by arguing that individuals are unified as cultures and have considerable capacity of self-knowledge, expression, and regulation. Meanwhile, Foucault (1977) describes the human subject as contested and shifting in the intersection of different discourses. In other words, subjects are constructed as discourses. Maclure (1995) contests this idea by asking: How can we dismiss the living oppressed subjects? In addition, it is important to consider that there are other non-discursive conditions of the subject that are real and urgent to change. We need to keep in mind that subjects are not exhausted in language or language games either.

In discussing the limitations of postmodernism, Cole (1994) disputes the idea of the contingency of our own subjectivity, which for him is logically diluted and practically disastrous. For him, the infinite textuality of the constituted subject with minute dependency and evasions is unsustainable because of its unrootedness. We too consider that it is not possible to think of the subject as having agency within the postmodern infinite textuality without falling into absolute relativism and from this to fatalism.

The postmodern engendered fatalism which Jenny Bourne (2002) calls the "game of despair" hinders any possibility of political action. For her, politics in postmodernism has been built on the notion of identity and difference that leads to the fragmentation of "selves,", a lack of the central features of personhood, the infinite differentiation among people, and lack of reasons to relate to others and actively resist capitalism. Following this postmodern critique to the more stable characterization of the self, we can see how this "gem" of postmodernism is reduced to rubble by causing its proponents to fall into the abyss of instability, confusion, anarchy, hopelessness, powerlessness, and solipsism.

Language and discourse. Postmodernists and poststructuralists transformed the role of language in society and in academia.

Derrida (1974) proclaims that language is everything. We consider that the postmodern and poststructuralist gem concerning language repositions it as constitutive and a link in socially organized human activity. Language can be action in itself as in speech acts. However, language games cannot cover all the possible and the most impacting actions to change the world for the better. We can say that through language we change the word, but not the world in all the dimensions that need to be changed.

There are other nonlinguistic conditions, characteristics, and actions of humans and of reality we need also to attend. They may be intertwined with discourses, but we cannot discount their own existence and impact on our lives beyond the linguistic interactions and constructions. Reducing everything to language games is sterile and irresponsible at best. Rikowski and McLaren (2002) point out that postmodernism's excessive reliance on discourse and its limitless games results in not paying enough attention to the structural constraints set by capitalism and its social relations.

Research, knowledge and epistemology. Concerning research, knowledge, and epistemology the gems held by postmodernists and poststructuralists include the rejection of the pretended neutrality of researcher, the acceptance of socially constructed knowledge (creation), not just discovery; and the questioning of the expert role, the important role of language for studying and understanding all human activity.

The issues with postmodern research start when inquiry results are reduced mainly to the transformation of self-narratives. The reasons are based on the ideas of multiple and very different realities, the lack of universality, consensus, certainty, and direction. Actually, the main changes are centered on the change of words and not in changing the world. Therefore, there is implied a dismissal of liberation projects, collective actions, and transformation of life conditions beyond the mere discourse about them. Consequently, having dreams of a better world and the required organization and collective struggles is discounted as impossible, or the product of romantic minds at best.

Postmodernists characterize knowledge as ambiguous, unstable, and uncertain; thus, language adapts better to these new characteristics of knowledge (Beck, 1993). Beck considers this characterization as an exaggeration. It is true that we need to adapt in accordance to the circumstances, but we also should employ reason as well as feelings and intuition. We need to set ends and means to achieve our goals in life. "Theory, understood as a loose interconnection of qualified generalizations, is crucial for daily living" (p. 7)

Educational Impact of These Oppressing Systems

Hope is crucial for radical changes to take place (Fromm, 1968; Freire, 1994). Unfortunately, fatalism is part and parcel of actors in neoliberal global capitalism, and in strands of poststructuralism/postmodernism that have fallen into absolute contingency. Fatalism is a pervasive common denominator of the neoliberal ideology as seeded in every sector of society including the educational arena. Like a sucktopus, fatalism extracts life, hope, and agency, and infuses the poison of hopelessness and despair (Freire, 2005). It manifests itself in a conditioned idea of an inexorable future. It is a very powerful tool for the stagnation of social movements that stymie, the possibility of thought outside the boundaries of the thinkable as authorized within these systems.

Fatalism facilitates dehumanization of people, especially those more vulnerable individuals in society, educational systems, and research processes: the poor, the subordinated, the young, the old, women, or ethnic minorities, to name a few. The commoditization under this trend is clear—everything and everyone has a price. Children are no longer human beings; they have become products in the form of test scores. According to this business ideology, what has become important is the performance of the school and not the meaningful learning of the children, and even less their well-being. Knowledge production, dissemination, and consumption have been corporatized. Educational research is also part of the cyclical corporatization trend whose products help legitimize the patronizing discourse that blames the victims, under the guise of scientifically-based research.

As part of the dehumanization process, teachers and children become disposable when they do not meet the goals and expectations of the system. They are treated as a means to achieve the ends of those at the top of the educational system, the government and its corporate profiteers. Humanization as Freire (1992, 2003, 2005) and Fromm (1968) propose is the principle that humans are ends in themselves and that the ends never justify the means to achieve them. Any system (social, educational, economic) that does not respect these principles is dehumanizing. Unfortunately, the NCLB is another frontal attack on public education aimed at privatization of schools when children do not meet the goal imposed on them and their teachers (Meier & Wood, 2004; Valenzuela, 2005). This dehumanization is not the main purpose of NCLB, rather it is a tool to create failure within the public school system, thus justifying the privatization of schools. As Chomsky in *The Corporation* (Bakan et al., 2003) argues, the privatization of public service is not given to a "nice" person but to an unaccountable tyranny.

The corporate (for profit) media have become part and parcel of everything that has to do with communication of information to the public. Ben Bagdikian's (2004) *The New Media Monopoly* demonstrates how media power is political power. He distinguishes two worlds: the 'flesh and blood world' in which we live, and the world created by the media. More and more, these two worlds are becoming separate. The incorporation of the media has shrunk to five mega corporations, creating an oligopoly. They have become adjuncts and allies of government and elites, helping them to promote their policies, and worse, covering up corruption, mismanagement, abuses, and lies, while at the same time obliterating dissent (Chomsky, 1989). The media go further, as Chomsky notes, establishing the boundaries of the thinkable. The corporate media are not only helping the elites and big corporations, but they themselves are lobbying and even writing the policies (e.g., energy, communications, NCLB) that favor their own agendas. Educational policies (an example being NCLB) are blatant examples of how media manufacture consent and obliterate dissent (Coles, 2003; Metcalf, 2002). Another example, of corporate media helping the government to promote policy is Armstrong Williams, who was paid $240,000 to comment on the benefits of NCLB and promote this policy on his television program (Rendall, 2005).

The corporatization of all areas of society, including education has resulted in what Chomsky (Chomsky 2000) refers to as an "assault on solidarity." He argues that corporations are totalitarian systems. "Corporations are not benevolent societies. The board of directors of a corporation has the legal obligation to be a monster. They are not supposed to do nice things" (p. 1), but rather, they are accountable to the stakeholders of the company, not to the people they are supposedly "serving." Profit is the bottom line. "The effect that we expect is the undermining of solidarity and collaboration and other 'subversive' notions of mutual support, solidarity, sympathy and caring for other people" (p. 2). He transcribes the declaration of Lehman Brothers about getting into education to make money. "Look, we've taken over the health system, we've taken over the prison system, the next big target is the educational system, so we can privatize the educational system, make a lot of money out of it" (p. 1). The bankruptcy of this company is a good testimony of the incompatibility of a social service, such as education and the business model, which really do not mix.

The oppressing systems described above have had tremendous impact on research in various ways. Postmodernists/post-structuralists and conventional researchers (qualitative and quantitative) use what Bakhtinians would call a "balcony" research approach. That is, the researchers basically observe and describe the world from above, from their own perspectives and categories, and for their own benefit first of all. These research practices do not include as a *sine qua non* condition to be socially responsive and hence of benefit for research participants. For instance, the achievement gap (between white and minority students) is nowadays heavily studied and addressed in policies; it is "out there" in the public discourse and a major concern for most educators. The NCLB policy, as Anyon (2005) argues, was tailored for bridging such a gap; however, as it is our daily experience in schools where the NCLB has a major impact, especially in poor minority urban communities, the gap is widening. Actually, this gap is created by misleading policies, which support corporate tests and textbooks that privilege white middle class experiences leaving behind all the others who do not share those experiences (Valenzuela, 2005; Meier & Wood, 2004; Nichols & Berliner 2007). Gloria Ladson-Billings' (2006) keynote address at the 2006 AERA conference argued that the focus on this achievement gap is misplaced; instead, we should focus on the "education debt" as the accumulated deficit in equity and equality in their education. To explain the difference, she draws on the analogy of "national debt" as different from a budget deficit. In other words, the problems with minority students' lack of achievement and school dropout cannot be explained by asserting the deficit of students and their families and cultures, but on accumulated deficits in the quality of education and other social services. Added to this is the vicious racism, classism, hegemony of standard English, and so on, most minority students face on a daily basis in schools. Actually, the *education debt* includes socio-political, moral, historical, and economic components. Thus, education researchers should embrace the task of working to expose the factors of the education debt and address bridging the infamous achievement gap. Today, most research on educational issues is just a holographic view of the same apparent problem with no attempt to challenge the system to address the disparity of quality education for poor and minority children.

Concluding Remarks

The previous section on denouncing the oppressing systems also establishes the main reasons why research as praxis (RAP) is so relevant today. It is important to allude here to Marx and Engels's (1970/1845) "11th Thesis on Feuerbach": "The philosophers have only *interpreted* the world, in various ways; the point is to *change* it" (p. 23). This idea of transformation is central to RAP—research in the public interest, which is sorely needed today in education as well as in many other domains. We celebrate that in 2006, the American Educational Research Association, under the presidency of Gloria Ladson-Billings, had as its annual conference theme "Research in the Public Interest." The authors of her co-edited book with William Tate Anyon, Ayers, Apple, Molnar, Cornbleth, among others) entitled *Education Research in the Public Interest: Social Justice, Action and Policy* concur that these are times for action to change policies that are harmful, and that these concepts should be at the center of the education research agenda. The following section on "Announcing Possibilities", following Freire's (2005) framework, includes the theoretical grounding of the RAP principles and the enactment of democracy and political action.

References

American Association of University Professors AAUP. (2006). Contingent appointments and the academic profession. In AAUP, *Policy Documents and Reports,* 10*th* ed. Washington, D.C.

American Educational Research Association. (2006). Standards for reporting empirical social science research in AERA publications. *Educational Researcher, 35*(6), 33–40.

American Educational Research Association. (2009). Standards for reporting on humanities-oriented research in AERA publications. *Educational Researcher, 38*(6), 481–486.

Anyon, J. (2006). What should count as educational research: Notes toward a new paradigm. In G. Ladson-Billings & W. F. Tate (Eds.), *Education research in the public interest: Social justice, action, and policy.* New York, NY: Teachers College Press.

Anyon, J. (Ed.). (2005). *Radical possibilities* New York, NY: Routledge.

Apple, M. (2004). *Ideology and curriculum* (3rd ed.). New York, NY: Routledge Falmer.

Apple, M. (2006). Interrupting the right: On doing critical educational work in conservative times. In G. Ladson-Billings & W. F. Tate (Eds.), *Education research in the public interest: Social justice, action, and policy* (pp. 27–45). New York, NY: Teachers College Press.

Ayers, W. (2006). Trudge toward freedom: Educational research in the public interest. In G. Ladson-Billings & W. F. Tate (Eds.), *Education research in the public interest.* New York, NY: Teachers College Press.

Bagdikian, B. H. (2004). *The new media monopoly.* Boston: Beacon Press.

Bakan, J., Crooks, H., & Achbar, M. (Writers). (2003). The corporation [Video]. In M. Achbar & B. Simpson (Producer). Canada: Distributed by Zeitgeist Film.

Bakhtin, M. M. (1986). The problem of speech genres (V. W. McGee, Trans.). In C. Emerson & M. Holquist (Eds.), *M. M. Bakhtin: Speech genres and other late essays* (pp. 60–102). Austin, TX: University of Texas Press.

Baudrillard, J. (1988). *Selected writings*. Oxford, UK: Polity Press.

Beck, C. (1993). Postmodernism, pedagogy, and philosophy of education. In EPS/PES (Ed.), *Philosophy of Education Society: Yearbook-1993.*

Berliner, D. C., & Biddle, B. J. (1995). *The manufactured crisis: Myths, fraud, and attack on America's public schools*. Reading, MA: Longman.

Bok, D. (2003). *Universities in the marketplace: The commercialization of higher education*. Princeton, NJ: Princeton University Press.

Bourne, J. (2002). Racism, postmodernism and the flight from class. In D. Hill, P. McLaren, M. Cole, & G. Rokowski (Eds.), *Marxism against postmodernism in educational theory* (pp. 195–210). Lanham, MD: Lexington Books.

Boyles, D. R. (2005). *Schools or markets? Commercialism, privatization, and school-business partnerships*. Mahwah, NJ: Lawrence Erlbaum Associates.

Broad, R., & Cavanagh, J. (2008, November 14). Swear Off 'Market Fundamentalism'. *Seattle Post-Intelligencer*. Retrieved from. http://www.commondreams. org/view/2008/11/14-6.

Brown, R. H. (1994). Reconstructing social theory after the postmodern critique. In H. W. Simons & M. Billig (Eds.), *After postmodernism: Reconstructing ideology critique* (pp. 12–37). London, England: Sage Publications.

Brown, T., & Jones, L. (2001). *Action research and postmodernism*. Buckingham, UK: Open University Press.

Chomsky, N. (1989). *Necessary illusions: Thought control in democratic societies*. Cambridge, MA: South End Press.

Chomsky, N. (2000, May 12). Assaulting solidarity privatizing pducation. *ZNet Daily Commentaries*, Retrieved in October 30, 2010 from http://www. commondreams.org/view/2008/11/14-6.

Cole, M., Hill, D., McLaren, P., & Rikowski, G. (2001). *Red chalk: On schooling, capitalism, and politics*. Brighton, UK: Institute for Education Policy Studies.

Cole, S. E. (1994). Evading the subject: The poverty of contingency theory. In H. W. Simons & M. Billig (Eds.), *After postmodernism: Reconstructing ideology critique* (pp. 38–57). London, UK, & Thousand Oaks, CA: Sage Publications.

Cole, M., Hill, D., & Rikowski, G. (1996). Between postmodernism and nowhere, for a critique of N. Blake 'Between postmodernism and anti-modernism: The predicament of educational studies. *British Journal of Educational Studies, 44*(1), 371-393.

Coles, G. (2003). *Reading the naked truth: Literacy, legislation, and lies*. Portsmouth, NH: Heinemann.

Cornbleth, C. (2006). Curriculum and students: Diverting the public interest. In G. Ladson-Billings & W. F. Tate (Eds.), *Education research in the public in-*

terest: Social justice, action, and policy (pp. 199–212). New York, NY: Teachers College Press.

Derrida, J. (1974). *Of grammatology* (G. B. Spivak, Trans.). Baltimore, MD: Johns Hopkins University Press.

Derrida, J. (1981). *Positions* (A. Bass, Trans.). Chicago, IL: The University of Chicago Press.

Dorfman, A. (1983). *The empire's new clothes: What the Lone Ranger, Babar, and other innocent heroes do to our minds.* New York: Pantheon Books.

Ellsworth, E. (1989). Why doesn't this feel empowering? Working through the repressive myths of critical pedagogy. *Harvard Educational Review, 59,* 297–324.

Emery, K., & Ohanian, S. (2004). *Why is corporate America bashing our public schools?* Portsmouth, NH: Heinemann.

Feuer, M., Towne, L., & Shavelson, R. (2002). Scientific culture and educational research. *Educational Researcher, 31*(8), 4–14.

Fine, M. (1997). Letter to Paulo In P. Freire, J. W. Fraser, D. Macedo, T. McKinnon & W. T. Stokes (Eds.), *Mentoring the mentor: A critical dialogue with Paulo Freire* (pp. 89–98). New York, NY: Peter Lang.

Foucault, M. (1972). *The archeology of knowledge and the discourse on language.* New York, NY: Pantheon Books.

Foucault, M. (1977). *Discipline and punishment: The birth of the prison* (A. Sheridan, Trans.) London, England: Harmondsworth Penguin.

Foucault, M. (1980). *Power/Knowledge: Selected interviews and other writings 1972-1977* (C. Gordon, L. Marshall, J. Mepham & K. Soper, Trans.). New York, NY: Pantheon Books.

Freire, P. (1992). *Pedagogy of the oppressed.* New York, NY, Continuum.

Freire, P. (2003). *El grito manso [The gentle shout].* Buenos Aires, Argentina: Siglo XXI Editores.

Freire, P. (2005). *Pedagogy of indignation.* Boulder, CO: Paradigm Publishers.

Freire, P. (1994). *Pedagogy of hope.* New York, NY: Continuum.

Fromm, E. (1968). *The revolution of hope: Toward a humanized society.* New York, NY: Harper and Row.

Giroux, H. (2002). Neoliberalism, corporate culture, and the promise of higher education. The university as a democratic public sphere. *Harvard Educational Review, 74*(2), 425–463.

Giroux, H. (2004a). Neoliberalism and the demise of democracy: Resurrecting hope in dark times. *Dissident Voice.* Retrieved from www.dissidentvoice.org /Aug04/Giroux0807.htm.

Giroux, H. A. (2004b). *The terror of neoliberalism: Authoritarianism and the eclipse of democracy.* Boulder, CO: Paradigm Publishers.

Hanley, L. (2005). Academic capitalism in the new university. *The Radical Teacher* (73), 3-7. Retrieved from http://www.jstor.org/stable/20710307

Herman, E., & Chomsky, N. (1988). *Manufacturing consent; The political economy of the mass media.* New York: Pantheon Books.

Hess, F. M. (Ed.). (2008). *When research matters: How scholarship influences education policy.* Cambridge, MA: Harvard Education Press.

Horn, R. A. (2004, April). *The new federal definition of scientific educational research: Implications for educators who engage in non-positivistic research.* Paper presented at the American Educational Research Association, New Orleans, LA..

Howe, K. R. (2009). Epistemology, methodology, and education sciences. *Educational Researcher, 38*(6), 428–440.

Jameson, F. (1981). *The political unconscious: Narrative as a socially symbolic act.* Ithaca, NY: Cornell University Press.

Kelly, J., Cole, M., & Hill, D. (1999, September). *Resistance postmodernism and the ordeal of the undecidable: A Marxist critique.* Paper presented at the British Educational Research Association Annual Conference, Brighton, UK.

Klein, N. (2007). *The shock doctrine: The rise of disaster capitalism.* New York, NY: Metropolitan Books.

Klein, N. (2008, October 27). Bailout profiteers. Online posted to http://www.naomiklein.org/articles/2008/10/bailout-profiteers.

Ladson-Billings, G. (1997). I know why this doesn't feel empowering: A critical race analysis of critical pedagogy. In P. Freire, J. W. Fraser, D. Macedo, T. McKinnon, & W. T. Stokes (Eds.), *Mentoring the mentor: A critical dialogue with Paulo Freire* (127–141). New York, NY: Peter Lang.

Ladson-Billings, G. (2006). From the achievement gap to the education debt: Understanding achievement in U.S. schools. *Educational Researcher, 35*(7), 3–12.

Ladson-Billings, G., & Tate, W. F. (Eds.). (2006). *Education research in the public interest: Social justice, action, and policy* (pp. 17–26). New York, NY: Teachers College Press.

Lankshear, C., Peters, M., & Knobel, M. (1996). Critical pedagogy and cyberspace. In H. Giroux, C. Lankshear, P. McLaren & M. Peters (Eds.), *Counter-narratives: Cultural studies and critical pedagogies in postmodern spaces* (pp. 1-40). New York, NY: Routledge.

Lather, P. (1989). Postmodernism and the politics of enlightenment. *Educational Foundations, 3*(3), 7–28.

Lather, P. (1991). *Getting Smart: Feminist research and pedagogy with/in the postmodern.* New York, London: Routledge.

Lather, P. (1998). Critical pedagogy and its complicities: A praxis of stuck places. *Educational Theory, 48*(4), 487–497.

Lather, P. (2008). New wave utilization research: (Re)Imagining the research/policy nexus. *Educational Researcher, 37*(6), 361–364.

Lyotard, J. F. (1984). *The postmodern condition: A report on knowledge* (G. Bennington & B. Massumi, Trans.). Minneapolis, MN: University of Minnesota Press.

Macedo, D. (2006). *Literacies of power: What Americans are not allowed to know* (Expanded ed.). Boulder, CO: Westview.

Macedo, D., & Goumari, P. (Eds.). (2006). *The globalization of racism*. Boulder, CO: Paradigm Publishers.

Maclure, M. (1995). Postmodernism: A postscript. *Educational Action Research*, *3*(1), 105–116.

Marx, K., & Engels, F. (1970/1845). *The German ideology* (International Publishers, Trans.). New York, NY: International Publishers.

McLaren, P. (1997). *Revolutionary multiculturalism: Pedagogies of dissent for the new millennium*. Boulder, CO: Westview.

Meier, D., & Wood, G. (Eds.). (2004). *Many children left behind: How the No Child LeftBbehind act is damaging our children and our schools*. Boston, MA: Beacon Press.

Metcalf, S. (2002, January 28). Reading between the lines. *The Nation*, 1–7.

Molnar, A. (1996). *Giving kids the business: The commercialization of American schools*. Boulder, CO: Westview.

Molnar, A. (2005). *School commercialism: From democratic ideal to market commodity*. New York, NY: Routledge.

Molnar, A. (2006). Public intellectuals and the university. In G. Ladson-Billings & W. F. Tate (Eds.), *Education research in the public interest: Social justice, action, and policy* (pp. 64–80). New York, NY: Teachers College Press.

National Commission on Excellence in Education. (1983). *A nation at risk: The imperatives for education reform*. Washington, DC: US Department of Education.

National Reading Panel. (2000). *Teaching children to read: Report of the National Reading Panel*. Washington, DC: National Institute of Child Health and Human Development.

National Research Council. (2002). *Scientific research in education*. Washington, DC: National Academic Press.

Neuman, S. (2002). *Scientific-based evidence*. US Department of Education. Retrieved from http://www.ed.gov/nclb/research/reyna.html. Accessed March 6, 2002.

Nichols, S. L., & Berliner, D. C. (2007). *Collateral damage: Testing corrupts American schools*. Cambridge, MA: Harvard Education Press.

Peters, M. A., & Burbules, N. C. (2004). *Poststructuralism and educational research*. Lanham, MD: Rowman and Littlefield Publishers.

Porfilio, B., & Yu, T. (2006). Students as consumers: A critical narrative of commercialization of teacher education. *Journal for Critical Education Policy Studies*, *4*(1). Retrieved from http://www.jceps.com/ ?pageD=article &article ID=56.

Raduntz, H. (1998, March). *Researching and rebuilding a Marxian educational theory: Back to the drawing board*. Paper presented at the Australian Association for Education Research, Adelaide, Australia.

Rahman, M. A. (1994). *People's self development: Perspectives on participatory action research: a journey through experience*. Dhaka, Bangladesh: University Press Limited.

Rendall, S. (Writer) & Goodman, A. (Director). (2005). FAIR on Bush admin funding of Armstrong Williams: "The government is running a domestic propaganda operation secretly targeting the American people" [*Democracy Now*]. In S. A. Kouddous (Producer). Retrieved from http://www. democracy-now.org/2005/1/1.

Rikowski, G., & McLaren, P. (2002). Postmodernism in education theory. In D. Hill, P. McLaren, M. Cole, & G. Rikowski (Eds.), *Marxism against postmodernism in educational theory* (pp. 3–12). Lanham, MD: Lexington Books.

Rorty, R. (1989). *Contingency, iron, and solidarity.* New York, NY: Cambridge University Press.

Rust, E. (1999). *No turning back: A progress report on the Business Roundtable Education Initiative.* Washington, DC: Business Roundtable.

Saltman, K. J. (2005). *The Edison Schools: Corporate schooling and the assault to public education.* New York, NY: Routledge.

Selingo, J. (2003, February 28). The disappearing state in higher education. *Chronicle of Higher Education, 49.*

Slaughter, S., & Leslie, L.L. (1997). *Academic capitalism: Politics, policies and the entrepreneurial university.* Baltimore, MD: Johns Hopkins University Press.

Slaughter, S., & Rhoades, G. (2004). *Academic capitalism and the new economy: Market, state, and higher education.* Baltimore, MD: Johns Hopkins University Press.

St. Pierre, E. A. (2002). "Science" rejects postmodernism. *Educational Researcher, 31*(8), 25–27.

Steinberg, S., & Kincheloe, J. J. (1995). Introduction. In P. McLaren, T. Hammer, D. Sholle, & S. Reilly (Eds.), *Rethinking media literacy: A critical pedagogy of representation* (pp. 225–259). New York, NY: Peter Lang.

Steinberg, S., & Kincheloe, J. J. (1997). Introduction: No more secrets-- Kinderculture, information saturation, and the postmodern childhood. In S. Steinberg & J. J. Kincheloe (Eds.), *Kinderculture: The corporate construction of childhood.* Boulder, CO: Westview Press.

Torres, M. N., & Mercado, M. (2007). The need of critical media literacy in the teacher education core curriculum. In D. Macedo & S. Steinberg (Eds.), *Media literacy: A reader* (pp. 537–558). New York, NY: Peter Lang.

Torres, M., & Reyes, L. V. (2005). *Legacy of the Bakhtin Circle for reorienting the philosophy, object of study, and teaching of human languages, CD Conference Proceedings, Jyväskylä.* Paper presented at the XII International Bakhtin Conference, Finland, July 18–22.

US Department of Education Office of Elementary and Secondary Education. (2002). *No Child Left Behind: A desk reference.* Retrieved October 27, 2010, from http://www.ed.gov/policy/elsec/leg/elsea02/html.

U.S Government Patent Policy Act of 1980, H.R. 6933 C.F.R. (1980).

Usher, R., & Edwards, R. (1994). *Postmodernism in education: Different voices, different worlds:* London, UK: Routledge.

Valenzuela, A. (Ed.). (2005). *Leaving children behind: How "Texas-style" accountability fails Latino youth.* New York, NY: SUNY Press.

Voloshinov, V. N. (1973). *Marxism and the philosophy of language* (L. Matejka & I. R. Titunik, Trans.). Cambridge, MA: Harvard University Press.

Yatvin, J. (2002). Babes in the woods: The wanderings of the National Reading Panel. *Phi Delta Kappan, 83*(5), 364-369.

Chapter 2

Announcing Possibilities with Research as Praxis: A Counter-Hegemonic Research Paradigm

Myriam N. Torres & Loui V. Reyes

In Chapter 1 we presented a critical examination of various oppressing systems that make research, specifically in education, an instrument for maintaining the status quo of exclusionary epistemologies and colonizing practices. In this chapter we are proposing Research as Praxis (RAP) as a counter-hegemonic research paradigm grounded on the idea that people of all conditions have the right to participate in generating knowledge and benefiting from it. Lather (1986) characterizes "research as praxis" as a type of emancipatory social science for understanding inequality and inequity in the distribution of social goods, for critiquing the status quo, and for working toward a more just society. We build upon this conception of research as praxis.

We are also inspired by and building upon the movement of Participatory Action Research. First of all, we need to contextualize and clarify why we are using the name Research as Praxis (RAP) instead of Participatory Action Research (PAR). The characterization of RAP is indeed based on the literature and authors of PAR as it has been pioneered in the so-called "Third World countries." The problem of using PAR in the United States today has to do with its widespread misunderstanding and/or co-optation by subsuming it as a "strategy of inquiry" within the qualitative paradigm(s) (Denzin & Lincoln, 2005). The defining characteristic "participatory" tends to be used as a "hook" to gain acceptance from research participants of top-down models and programs (Dorston & Miranda, 2000; Contreras, 2000; Falabella, 2000), a practice which has become common in world organizations. In addition, "participatory" is often confounded with "participant observation", a method of ethnographic research. "Action," the other defining characteristic of PAR, is often despoiled of its transformative and liberating ideals and reduced to instrumental purposes. Consequently, action research has become a technique or "method" for "problem solving" such as implementing social programs or "doing something" about solving an identified problem.

Mariño (1990) discusses the situations where action becomes synonymous with "applied" research in which such action (intervention) actually prevents engagement in transformative action for social change. Our goal is the recuperation of the original principles and wisdom of PAR, situating them in the context of the U.S., postmodernist strands, and the economic globalization of market ideology in society in general and education in particular. We believe, perhaps naively, that by using the term "Research as Praxis," we can recuperate and further advance the philosophical, political, and social underpinnings of Participatory Action Research (PAR). In so doing, we situate this paradigm in a language that is conducive to the original conception of PAR as an endogenous science resulting from people's movements of liberation and transformation.

Concerning the origins of PAR, First World authors such as Kemmis and McTaggart (2005), Masters (1995), Brown & Tandon (1983) track the development of this type of research and seem to suggest that the work of Third World authors and people's movements simply followed the wave initiated by First World authors. Certainly, the history of the PAR movement is quite different depending on who accounts for it. Third World authors (e.g., Rodriguez-Brandão, 2005; Freire, 1992; Fals-Borda, 1976, 1985;

Rahman, 1994; Nariño, 1990; Vio-Grossi, 1978, 1983) document multiple origins in contrast to the supposed linear development described by Kemmis and McTaggart (2005). We consider this phenomenon as "First World centrism," which is visible in many other dimensions of society. A propos, Fals-Borda (1970, 1985, 1991, 1998a, 1998b) explains the multiple origins alleging that PAR is endogenous to people's movements and hence has emerged almost simultaneously in various countries of the Third World, and also in marginal communities of the First World, without apparent communication among them. This dynamic is not a coincidence; they all share past and present experiences of colonialism, oppression, and exploitation at the economic, political, and intellectual levels. RAP has its origins in the popular social movements during the 1960s through the 1970s, especially in the Third World countries (Rodriguez-Brandão, 2005). Actually, RAP inquiry has originated in the convergence of social movements and socially responsive academic work.

RAP as a Philosophy of Life and Work Ruptures with Conventional Research Approaches

Starting the work of recuperation of PAR in the context of the United States, and re-baptizing it as RAP, we should begin by saying that RAP is an existential experience of life and work, which Fals-Borda (1985, 1991a; 1995) calls *vivencia*. *Vivencia* means "inner-life experience" linked to finding fulfillment as human beings committed to social justice and civic responsibility. RAP as *vivencia* involves research, education, and sociopolitical action through grassroots organizations aimed at constructing countervailing power for and by the oppressed and exploited. RAP becomes, thus, a philosophy of life and work, as well as a methodology, with a renewed commitment to improving life conditions of the most marginalized communities in society, and to transform social oppressive structures. This type of work clearly clashes with the academic establishment that calls for a separation of research, teaching, and service activities, and most importantly with the separation of reason from moral commitment and social responsibility as part of the research activity. The convergence between academia and people in the communities, as proposed by the pioneers of this new paradigm, might make academic work more socially responsive and down to earth. At the same time, community work may become more reflective and intellectual, which leads to the enhancement of popular knowledge.

PAR pioneers Hall et al. (1982) and Fals-Borda and Rahman (1991) and their collaborators challenge the monopoly of know-ledge production, which they consider as anchored in enclosed academic circles by self-appointed institutional guardians under the guise of rigor, quality, and scientism. This is exactly what is happening with the trumpeting of "Scientific Research in Educa-tion" (SRE) from the National Research Council (2002). RAP work breaks away from this monopoly of knowledge production by recognizing popular knowledge and valuing it at the same status as academic knowledge. Recognizing the capacity of common people to name and explain their worlds and valuing their know-ledge produced is a way of democratizing research. However, the search for knowledge by RAP investigators is not merely intellec-tual activity but a search for answers to such questions as: know-ledge for what purposes? For whom? By whom? Why? What is transformed? And in whose interest?

RAP as a Distinctive Paradigm of Research with Human Beings

Based on PAR authors, the RAP paradigm can be characterized as breaking with the conventional subject-object relationship to subject-subject dynamics. Rodriguez-Brandão (2005) refers to this shift as going from "object of my research" to "subject of our re-search." In this transformation research, participants are prota-gonists and the outside researchers become supporting actors. Genuine and active participation in the whole process of research creates the conditions for recognizing, valuing, and enhancing popular knowledge and science (Fals-Borda, 1985, 1990). This type of research paradigm involves both academic and popular science and includes not only the study of reality but the apprehension of reality. It is therefore also educational. RAP involves political action toward building countervailing popular power for transforming the life conditions of participants and the more marginalized sectors of society. In other words, RAP is a liberating movement. As Mariño (1990) clarifies, RAP type of work is not just a means for solving problems but for learning to 'apprehend' reality in order to transform it in the public interest.

In studying participants' own reality, the focus is not on isolating a variable to be able to study it scientifically. The focus is, as Fals-Borda (1998a) highlights, the wholeness of reality and the fluidity of the cultural, social, economic, political, and educational dimensions. Therefore, we need to study a given issue in reference to the local and broad context in order to understand that issue and act upon it. The holistic nature of any socio-humanistic phenomenon makes RAP an existential experience *vivencia* (Fals-Borda, 1995, 1991). This term refers not only to work but also to satisfying life and human fulfillment. Characterizing RAP as a *vivencia* implies that it is an *open system* (Fals-Borda, 2002) which is conducive to authentic participation to achieve not only growth but power. It is obvious that this type of research is carried on *by* the people, *with* the people and *for* the people; therefore, it is not neutral, but on the side of the exploited and oppressed, who are the victims of ravaging capitalism, neoliberalism, and market-driven economic and political domestic and foreign policies (Fals-Borda, 1998b).

In this vein, RAP is a heretical movement, as was commonly acknowledged by the participants in the 8th Congress of Participatory Action Research of 1997 held in Cartagena, Colombia (Fals-Borda, 1998b). It goes against the academic research establishment and even against the public notion of scientific research. There were many theoretical frameworks for the heretical characterizations of this paradigm, from existential phenomenology, dialogism, and ethno-methodology to social philosophy and science. Participants in the congress dared to consider this PAR/RAP heretical movement as closer to modern physics than social and educational research based on the positivist paradigm. Modern physics is based on Heisenberg's *indeterminacy principle* relating to subatomic matter characteristics, which Wallerstein (1998) calls "social scientism" of modern physics. As we know, this principle refers to the changing nature of subatomic matter (waves or particles) depending on the instruments of observation and measurement. Similarly, in RAP vivencias, it is recognized that people are indeterminate and their reactions depend on the context and on the instruments of observation and measurement. The goal in RAP is not the accumulation of a decontextualized and ahistorical set of theories and principles of practice but rather to gain knowledge in a collective dialogical process aimed at transformation of reality toward the improvement of human conditions at local and wider levels.

The principle of indeterminacy is at the center of Thomas Kuhn's (1962) argument concerning revolutions in scientific paradigms. Based on this Kuhnian notion of scientific paradigms, de Souza (1990) maintains that PAR/RAP is a *new paradigm of research* with its own philosophical principles, theory, methodology, and procedures. It builds local context theories from joint learning, action, and dialogue. Therefore, it is not a type of research directed to testing theories (Fricke, 2006), nor is it an applied science in which the intervention, most of the time, prevents real collective action for liberation (Mariño, 1990). RAP does not always start with research and end with action. It is a dynamics between theory and action that enhances both (Fricke, 2006). RAP is also a way to integrate the educational process into the civic society by anchoring the schools in the hearts of the community (Niño-Diez, 1998).

RAP Principles: Why Do We Need Principles in RAP?

Are these principles a way of boxing in the RAP paradigm? Who are we to define these principles? Are we falling, hence, into the foundational realm? We argue that the question is not that of having or not having principles. The question should be: What kind of principles? Who benefits from the use of those principles? As stated above, RAP is a philosophy of work and life, rooted in radical democratic participation, both in the research process and in the use of the knowledge in the public interest. For example, RAP relives the principle of radical democracy; however, its enactment will require the deliberation of the part of research participants to determine the specificities of such democratic participation.

Before presenting the main tenets of RAP, let's reflect on what could happen if RAP did not have principles to guide the work of both researchers and participants? Pretending to be authentic and congruent with a general idea of democracy, we could easily fall into a *laissez-faire* situation, which leads us inevitably to an absolute contingency. More specifically, everything depends totally on the local context and conditions. Falling into absolute contingency implies that we cannot reach consensus because everyone has unique circumstances. This trap paralyzes our state of being, preventing us from engaging in liberating causes and social movements because it is considered impossible to achieve any significant degree of agreement with others; therefore, collective understanding and actions are impossible. Hence, solidarity is more an illusion than reality for working collectively. The problem is that stance of absolute contingency ends up supporting the status quo of the hegemonic ideology. This dynamic is what Cole (1994) names "The Poverty of Contingency Theory." Since the liberating causes and movements are paralyzed, they are precluded from questioning this hegemonic ideology and, even worse, from acting as a countervailing power.

This absolute relativism is the problem that some mainstream strands of postmodernist thinkers pose to RAP's principles and goals. Their entrapment in contingency has silenced liberating voices, which in turn allows the hegemonic forces, through an appealing postmodern rhetoric, to pursue their agendas without being challenged.

The previous reflection on the viability of RAP principles gives us the justification for its existence and practicality. We distinguish three major principles that form the philosophical base and guide the RAP work. They are:

1. radical participatory democracy;
2. collective action for transformation toward a better world; and
3. commitment to work for social justice in solidarity with marginalized communities.

Below is a brief description of these principles, followed by an in-depth conceptualization of praxis and the principles of RAP.

First Principle: Radical Participatory Democracy

This is the kernel of RAP–type of work, which leads to an epistemological break in the researcher/researched dyad. It implies a rupture from the conventional asymmetrical subject-object to a horizontal dialogical subject-subject relationship. It is dialogical and hence demands that research participants become co-researchers involved in the decision-making process at all steps in the research process, from the selection of the research topic to the use of the knowledge and the decisions to act upon it. This involvement germinates participants' empowerment and self-reliance. Therefore, the outside researcher(s)' uppermost task is to create the conditions for such a radical democratic participation to take place so that the popular knowledge converges with academic knowledge, and both are equally valued. These conditions and relationships harness countervailing power for transforming oppressing and colonizing social conditions and structures.

Second Principle: Collective Action for Transformation toward a Better World

The participants' countervailing power manifests itself in the collective action for transformation (Rahman, 1994). Collective action requires some advanced degree of consciousness-raising and solidarity. This action for transformation is led by the collective hope of a better world as dreamed of by participants and guided by public interest or common good.

Third Principle: Commitment to Work for Social Justice in Solidarity with the Marginalized Classes

Researchers in RAP vivencias need first to understand their role as "animators" (Fals-Borda, 1985, 1991) and forgers of the conditions for radical democratic participation of the people in the study toward transforming their realities. This commitment in RAP work becomes an existential experience, or as Fals-Borda (1991) calls it, a "vivencia," i.e., a philosophy of life and work. A vivencia is holistic (involves the whole person: cognitive, personal, social, ethical, and political) and includes interplay among research, education, and communitarian work. Before going in depth into RAP principles, we consider it very important to conceptualize what we mean by praxis.

Philosophy of Praxis

"The philosophers have only *interpreted* the world, in various ways; the point is to *change* it" (Marx & Engels, 1970, p. 123)). This is at the core of what it means to do RAP work. Praxis as a theory has a long history. Aristotelian philosophy is considered praxis oriented (Eikeland, 2006). According to Eikeland, Aristotle developed a theory of *phronesis*. We consider that this theory gives us a broad picture of the complexity of praxis as the human activity *par excellence*, which is central to understanding RAP principles. Praxis contrasts with the instrumental and analytical way of thinking about theory-practice relationships, which divides and creates a hierarchy of labor while compartmentalizing reality, including human beings. Thus, wholeness is a distinctive and a *sine qua non* condition for understanding humanness via praxis as the human activity *par excellence*.

Aristotelian Phronesis and the Understanding of Human Praxis

Phronesis for Aristotle is an intellectual and ethical virtue. As an intellectual virtue, *phronesis* is the search for truth. Virtue is what makes anything work at its best. Unlike other intellectual virtues such as Sophia = theoretical wisdom; *nous* = intuitive intelligence; *episteme* = science; *tekhne* = technical reasoning; *deinotes* = cleverness; and *eustokhia* = quickness of mind, that could be either good or bad, *phronesis* must always be good. For Aristotle, the activity of the intellect is lingual–reasoned speech or *logos*. For example, *episteme,* as an intellectual virtue, refers to the theoretical knowledge that is already complete and articulated in language and is independent of actions and interventions. *Episteme* thus does not have the same meaning in modern science (Eikeland, 2006).

Phronesis, as an ethical virtue, is a disposition to act rightfully. It requires perfection by practice and an ensouled body. Other ethical virtues are courage, friendship, justice, and temperance to name a few. Phronesis is nothing without the other ethical virtues. At the other extreme of the continuum are the vices, incompetence, excesses, and deficits. Whereas *phronesis* and *tekhne* are both intellectual virtues and both suggest action; they differ in that phronesis uses deliberation, while *tekhne* uses calculations. Deliberation in phronesis is oriented toward justice and perfection. The deliberative process involves the examination of concrete situations weighing different aims and arguments as it seeks what to do. Phronesis' deliberative process is different from other deliberative processes such as *rhetoric, epistemic,* and *cleverness* in that in phronesis there are no hidden agendas as there may be, for example, in rhetoric (Eikeland, 2006).

Tekhne, as understood by Aristotle, has a place in his philosophy, but it represents only a minimal part of the intellectual activity. Today, however, the meaning of *tekhne* has become the meaning of educational practice, and even the meaning of education. In other words, educational practice and educational research have been reduced to instrumental reasoning (Habermas, 1987) or technical rationality (Schön, 1983), where the manipulation of the effects is what counts. The dominance of technical rationality reduces research to merely technical and methodological matters and suppresses philosophical discussion on important issues such as the purposes, power, control, and politics underlying this instrumentalist vision of research in education.

The Aristotelian understanding of phronesis helps us to illustrate the wholeness and complexity of humanness and human activity, which is at the core of RAP type of work. The focus on mostly or solely instrumental action, as is the case with several trends of action research, leads us to dismiss the richness, and the interactive and interdependent dynamics among cognition (reason) moral obligation (ethics) and political action, which all converge into the notion of *phronesis*.

Marx and Marxist Contributions to Understanding Human Praxis

For Marx, according to Sánchez-Vázquez (1977), praxis becomes the theoretical foundation of philosophy, its consciousness, and its instrument aimed at transforming society and nature, and in turn the human nature. Praxis is at once theoretical and practical. It is the unity between theory and practice in a dialectical relationship. Philosophy cannot transform the world by offering an interpretation of the world, but praxis can make this transformation. Praxis is at the root of knowledge, and it is at once object and end of science. Marx and Engels (1970) critique Feuerbach's "vulgar" materialism concerning the objectification of reality through contemplation (Thesis 1), not as a human conscious activity, which obviously involves subjectivity but it is not limited to it. Research that is not merely a contemplative but a transformative activity changes the world and in turn transforms human beings through human labor. Marx dignified human labor and through labor humanized nature. In other words, human beings are dignified by their labor when it transforms nature, and then humans are transformed as a consequence. However, when the products of

their labor are only external, that is, they have no positive reper-
cussion on their life conditions, labor becomes alienated as are
workers. In brief, human labor can humanize or dehumanize. The
revolutionary praxis that Marx promotes is precisely the humanization of labor and therefore of humans, as opposed to capitalism,
which is based on dehumanized, alienated labor. We find it useful
to elaborate definitions that highlight the distinctive characteristics of praxis. First, activity is an action on specific objects and
distinguishes itself from praxis, a human activity *par excellence,*
because praxis is guided by an ideal result and therefore gives this
human activity both a conscious and an intellectual character.
Second, labor is also one of the human activities *par excellence.*
Therefore, it is a fundamental human praxis that happens in
concrete material social conditions. Labor should be a productive
activity for satisfying human needs; hence, it humanizes tools and
products such as artistic and scientific activities. Labor not only
transforms the object but transforms humans—as social beings—
and their economic, social, and political relationships. Political
activity pursues ends according to the interests of the social
classes and is grounded in a deep and critical understanding of
reality. From this perspective, a conscious and clearly oriented
organization is needed in order to develop strategies and tactics to
advance the transformation of society through a revolutionary
praxis. For Marx, the proletariat is the agent of this revolutionary
praxis.

Engaging in revolutionary praxis requires us to understand
Gramsci's (1971/1950) notion of hegemony as rule and domination
by consent. Hence, understanding reality includes those agendas
and manipulations of the forces of power to normalize and natural-
ize inequity, injustice, exploitation, and oppression. Even common
sense is manufactured with hegemonic ideas. Praxis as human
activity *par excellence* helps us construct counter-hegemonies, thus
transforming our hegemonic common sense into "good" sense as
Gramsci maintains. Dialogue, as understood by Freire, helps in
this pursuit. The praxis of dialogue is a counter-hegemonic way of
communication. Actually, praxis happens within dialogue, not just
follows it.

Following Marx's philosophy of praxis, Hoffman (1975) advances from the premise that praxis does not only contemplate the universe but transform it and that praxis implies action, commitment, and social change. We, as humans, are part of the world we study and we cannot theorize in some kind of detached neutral manner. Thus, epistemology as understood traditionally as a theory of knowledge, does not have sense in a frame of praxis. What is true and what is false can only be demonstrated in the course of praxis itself. In place of the positivist division of theory from practice, objective from subjective, there is "praxical unity" (p. 19). It is critically and passionately concerned with social change. Marxism regards praxis as an authentic dimension of human activity. There is no human nature that cannot change. Hoffman also considers that "Marxism is thus not only the theory of Karl Marx but it is the theory of Marx steeled and tempered, enriched and developed by decades and decades of vital historical experience" (p. 22).

Along the same stream of thought, Bernstein (1971) indicates that Marx wrote "The German Ideology" a year after he wrote the well-known theses on Feuerbach's vulgar materialism (1845). These theses concern the meaning and significance of *praxis*. This concept is central to his thought and key for understanding his analysis of the structure and evolution of capitalism, "social interrelationships," emphasis on the means of production, and "revolutionary praxis."

We need to recognize that not only Marx and Marxists point to the problems of capitalism which negatively affects so many people, except for the big capital holders. Capitalists do so, too. Stephen Mihm (2009) writes about Hyman Minsky's prediction of the current economic meltdown more than a decade ago. Mihm's article is one of very few direct criticisms of the heart of capitalism that we can find in the corporate media, which prefer to blame the victims rather than addressing the roots of this crisis in the very nature of capitalism. Mihm points out Minsky's prediction of the current crisis based on his studies of the financial system within capitalism. Minsky considers that "instability... is an inherent and inescapable flaw of capitalism" (cited by Mihm). Minsky examined the financial system and its cycles and found that in difficult times, both institutions and individuals try to do business careful-ly. This discipline leads to success, and "success breeds a disregard of the possibility of failure" (Minsky cited by Mihm). Consequent-ly, speculation unravels until it gets out of control.

Minsky (1992) focused on the financial system from a theoreti-cal and historical perspective and developed the "Financial Insta-bility Hypothesis," which, as Mihm (2009) notes, fell onto deaf ears. These ideas were and are today opposed to the dominant orthodoxy that maintains that free-market capitalism is a stable basis for the economy. Despite Minsky's (1992) pessimism in counteracting such capitalist orthodoxy with appropriate and timely measures, he considers that this instability can be some-what controlled by regulations. He explains: "The financial insta-bility hypothesis is a model of a capitalist economy which does not rely upon exogenous shocks to generate business cycles of varying severity. The hypothesis holds that historical business cycles are compounded out of i) the internal dynamics of capitalist econo-mies, and ii) the system of interventions and regulations that are designed to keep the economy operating within reasonable bounds" (p. 9). Even though Minsky's critique goes directly to counteract the false premises of capitalism, his solutions remain within the same system. The capitalist orthodoxy seems to bind the thinking even of its detractors.

Participatory / Radical / Grassroots Democracy in Research

This is the most distinctive and differentiating characteristic of RAP. The discussion about the notion of *"participation"* can be rooted in Rousseau, Owen, Mill, and the anarchists Proudhon and Kropotkin, as well as Dewey (Fals-Borda, 1998b). According to Fals-Borda's analytical synthesis, participation is radically defined as "a struggle against political and economic exclusion from exercising control over and access to public resources. This is in stark contrast to the liberal definition of participation which easily falls into demagogy and manufacture of consent. Radical participatory democracy involves symmetrical relationships among participants in the RAP process. It is rooted in the traditions and real histories of common people. With this type of grassroots participation people move from bottom up and periphery to the center (Fals-Borda, 1985). In the same tone, Freire (2005) characterizes *radical democracy* as active and symmetrical participation by ordinary people in dialogical understanding of their realities to name and envision a better world, and work to achieve that dream. This type of grassroots participation has spread out and become a landmark of what has been called the "participative family" (e.g., participatory research, participatory action research, participatory evaluation, participatory budget planning, and participatory rural appraisal). Pilger (2007) distinguishes between liberal democracy and grassroots democracy. He considers that the former was created long ago by and for the elites, while the latter is never handed down; hence it is always fought for and struggled for by real people; it is bottom-up democracy.

Vio-Grossi (1983) warns us that when talking about participation, we should look at the potentialities and limitations in specific contexts and groups. He points out how democratic participation has become perverted in order to serve the interests of those in power who manipulate participation by top-down decisions and reduce it to an acritical participation of people. Mariño (1990) humorously mocks this type of top-down participation as: "I participate, you participate, and 'they decide.'" Freire (2005) asserts that a democratic state is one that respects the freedom of its citizens but does not abdicate its role of regulating social relations for equitable access to social goods. Anisur Rahman brought this idea of *participation* to the ongoing movement of action research, to distinguish PAR from main-stream action research (Fals-Borda, 1998b). Most PAR Third World investigators critique the type of action research movement pioneered by Kurt Lewin because they think it becomes instrumentalist in the service of the status quo, especially when more transformative and liberating actions are rendered unnecessary. In order for people to make bottom-up radical participatory democracy work, they need to organize themselves for purposeful action toward gaining countervailing power. According to Rahman (1991a, 1991b, 1994), traditional notions of organization create and maintain formal power which works against people's power. Organization within the context of radical participatory democracy should be a means for people's participation toward building their own power against exclusion, exploitation, and oppression and toward a better world. People's power transcends people's organization (Rahman, 1994). We may add that the utopia of a better world should be the ultimate goal of people's power.

In the historical analysis of the participatory research movement in Latin America, Rodriguez-Brandão (2005) situates participatory research as a dynamic moment in the action flow of a popular social movement. Popular participation must take place preferentially throughout the investigation-education-action process. From his perspective, research is not the beginning or even the center of this process, but it is a moment in the flow of popular social action. Research is anchored in the grassroots movement. Following the same rationale, Fals-Borda (2002) insists on a grassroots education-plus-research combination to transform the sterilized academic research by inviting academic researchers and school teachers to integrate their efforts and work with the community toward carrying out a true educational process while doing research and field work.

Democracy in the world and in the United States, in particular, has become merely rhetoric. When the ruling class acts in cahoots with corporate power and the government, they become obnoxious, blatantly dictatorial, and shameless corporatocrats (Perkins, 2004, 2007; Chomsky, 2000, 2003). Everything is coordinated to erase true democracy and use it as a catchword of propaganda of market agenda. The neoliberals' and conservatives' *alliance* (Apple, 2004, 2006) based on a minimal agreed upon agenda—*profit*—has domestically and globally triumphed through a comprehensive, coordinated, and well-funded campaign, employing the corporate media megaphones. In their pursuit of profit, humanness becomes irrelevant. RAP, which is rooted on radical participatory democracy, can represent a powerful venue to counteract corporatocracy if we engage in multiple fronts, both inside and outside the different systems.

Epistemological Break

A direct implication of radical democracy is what Fals-Borda (1985, 1991a) calls an "epistemological break," which means a radical change in the relationship between researchers and research participants, from subject-object to subject-subject. That shift implies recognition of people's endogenous intellectual and practical creation of knowledge and power. People's endogenous understandings and power emerge from the study of cultural traditions and life experiences within the context of resistance to hegemonic ways of science-making (Rahman, 1991a, 1994; Fals-Borda, 1985). Thus, the traditional gap between academic knowledge and popular knowledge narrows. The role of the outside researcher (often coming from academia) transforms itself to that of a co-researcher working alongside the working classes.

The epistemological break also involves a rupture from analytical thinking and methodology (one variable at a time) to a "holistic epistemology" (Fals-Borda, 1998b). It implies a departure from the sole emphasis on the cognitive part of knowing to involving ethics, values, commitments, and social responsibilities. As Fals-Borda (2002) puts it, RAP type of research is a break from the Cartesian heritage of separating the mind's work from everything else. Further separation happens when we embrace "commitment" as the hallmark of the role of the outside researcher(s). Thus, as Fals-Borda (1998b) highlights, in RAP type of work, "*What is* can only be defined in the context of *what should be*" (p.163). *What should be* is decided by participants in dialogue within the context of a democratic definition of a better world.

Concerning action research, Fricke (2006) summarizes the core characteristics of the epistemology of Action Research (AR), which in the European tradition overlaps much more with those attributed to RAP: One is the democratic dialogue between the researcher and practitioners for joint reflection and understanding based on work experiences as the basis of participation. Thus, for Fricke, action research is realized through the values of democracy. The ultimate goal is transformation through action, which is the basis for valuing and evaluating the action research project as opposed to the conventional research's concerns with "fixed theoretical criteria" of validity and reliability. Fricke (2006) characterizes the relationship between theory and practice within action research in the following terms:

1. Action research does not lead us to an accumulation of knowledge;
2. Theory is not applied to practice but developed from local context. It's a learning process of both the researchers and the practitioners;
3. There is no individual or group copyright in AR;
4. Theory is not external to practice; it's developed from within social contexts and in joint learning;
5. AR researchers work both inside and outside social change processes (p. 171).

These characteristics of action research are in stark opposition to more conventional academic research.

Breaking with the conventional epistemology also means, as de Souza (1990) claims, that action is epistemologically relevant; that is, action is the subject of knowledge in the context of radical democratic participation of common people. To attain understanding, they need to engage in collective dialogue about the action and all its antecedents, consequences, and participants' roles. In doing so, they transform themselves as both agents and subjects of history.

Dialogue for Promoting Collective Studies and Understanding of Our Realities

Dialogue and dialogism is a philosophy in which ontology, epistemology, and axiology are confluent in the dynamic of being human and being engaged in socially organized activity. From this perspective, being human is being in relation *with* others and in dialogue with others to understand the world (Bakhtin, 1986a; Freire, 1992). Thus, knowing (an epistemological activity) is constitutive of being human; it defines and enhances our humanness. It is not an ancillary activity. A human being is a living process, not an essential abstract entity. This living process is inscribed in values and worldviews, which are deeply axiological. We cannot compare on a one-to-one basis these philosophical principles of dialogism (ontology, epistemology, and axiology) of RAP with those of other paradigms, as Guba and Lincoln (1989) did when comparing qualitative and quantitative research paradigms. Dialogism as characterized by both Freire and Bakhtin does not support these philosophical areas of the conventional philosophies underlying research.

Dialogue, according to Freire (Shor & Freire, 1987) happens in a specific context and historical circumstances. For Freire, dialogue is not just an amicable encounter for social niceties. Rather it is a profound encounter among humans, "to achieve the goals of transformation; dialogue implies responsibility, directiveness, determination, discipline, and objectives" (p. 102). Dialogue also includes a critical understanding of the world in which we live and the forms of collective action aimed at making the world better.

The principles of dialogism articulated by both Freire (1992) and Bakhtin (1986a) can only happen in a situation that is radically democratic, such that dialogue is historical and contextual. For both, dialogue requires horizontality in power relations and mutual trust, which is in itself constructed through dialogue. Dialogue is the encounter of people in order to understand the world and shape it (Freire, 1992). Given that being human means to be in relation to others, the notion of otherness is inherent to dialogue. The relation with the external world is mediated by the relation with other human beings. "At first I am conscious of myself only through others: they give me the words, the forms, and the tonality that constitute my first image of myself" (Bajtn, 1982, p. 360). Consequently, for both Freire and Bakhtin, self-sufficiency is incompatible with dialogical beings, given their incomplete and dynamic nature. Humans are always evolving either to become humanized or dehumanized (Freire, 1992). Their engagement in dialogue needs to be aimed at humanization and hence at understanding and shaping a better world. When an apparent dialogue aims to manipulate participants and make them believe that they are participating in decision making when they are not, we have, according to Freire, an antidialogue. Dialogue has been used as a buzz word to rally people's support for policies that actually go against their own interests. The so-called task forces go into the community they are working with, pass out surveys, or get people to talk; they collect the information, and then they make the top-down policy decisions. This dynamic happens at all levels including academia. A relevant example has to do with the development of standards for reporting research in the AERA publications (American Educational Research Association, 2006, 2009). One of the authors attended one of the sessions where the standards were discussed by the AERA members and conference attendants. The final report does not really reflect the many arguments presented by those opposing the measure.

With similar philosophical perspective, yet situating dialogue into the educational realm, Mercalfe and Game (2008) help us to distinguish between verbal exchanges and genuine dialogue on the basis of relational qualities. For them, genuine dialogue implies that participants meet to do things together and act responsibly to keep the dialogue going and open "beyond self-centered biases and desires" (p. 251). In contrast, a verbal exchange is centered in the subject standing alone with his/her own positions and desires. The authors use Buber's (1970) notions of *I-it* and *I-thou* to draw the differences between exchange (I-it) and dialogue (I-thou). 'I-it' is the Hegelian (ideal, transcendental) subject standing alone that sees the world in terms of his/her "own position and desires." The world's state of affairs becomes a means to the subject's ends, and hence challenges are considered threats. The goal of knowledge acquisition is to increase control of threats and of resources. In contrast, the *I-thou* relation indicates that the *I* is not fixed but always becoming. The world is not a set of external matters but is constitutive and reshaped in our relationships and dialogues. People find their potential by relating to others; hence changes occur relationally, without arising from a subject's desires. These authors clarify the role of dialogue in educational theory in the following terms: "If educational theory loses its ability to recognize dialogue, it loses its ability to understand education as a transformative rather than a simple accumulative process" (p. 346).

As exposed in the previous sections, the principles of dialogism are embedded in RAP. Bakhtin (1986c), in his essay on Methodology of Human Sciences, delineates the difference between doing research in natural sciences from doing so in the human sciences. Research in human sciences, Bakhtin claims, deals with human subjects who are expressive and dialogical beings as opposed to objects who are the focus of the study in the natural sciences. Given that the object of the human sciences is the expressive speaking *being,* it follows that language is the primary data of all human sciences.

Bakhtin (1986c) goes on to differentiate between *knowledge production,* as the result of natural sciences research, and *understanding,* which he considers is the outcome of human sciences research: "The exact sciences are a monological form of knowledge: the intellect contemplates a thing and speaks of it. Here, there is only one subject, the subject that knows (contemplates) and speaks (utters).... But the subject as such cannot be perceived or studied as if it were a thing, since it cannot remain a subject if it is voiceless; consequently, there is no knowledge of the subject but dialogical" (Bajtin, 1982 , p. 383). For Bakhtin, understanding is dialogical, "All true understanding is active and already represents the embryo of an answer. Only active understanding can apprehend the theme (the meaning of the utterance); it is only by means of becoming that meaning can be apprehended.... All understanding is dialogical" (Bakhtin, 1986c, p. 159).

Concerning the criteria of validity in research, Bakhtin (1986c) assigns *accuracy* for the natural sciences, and *depth* for human sciences. In the natural sciences, the object of research does not respond to the cognizant subject. In contrast, in the human sciences, the basic criterion of validity is *depth*, which comes from the engagement of dialogic partners in understanding the social reality at hand. This understanding does not imply that dialoguers lose their individual perspective: "In the human sciences accuracy consists in overcoming the other's strangeness without assimilating it wholly to oneself (all sorts of substitutions, modernizations, no recognition of the stranger, etc.)" (Bakhtin 1986c, p. 169). This assessment implies that dialoguers remain as equally signifying consciousnesses.

Building Solidarity in Collective Dialogical Research

Solidarity is not really part of the commonsense strategy for resisting exploitation, discrimination, and assault on people's rights in the public discourse and government policies. Chomsky (2000) considers that the lack of solidarity is systemic. He points to the "assault on solidarity" by privatizing education, so the ethic of care for others is totally undermined when education is falling into the private motif: "Gain wealth, forgetting all but self." We need to stop that, he argues. Carol Schachet (2008) notes that solidarity is not a word in the popular vernacular language in the United States, but it is a core ideal in activism and radical philanthropy. She highlights two meanings of solidarity that are always changing with the circumstances: First, solidarity as fraternity or togetherness in a group; and second, solidarity as connecting with other people in support of their struggles for a more humane, peaceful, and just world.

Maccani (2008) talks about his own experience of learning solidarity from the Zapatista Movement of indigenous people of the South of Mexico. Their take on solidarity is "everything for everyone," including all the people who are fighting for justice, land, work, education, health, and the rescuing of human dignity as the prime value of society. The "sub-comandante" Marcos of the Zapatista Movement refers to charity practices as a "Cinderella Syndrome." The Zapatista Movement has declared their commitment to fight neoliberalism or the "Empire of Money," which for Zapatistas represents the Fourth World War (considering the 'Cold War' the Third World War), in which the main enemy is everything humane. In the same vein, Naomi Klein (2007) in her book, *The Shock Doctrine: The Rise of Disaster Capitalism* concludes that for most people in the Southern Hemisphere, neoliberalism is considered the "second colonial pillage." Maccani points out that the Zapatista movement is committed to fighting and denouncing neoliberalism while enhancing humanness. They have declared themselves in solidarity with all the people fighting for an end to globalization of exploitation, the usurpation of territory, resources, and labor for the sole benefit of a few multinationals. In the United States, we could see sadly, yet clearly, that the members of the Congress, allied with corporate elite, opposed the 'stimulus package' of President Obama as well as health care reform. They worked tenaciously to strip from the package the measures that aim to benefit directly "main street" people, because some call it "socialism." In other words, being in solidarity with the people, in an economic crisis, as should always be the role of a democratic government, is by default a bad policy. Unfortunately, those who opposed anything more humane and truly democratic, have larger megaphones in the corporate media than those screaming for social and economic justice.

It is important to distinguish solidarity from charity. Greer (2008), talking about solidarity and philanthropy, remarks that the current tendency is to solve public problems with private solutions. This approach leads to the expansion of philanthropic organizations that channel the charitable donations from people, organizations, and corporations to those more in need. She considers charity a "creature of capitalism." However, she advocates for a type of "radical philanthropy" to support institutions that organize people and on behalf of the people to put pressure on the government to adopt a social justice agenda to work toward a peaceful and sustainable life in community.

Sometimes these humanitarian organizations are only a façade to move money from the United States government into certain political organizations in other countries. A recent well-known case is the nongovernmental organization euphemistically called "Endowment for the Humanities." This organization channeled money from the CIA-US government to the Venezuelan Opposition Party to carry out the 2002 coup d'état against the democratically elected President Hugo Chavez of Venezuela. Almost everybody in

Latin America knows the role of the CIA in carrying out these types of maneuvers and knows that among the Peace Corps there are informants, especially when the government of the host country is not liked by Washington politicians and the establishment. Recently there was a scandal in Bolivia in which the US embassy asked at least two Fulbright scholars as well as Peace Corps volunteers to spy on Cubans and Venezuelans in Bolivia (Schaick et al., 2008).

At any rate, solidarity is a *sine qua non* condition for RAP work. Fals-Borda (1985) summarizes and compares the collective struggles by ordinary people in three Latin American countries (Mexico, Colombia, and Nicaragua). One major lesson learned from that study was that achievements were proportional to the degree of solidarity and strength of the collectives. These are built by engaging in collective research in the critical recuperation of their own history through popular expression such as folklore, music, art, craft, and theater. Collective research also includes collective dialogue in community assemblies. Radical participatory democracy implies that collective insights belong to the community and should serve it first.

To illustrate what we mean by solidarity, we use a metaphor of a wheat sheaf. A wheat sheaf is a bundle of wheat stems. Each stem or a small group of stems can be broken very easily. The more stems in the sheaf, the more difficult it becomes to break them. Through history, we can see that radical social changes have been the fruit of social movements with shared goals and commitments. The collective element in the social movement is the sheaf, which is difficult to dominate by the forces that maintain the status quo. It is important to clarify that individuality is not lost in the collective, for each individual (stem of wheat) plays a role in maintaining the collective (sheaf) together and strong, and in moving together toward achieving their shared goals. In brief, building solidarity implies shared goals and commitment to working toward a better world (more just, equitable, peaceful, and sustainable), and for recuperating human dignity and putting human fulfillment before profit and material gain.

Convergence of Popular Science with Academic Science

An important task before us is to acknowledge that there are at least two knowledge generation streams that need to be valued equally, i.e., the academic science and the underprivileged popular science (Rahman, 1994). The popular science is an informal endogenous process that should be systematized and written down to inform academics and ultimately to serve the people's interests. This idea does not mean that any and all popular knowledge is for the people's interests because, as Mariño (1990) points out, popular knowledge is often impregnated with the dominant ideology and strategies that anesthetize people's thinking. The idea behind RAP type of work is that both academic knowledge and popular knowledge have limitations. Therefore, their dialectical interrelationship is important for the enhancement and social relevance of both types of knowledge.

RAP work embraces and promotes the convergence between academic knowledge and popular underprivileged knowledge, thereby producing knowledge and theories as interplay between academic science and popular science. RAP produces theories and applies theories, many of them constructed by the same research participants as they study their reality. "This effort has resulted in benefits for both. Such a discovery is again nothing new. But it has served to cut some pigtails of arrogance from autistic academicians still in ivory towers" (Fals-Borda, 2002). We may question how RAP is reported. Given the fact that RAP is aimed at transforming oppressive conditions of underprivileged people, the results are reported systematically during the course of the research process to the research participants. Fals-Borda (1990, 1985) proposes what he calls a "systematic devolution of results." The purpose of the systematic devolution of results to the research participants and community is not only to inform them but to educate and strengthen the history and ties among the members of the community with a vision toward its transformation. The results should be presented in a form and language that is accessible to all the parties involved. Fals-Borda (1985) identifies at least four levels of communication of results for the final report of RAP type of research emulating stereophonic channels:

1. symbols and pictures without printed words;
2. visual and written as an illustrated booklet;
3. materials with a view to training community leaders and cadres; and
4. paper with complex analytical discussion for cadres and intellectuals. Fals-Borda warns us about the need to consult and get approval from the research participants about the content and format of the various reports and the use of those results for the public interest starting with the participants themselves.

RAP Involves Collective Action and Transformation for Social Justice

RAP work is incomplete if the project does not include collective action toward improving the living situations of participants as well as their own understanding of their worlds in particular and other communities of people with similar situations in general. This work is inspired by Marx and Engels' (1970) 11th Thesis, according to which the point of studying and interpreting the world is to transform with the people and for the people's benefit.

Action in RAP is not just any action but the one identified above as the human activity *par excellence, praxis.* Therefore, engaging in action is more than just "doing things," it is doing them as intellectual, ethical and political activities aimed at transforming consciousness, life, material, and social conditions toward building a better world from the bottom up.

Why collective action and not just action? In the previous section about solidarity, we described using the wheat sheaf metaphor to explain how people, when united, are able to change social structures, which as individuals they may not able to do. As Howard Zinn (Zinn & Macedo, 2005) attests, history helps us understand how real social change for the betterment of most people occurs: it comes as a result of grassroots social movements. Many examples of Participatory Action Research *vivencias* in the Third World are testimony of collective actions (Fals-Borda & Rahman, 1991; Fals-Borda, 1998; Rahman, 1994; Rodriguez-Brandão, 2005).

There are some important concepts to be clarified in order to deepen the understanding of collective transformative action. We need to ask: Why is it ethically necessary to benefit people, in other words, to privilege public interest (common good) over private interest? Why should RAP practitioners facilitate the empowerment of people, not just alleviate their conditions? The building of countervailing power by radically democratic participation of people leads to transforming their worlds; that in turn means the improvement of living conditions in tandem with self-development and self-reliance (Rahman, 1994; Fals-Borda, 1991, 1985).

Public Interest and Public Good as Ultimate Goal of RAP

In this country, where the dominant culture and political and economic systems privilege private interests over public interests, understanding the latter concept of the common good is not easy. The irony is that most of the time the private interests are not necessarily those of individuals comprising the general public but of those who hold the economic, political, and military power.

Looking at the relationship between research and public interest, we should remember Du Bois (Ayers, 2006, p. 42): "Science is a great and worthy mistress, but there is one greater and that is humanity which science serves." This statement embodies the meaning of public interest in RAP, which points to the ultimate goal of research: service for the common good. Taking the stance of doing research for the public interest is a political act; there is no room for neutrality in RAP type of work. As Ayers (2006) points out, research for the public interest addresses issues of social justice by building resistance against inequities, oppression, and dehumanization and by challenging orthodox elitist or supremacist thinking by seeing other human beings more fairly and fully.

The philosophy of public interest, in the context of RAP, is rooted in the principles of radical participatory democracy and distributive justice, which involves inclusiveness and egalitarianism. Participatory research as envisioned by Streck (2007) is part of a movement of values, culture, and people toward achieving their goals. Participatory research is a public action and helps constitute the public sphere, overcoming the deficiencies of representative democracy. It helps the community to see and listen to itself, which is the fundamental condition for the existence of the public sphere. This is done through dialogues and deliberations in public assemblies to reach consensus for change based on grass roots research and the hopes and dreams of common people. The RAP investigator has a public responsibility to the people he or she is working with in focusing on the social dimensions of research rather than falling into methodizing or self-legitimizing discourse. In this same vein, Cardoso (1998), who was president of Brazil, promoted the idea of integrating academic knowledge with social dimensions as foundations of political activity in order to govern for the public interest. Otherwise, he argues: "politics becomes a technique and the world of practical 'consequences' prevails over the goals of common well-being" (p. 15).

Reviving public interest in research, especially in educational research, is now not only important but urgent. It is not a conspiracy theory that universities are being taken over by corporations to influence what is worth researching. They give the researchers the money, and they want the results to benefit their businesses. Meanwhile as we examined in academic capitalism, in Chapter 1, public interest is forgotten, as is academic freedom. In addition, the state continues to cut its financial support.

One of the authors (here referred to as faculty member 2) was involved in the following paraphrased exchange in a research council committee meeting at the higher level of the institution she works for.

Faculty member 1: This office is given these small grants as seed money to be awarded to faculty to start their research and then write grants to get money from foundations or government agencies. At the end, this university needs to receive back the monies it is giving with these grants and more.

Faculty member 2: It is good that this office is giving this small economic support to some faculty who would have no support otherwise, because their interests and the nature of their studies do not fall into the type of projects easy to get funded. But what about the public interest, the service to the people of this area, since the vision of this university is to serve the people of the state?

Faculty member 1: Of course the research done will benefit the people of this state as all research does, directly or indirectly.

Examining this verbal exchange, it is evident that F1 is assuming that any type of research will benefit people. This noble goal has been the excuse to justify the abuse of research participants (e.g., the Tuskegee syphilis experiment) or channel public money into private hands as often happens with pharmaceuticals research (Epstein, 1998). There were few opportunities to bring up the issues not only of public interest, but faculty research interests as the driving force for engaging in research; most of the agenda in this committee is driven by financial issues: how much money the faculty of this or that college is bringing to the university. There even was a party organized by this same office to celebrate the millionaires (meaning the faculty who brought millions of dollars to the university by writing and securing grants). We all know that the issue is not that of writing and getting a grant. The issues are: What is available? For what type of research? And who will be the most benefited? In Chapter 1, we exposed the restrictions on educational research brought up by NCLB and how research in the public interest is tremendously limited as to funding from governmental agencies. Many foundations are falling also into a vague and narrow view of the purpose of research.

We consider that with RAP, the issue of public interest is brought back and clarified for people, even educated people. RAP sets the conditions for the enactment of a public sphere where there is participation of common, historically marginalized people in the study and deliberation of their problems and solutions pertinent to their lives. Rodriguez-Brandão (2005) characterized *participatory research* as social research for the creation of knowledge carried in solidarity by researchers or militants and the common people. He identifies four distinctive purposes for participatory research:

1. as a means of understanding social issues to work on through participation;
2. as a dialogical instrument that provides political education;
3. as a vehicle to progressive construction of popular knowledge and ultimately popular science; and
4. as a way of empowerment of members of popular movements through popular education.

He further cautions us that limiting oneself to the first objective is limiting oneself to the colonizing idea of participation: communities participate in parts of the research project with no effective input in the direction of the research. Limiting oneself to the first two goals is a major gain since they are educational and co-responsible in social life, but those goals represent only halfway because they do not include a commitment to progressive decolonization and popular empowerment. Unlike Europe and the United States, Latin American participatory researchers dream of building other ideological and political alternatives for construction of knowledge guided by these central questions: Who knows? Whose knowledge? What for? Rodriguez-Brandão acknowledges that the approaches to participatory action research most widely disseminated and persistent were those of Paulo Freire and Orlando Fals-Borda.

Building Countervailing Power

RAP work spearheads the building of a popular counter-hegemony, based on grassroots power and organizations and aimed at challenging asymmetrical relations of power that legitimate oppression, exploitation, and manipulation. As de Souza (1990) points out, these social movements expand both academic and popular knowledge, facilitating their integration and their socio-political relevance for the enhancement of people's power. We need to start with the needs of the community or groups to ensure democratic participation in dialogues for understanding their situations. This understanding implies the identification of oppressive forces and their ability to control resources and minds in such a way that limits imagination and the possibility of 'thinking out of the box'. Otherwise, oppression leads to hopelessness. Understanding our own situation also implies consciousness of the threats (endogenous and exogenous) that oppressive forces represent or create. Looking at the history of the so-called democratic states, we can join with de Souza (1990) in asserting that any reform or social change that is top down, without people's participation, will result in actions against the people themselves. A case in point is the worldwide food crisis as documented by Grassroots International (2009), which has been aggravated by top-down solutions. The United Nations endorsed a proposal by more than 400 scientists from 80 countries, in which they argue that the solution to the food crisis should be agro-ecological: sustainable policies and practices to replace the "green revolution" promoted by corporate agribusiness, which have failed completely in Latin American, Asia, and Africa. The top-down green revolution resulted in big business for the transnational corporations (e.g., Monsanto) that controls the seeds, fertilizers, herbicides, and technology in general. Small farmers, family farms, and poor farmers could not keep up with the cost and pace, and/or obtain good crops; consequently, they lost their lands as well as their ability to feed themselves and their families. Unfortunately, the U.S. Senate passed in spring 2009 the Global Food Security Act with bipartisan support as well as the support of the biotech industry and corporate agribusinesses (Grassroots International, 2009). This situation is once again a case where public interest—actually basic needs of people such as food and shelter—are put at risk for the benefit of transnational corporations.

People's critical understanding of who or what causes and/or benefits from their problems is central in order for them to recognize the need for solidarity, hope, and commitment to sustain collective work for radical social transformation. People must become fully aware of the power of communal organization for collective action toward building people's self-reliance. Then they are motivated to organize themselves and connect with other peoples' organizations at local, regional, and global levels. Organization for collective action is a strategic work. The building of countervailing power in groups and communities should be carried out through sustained study, participation, and collective actions with common objectives that benefit the organization and society at large. By and large, countervailing power is the result of the interplay between education, research and communitarian work. Fals-Borda (1991) offers strategies that have been proven successful in his extensive work with participatory action research for establishing peoples' countervailing power:

1. Collective research: This type of research should be systematic and based on meetings, socio-dramas, public assemblies, committees, fact-finding trips and so on. This dialogic strategy replaces surveys or observations (fieldwork). Confirmation is obtained from the important values of this research such as discussion, dialogue, argumentation and consensus in the investigation of social realities.

2. Critical recovery of history: This activity involves digging in the collective memory to recover the experiences of the past, useful for the defense of the interests of this community. This process increases awareness through interviews and eyewitness accounts, for example, by older members of the community; imputation and personification are other techniques to stimulate the collective memory.

3. Folk culture should be valued and applied through art, music, drama, sports, traditions, beliefs, myths, storytelling, and playful activities.

4. Production and diffusion of new knowledge: RAP strives to end the monopoly of the written word; therefore other formats have been incorporated: auditory or visual communication; images, sound, painting, gestures, mime, photographs, radio programs, popular theater, videotape, audiovisual materials, poetry, music, puppets, and exhibitions. Other forms of organization and

social action are trade unions, leagues, cultural centers, action units, and schools. "There is an obligation to return this knowledge systematically to the communities and workers' organizations because they continue to be the owners" (Fals-Borda, 1985, p. 9). They should determine the priorities and the conditions for their publication and diffusion. There should be a mutually understandable conceptualization and categorization between the external and internal agents. The RAP researcher may also use other research techniques derived from sociological and anthropological research such as open interview, census or simple survey, direct systematic observation, field diaries, data filing, photography, cartography, statistics, sound recording, and archives.

We cannot be so naïve as to think that we can overcome the global imperialist corporatocracy (corporations, government, and media) as Perkins (2004, 2007) calls it, at the local community level alone, but we must maintain strong connections and communication with other national and transnational organizations and affinity groups. Furthermore, Generation Five (2008) warns us that "the goal of dismantling oppressive structures is shortsighted, and perhaps impossible, if we are not also prepared to build alternatives" (p. 4). This strategic work serves several purposes:

1. large numbers of people connected somehow equal more countervailing power against the corporatocracy;
2. better utilization of resources including information;
3. the shared victories tend to energize many other communities and organizations amidst so many defeats.

Susan George (1999), at the Conference on Economic Sovereignty in a Globalising World, calls us to look at the advantages that we have against neoliberalism and what we need to do immediately:

> Look at it this way. We have the numbers on our side, because there are far more losers than winners in the neo-liberal game. We have the ideas, whereas theirs are finally coming into question because of repeated cris-

es. What we lack, so far, is the organization and the unity, which in this age of advanced technology we can overcome. The threat is clearly transnational so the response must also be transnational. Solidarity no longer means aid, or not just aid, but finding the hidden synergies in each other's struggles so that our numerical force and the power of our ideas become overwhelming.

Collective People's Self-Reliance

Building self-reliance is necessary for building countervailing power. We refer to self-reliance not as a psychological process but also as a collective social transformation. This self-reliance, as conceptualized by Rahman (1991b, 1994), opposes what he calls "delivered development," which is top-down and has many strings attached that end up preventing the actual development of communities targeted with externally funded projects. Building self-reliance requires radical democratic participation of the communities in the decision-making processes that affect their lives. As Streck (2007) points out, the fact that people participate in city budget planning has a tremendous educational impact on the participants and constitutes a pathway toward consciousness-raising of their rights and responsibilities as members of a democratic state.

In the process of developing self-reliance, people's participation in decision making and in communal actions leads them to value their own collective capabilities. Rahman (1991b) and Mariño (1990) caution us against the idea that popular knowledge is always right and the people's actions are always beneficial to themselves. Thus, we cannot ignore inherent and internalized hegemonies by which unjust social structures and maladies are reproduced as natural and normal ways of being. As noted above, popular knowledge and academic knowledge need to converge to move people toward embracing social responsibility. We can draw examples of this growing self-reliance from the work in "Other Africa" as presented by Rahman (1991b), where people have lived under the inefficiency and limitations of "delivered development." In many countries and communities they have organized themselves from within, consciously excluding the imperialist corporatocracy of the world organizations. They have developed true self-reliance. RAP type of work involves careful and participatory planning of the type of development that people want and that benefits the public interest. This dynamic requires strategic work to protect the common good from both inside and outside forces that favor private vested interests.

Strategic Work

The starting point of any dialogue and action should be grounded in democratic ideals, simply because it may be difficult to disagree with them. In RAP, strategic work needs to be directed at addressing the overwhelmingly powerful repressive forces in order to build and nurture morale, hope, and solidarity. Otherwise we can easily be shocked and paralyzed into inaction. Since the forces of power are everywhere sucking all the dimensions of human and social life and activity, we need to be networking with all the like-minded local, national, and international organizations. We also need to build what Apple (2006) calls "tactical alliances," which may be with organizations that have differing ideologies but which coincide on specific goals that help us move further and faster in making crucial changes. This idea of alliances is a countervailing strategy that goes against the doctrine of competition promoted by the market fundamentalism of the neoliberal globalization. At the heart of the strategic work in RAP is the building of unity and solidarity organized around common goals of the people, for the people, and by the people. Max-Neef (1998), in talking about development of societies on a human scale as an alternative to developmentalist programs imposed by the imperialist neocolonizing forces, provides a powerful strategy against these presumed insurmountable forces. He uses a metaphor that envisions a "swarm of mosquitoes" against the rhinoceros. Even though there appears to be a huge disproportion of forces, the mosquitoes are able to disturb the rhinoceros enough to force it into retreat. The moral of this metaphor is that people in large numbers, in unity and solidarity, can disturb and overwhelm even the most powerful people and their corporate allies.

This type of strategic work may be done better outside the system, based on unity, solidarity, and numbers. We also need to work inside the system. We know that no system is completely impenetrable and that systems are vulnerable as we ourselves are. We need to open spaces in which changes can happen; this can become a powerful way to prove the effectiveness of our work at different levels.

Based on this principle of participatory democracy, Chambers (1998) has developed an approach called "Participatory Rural Appraisal" (PRA), which has moved to large-scale studies. This work on a large scale serves as a conduit to existing conventional organizations and institutions. Coming from different traditions, should we seek convergences and springboards for action? If so, could the concept of "responsible wellbeing" and "whose reality counts" provide a common ground? We have participatory methodologies that are popular, powerful, and self-spreading. Synergies have generated new ways to achieve established goals, e.g., visual forms of analysis.

Possibility of a Better World: Counteracting Fatalism by Recuperating Hope

The hegemony of the superpower mentality has had far-reaching implications, not only at the social, economic, and political levels but also the emotional and intellectual levels of people. The colonization of people's minds is thoroughly entrenched, yet invisible and unconscious for the most part. Even when people become aware of how bad their situations are by critically studying their reality, they often are incapable of imagining the possibility of change, and even less their collective power to bring about this change. Too many people have been brainwashed by the hegemonic forces of propaganda, stripping from them their agency as acting members of a working democracy. Here is where we as educators committed to social justice have the opportunity to promote what

Kohl (1998) calls *The Discipline of Hope.* Using the history of successful collective actions and movements helps to realize the possibility for building people's countervailing power. Part of the fatalism into which people fall comes from a myopic view of the world, which sees only binaries such as black and white, positive and negative, and capitalism versus socialism (which for many equates to communism). This limit to their imagination, imposed by the neoliberal forces of propaganda, is not accidental or benign but intentionally and systematically crafted.

We consider that through dialogue and study of the forces that lead us to feel hopeless and consequently fall into fatalism, we may be able to counteract it and therefore recuperate hope, which is this case is an "educated hope" as Giroux (2008) calls it. Educated hope contrasts with the naïve hope that ignores the constraints of hegemonic power. To illustrate this distinction, we may use the election of the first African American president—Barack Obama. Gonzalves (2008, Nov. 5) explains: "There's hope—not because one man was elected—but because the election realigns the political establishment, creating opportunities for us to bring pressure to bear on an Obama administration to make real change." Concerning the same event, the "scapegoat" of the Republican presidential campaign, Bill Ayers, invites us "to agitate for democracy and egalitarianism; press harder for human rights, learn to build a new society through our self-transformations and our limited everyday struggles" (Ayers, 2008).

At any rate, as educators we should be prepared to provide a hopeful education and hence a hopeful vision of education and society. This concept implies that we start studying in depth the roots of hopelessness, injustice, inequality, silencing, screaming without being heard, intimidation, multidimensional, and multilevel oppression based on race, ethnicity, class, gender, first language, non- 'standard English', country of origin, sexual orientation, to name a few. This vision of education may be Paulo Freire's long-lived struggle for a better world, one that is less ugly, more humane, sustainable, and peaceful.

All in all, we may need to start asking ourselves: Why do we need hope today more than ever? How do we justify that human need? A long time ago Erick Fromm (1968) described and explained the dark side of industrial capitalism and its technology as destructive of humanness when they drive and control vital dimensions of society. The drive for efficiency and profit does not take into account its de-humanizing effects. For him, the ends of the progress of society should be the overall well-being and enhanced quality of life for all human beings rather than the current economic efficiency model which promotes unlimited production and consumption as an end in itself. He considers that hope is central to achieving radical changes that lead to human well-being and life affirmation. Machines, computers, and media can help the growth of humans but cannot replace interpersonal relationships, human judgment, and social responsibility that build a social system oriented to life. Progress, the promised land of capitalism, is based only on economic terms, which do not unveil the tremendous and often skyrocketing inequities between rich and poor. Fromm proposes, in *The Revolution of Hope*, that progress should be based on values at a human scale for human fulfillment. The genuine human experience is not based on data, senses or intellect but rather on communion in the search for meaning and *telos* of existence: "Human experiences culminate in the statement that freedom is a quality of being fully human" (p. 91).

Hope is an ontological necessity claims Freire (1992, 1994, 1998, 2003, 2005, 2007). It is an important factor to be able to live as humans in a specific socioeconomic and historical context. We need technology and science, but we also need dreams and utopias, he points out. For him, a dream is a lucid perception of change, a vision of a better world that does not yet exists. It should be based on strong convictions and commitments to transform unjust structures. It requires persistence, consistence, and coherence between talk and action. The utopia of a better world implies collective work for achieving such a transformative dream. Hope is a human necessity that cannot be conceived *blindly*, waiting for someone else to protect us from our miseries and problems. Nor do we want to fall into *naïve* hope by believing that individually we can do our own little share to solve the problems of the world.

Naïve hope is rooted in the ideology of individualism, which is entrenched in capitalism, as well as the dominant ideology and constantly nurtured by those who benefit from the status quo: keeping us isolated and fearful of other ideologies and concepts deemed evil such as collectivism, socialism, rebellion, and radicalism. Naïve thinkers use a binary vision of change—either/or thinking—cling to the ideal of individual autonomy or fall into socialism, which for them is the same as communism. The signs of hopelessness, according to Freire (2005), are manifested in the incapacity of our officials and society as a whole to solve the problems that threaten life, earth, and human survival. We see that blatant impunity, corruption and manipulation of people's minds and hearts is the most effective way the system is teaching hopelessness. We continually hear teachers who are conscious of the intensity of this problem but who believe that there is no way to fight and win against those in power, because "they are so powerful."

Hope, as conceived by Freire (1992, 1994, 1998, 2003, 2005), Fromm (1968) and Giroux (2004b) should be educated. Educated hope implies consciousness-raising, or the capability to change the world by understanding how it works and defining the ways to intervene. Giroux (2004a, 2004b) considers educated hope as that expressed in the language of resistance and possibility, which requires a militant utopianism and optimism. Educated hope then is a radical democratic utopianism (utopian thinking) that proposes multiple alternatives grounded in broad-based participation of people in popular decision-making. Hence, hope is collective, social, and individual. It is anticipatory and mobilizing and pregnant in dialogue and not messianic or therapeutic.

Educated hope should be the basis of social organization and the core of education goals as well as the backbone of political and pedagogical action. Freire (2005), in his *Pedagogy of Indignation,* helps us to liberate ourselves from social censorship when we have valid reasons and a moral obligation to feel indignation before the systematic, massive, and shameless violation of human rights, the violence and exploitation that cause so much suffering of so many people around the world. Hegemonic discourses attack these feelings, labeling them as signs of weakness or personality disorders. Freire urges us to move from indignation to hope, from denunciation to annunciation. This move is dialectical, not linear. A dialectical move implies the establishment of a dynamic interdependence between these two opposing sentiments. Hopefully, this dynamic engenders ongoing social change. Concerning political action, Freire (2005) calls on us to fight with indignation but with respect, enthusiasm, and perseverance against the powerful oppressors and on the side of people who live in destitution. This collective action should be organized from the grassroots up by groups and communities. The fuel for action is people's desires and needs aimed at transforming society by improving their own life conditions for themselves and for others. We cannot just react to the increasing abuses of the corporatocracy. Adaptation should be only a temporary condition, a strategic step to embrace a more comprehensive struggle. These collective struggles may be situated, as Giroux (2004b) asserts, at the living and conscious experiences of ordinary people, "el pueblo." For him, these collective struggles are not just political movements but pedagogical interventions. We need to merge politics, pedagogy, and ethics, and open public spheres at all levels, inside the educational institutions and outside them. We, as educators, need to rescue utopian thinking, and to subvert dominant meanings by replacing them with the discourse of human rights and dignity aimed at transforming world power. Power, both economic and political, is to be put at the service of social programs and projects to make possible the utopia of a better world, where human fulfillment and well-being is privileged over profit and wealth accumulation in the hands of few people and of few countries.

For Freire (1998), joy and hope are necessary in educational practice to avoid succumbing to hopelessness and a consequent dehumanization of students' and teachers' lives and future. As critical educators, Freire (2005) urges us to embrace a pedagogy of hope and to say *no* to fatalism, not just with words but intellectually and in our activities. Children, he says, also can intervene in changing the world. We need to provide them with opportunities for reading and writing the world, to study and understand the factors that have produced and maintained world conflicts, human suffering, and lack of decent social services, including education. However, we must not be fatalistic. We often find teachers and other adults working with children, who think that in order to protect their children or students, they must prevent them from studying and understanding the real problems of the world. They allege that children should not be exposed to negative events and information, since many of them are already abused at home. They ask: Why do we need to make them feel bad and concerned about matters beyond their control? A good response to these overprotective adults, who prevent the reading and writing of the world by their children, is to cite references of many successful teachers who have assumed the ethical work of preparing students for intervening and reshaping the world so that it is more just, peaceful, life sustainable, and democratic.

One illustrative experience of how to nurture hope while examining critically the issues at hand, is Maria Sweeney's (1999) fourth-grade critical literacy classroom. Before the NCLB, under more flexible and holistic curricular conditions, she studied with her 4th-grade class the issues concerning the apartheid problem in South Africa. Students watched a video on the subject, and from there, they became engaged in many different ways. Students conducted research on the history of apartheid on their own, studied the geography of South Africa, integrated mathematics for studying the economy and related topics, which included mathematical relations and concepts. They wrote poems, songs, raps, and other genres to express their feelings about what they were learning. In this democratic and encouraging environment students decided to write a play as a form of social action to teach other students about this significant social problem. They did it in a very democratic and participatory way that included music and arts. Some parents were also involved in the design of sets and shared their knowledge about apartheid. What we glean from these class activities is the involvement of students, self-directed inquiries, readings, writings, and actions. It is the classroom of which we all dream when referring to democratic education for reading the word and the world. The children of Sweeney's class became prepared mentally and emotionally to face social problems with democratic hope and commitment to intervene in the world for social transformation. Contrary to common practice, this teacher did not overprotect or handicap students from participating in reading and writing their worlds.

Like Sweeney's classroom, Kohl (1998) describes from his experience the "schools of hope" as follows:

> Schools of hope are places where children are honored and well served. They have a number of common characteristics, no matter where they are to be found across the country. They are safe and welcome places, comfortable environments that have a homey feel. They are places where students can work hard without being harassed, but also places where the joy of learning is expressed in the work of the children and their sense of being part of a convivial learning community. They are places where the teachers and staff are delighted to work and are free to innovate while at the same time they are willing to take responsibility for their students' achievement....Parents feel welcome and often have a role in school governance. Community volunteers are abundant. Hope, projected primarily through the children's learning, is also manifest in how the physical environment of the school is treated with respect (p. 332).

We consider that this type of school is what our children deserve. Giving children less than this type of school environment and education is putting at risk their future and that of our nation.

Commitment to RAP Involves Ethically and Socially Responsive Work

"My mind and heart are with this group of people." This expression, if genuine, is the type of commitment necessary for embracing RAP work. As indicated above, RAP is an interplay among research, teaching, and community work, which makes the work of the researcher not only more complex but highly demanding on the grounds of ethical and social responsibility. In addition, as RAP is rooted in *participatory democracy*, the investigators have roles that are unique to this type of research approach.

Right and Duty to Change the World

As RAP practitioners, we need to ask ourselves: How can we struggle to make the world better? In the name of whom or what do we fight? Whose agenda counts? Whose knowledge is important? Following Freire's (2005) philosophy of work, our inviolable ethical principle is to respect the dignity and fulfillment of human beings over the ethics of the market based on profit, economic growth, and efficiency. Our struggles are aimed at transforming dehumanizing social structures and practices to overcome injustice, violence, exploitation, and environmental degradation. The underlying assumption is that there is a possibility to change the world for the better. However, who decides what a better world is? RAP work involves a bottom-up decision-making; that is, research participants need to come to terms concerning their vision of a better world. Their dreams and needs are at the center of that decision.

There is no real commitment when researchers miss opportunities to fight for changes that benefit the people with whom they are supposedly working in solidarity. Such a failure seems to be tied to lack of coherence between what one preaches and what one does. Freire (2003, 2005) insists that for educators and researchers, coherence is essential for personal and professional disposition. Therefore, they need to monitor themselves to consistently enhance it.

The work of the RAP inquirer is along the same line as that of the *public intellectual* that Molnar (2006) refers to, as academics working in the public interest. Molnar explains that very often a public intellectual falls into dilemmas between being faithful to the academic establishment while maintaining his other moral obligation to work in the public interest. He considers that the dilemma is especially acute for the untenured professor since there is risk in participating in research and service that is meaningful and socially responsive while at the same time one must time gain credit toward tenure and promotion. The load may be so overwhelming that untenured professors cannot do both because the academic structure most of the time does not support the work of the public intellectual. In the case of the tenured professor, Molnar (2006) addresses the issue of *careerism* where the professor needs to comply with the institution's expectations as to what is appropriate to the associate or full professor level. They might prefer to navigate the system by "whispering in the ear of power" and aligning their research interests to funding sources and opportunities. He adds that "they then 'trim' their views to better tack into the prevailing winds" (p. 65). Molnar points out that the 'real' work of the public intellectual is not only not rewarded, it is often at best tolerated, at worst devalued, dismissed, or sabotaged. The environment can become so hostile that as Fals-Borda (Cendales et al, 2005) recounts, his pursuit in doing research in the public interest forced him to resign a high academic position at a public university.

Pursuing RAP type of encompassing work implies that we make the choice in favor of the public interest. Fals-Borda (1995) argues that research in human and social phenomena, including education, does not make sense if it does not help its members to enhance and find meaning in their lives while engaging in action that promotes justice, equality, peace, and prosperity for all. RAP is a way to respond and engage people in that pursuit. It implies that these RAP researchers must commit to ethical and socially responsive work on the side of the poorest and most vulnerable people (who increasingly are becoming the majority of the world's population) in order to claim their rights and human dignity. For Fals-Borda (1995), this type of committed research helps to "unveil the conditions of their oppression and exploitation...assist in overcoming the constraints of savage capitalism, violence, militarism, and ecological destruction...endeavor to understand, tolerate and respect different genres, cultures and races, and to heed the voice of others" (p. 6). Therefore, "There is no need to make any apology for this type of committed research" (p. 5) in order to qualify as scientific and valid knowledge.

Researcher's Roles in Democratizing Research and Making It Socially Responsive

As indicated above, RAP is the interplay of research, education, and communitarian work. Therefore, the role of the external researcher is not that of setting the agenda, designing, planning, conducting and reporting the study as he/she does in conventional research. Given that RAP is rooted in radical participatory democracy, the role of the external researcher changes accordingly. Radical participatory democracy calls for treating research participants as human beings, owners of their own knowledge, having agency, and therefore they need to be able to study their own reality and participate actively in its transformation for improving their own understandings and life conditions. Hence, the role of external researchers is that of shared decision-making and being socially and culturally responsive to the issues, interests, and needs of the group or community, whose members become co-researchers and co-actors in the given RAP project.

Bishop (2005) developed what he calls a "participatory approach" to culturally responsive research and knowledge creation, as he engaged in research with the Maori indigenous people in New Zealand. Referring to the researcher roles, he points out that conventional roles are not pertinent for participatory researchers: "For the researchers (professionals and ordinary people) this [participatory] approach means that they are not information gatherers, data processors, and sense-makers of other people's lives; rather, they are expected to be able to communicate with individuals and groups, to participate in appropriate cultural processes and practices, and to interact in a dialogical manner with research participants" (p.120).

Doing a comparative synthesis of PAR/RAP experiences in three countries, Colombia, Mexico, and Nicaragua, in the 1970s and early 1980s, Fals-Borda (1985) identified, among other features, several crucial characteristics of the roles played by external and internal researchers, whom, later on, Fals-Borda (1991) calls "animators." By animation he means the support and assistance to participants in identifying their purposes and visions, as well as strategies for carrying out the study and the subsequent collective transformative actions. These very distinctive roles are radically different from those of conventional researchers. We bring those insights as inspiring examples of how RAP researchers' roles are played out in a specific conjuncture of social and historical circumstances and not as standard trans-situational and trans-historical roles. We need to remember that the roles of researchers in RAP projects include also educational and communitarian work, but from a radical participatory perspective.

Given that the communities in all three countries were large in population and spread out geographically, Fals-Borda (1985) identified internal (activists) and external agents (experts) united by one common goal—social transformation by means of building people's countervailing power in terms of intellectual, social and economic objectives. The permanent referent was always the interests, needs, and dreams of people of the target community. External and internal agents needed to work to overcome the patterns of thought and action traditionally incompatible between these two groups. They needed to work together as organic cooperators. Community members, including the internal agents, had detailed and varied understanding of the problems and concerns they faced at the micro-level of the community's collective experiences and popular knowledge. External agents provided technical abilities and understanding of the macro-context for connecting and/or explaining many problems of the community as well as strategies for solving them. Both types of agents had the responsibility for building and supporting relationships in the community and among themselves for producing knowledge, improving material conditions of the community, and overcoming political problems. The key strategies for achieving these objectives were: pluralist ideology, permanent validation in practice of people's knowledge and efforts, and participatory democracy.

External researchers played very important and necessary roles (technical, theoretical, macro-analysis) in those communities, but not to the level of understanding and solving the actual problems of people in the communities. External agents played an important role in animating community members to participate in the various community–generated activities. External researchers also created and maintained the conditions for radical participatory democracy; thus, community members not only received support for their causes but also obtained intellectual tools and self-affirmation of the legitimacy of their struggles and experiential knowledge. Despite the pivotal role of external researchers, they became aware of their responsibility for avoiding dependency of the community on their active participatory roles and instead promoted community autonomy to take control of their own development as community collaborators and researchers. External agents should work from the beginning toward becoming redundant (Fals-Borda, 1985).

Internal and external researchers realized that they needed to work toward overcoming fear and powerlessness in many members of the community they were working with. By working in circles and/or assemblies, people found common ground and discovered for themselves their potential for change, which legitimized their struggles. As they felt that their concerns were heard and shared, they started developing externally oriented countervailing power activities by organizing neighborhood committees, community action groups, and cooperatives. The RAP type of experiences, collective understanding, and actions were empowering and transformative for most members of the target communities and the community at large. In brief, these experiences can be characterized as "indefinite, plastic, and open" (Fals-Borda, 1985, p. 39).

Of course, crises and tensions also arise in RAP vivencias. Fals-Borda (1985) describes the tensions between and within internal and external agents and how people from the community observed these quarrels with amusement. What they expected from the agents was support and advancement of their causes. It became clear that agents should avoid sectarian attitudes. There were also crises in entire projects, to the point that "death and resurrection" of open-ended projects and activities are part of this type of work. Consequently, persistence and resilience are important components of the evaluation of the experience and its success.

As a final note, we have not forgotten to address how to determine validity in RAP projects. Chapter 3 is entirely devoted to that topic. We consider that the task of determining criteria of validity in RAP vivencias relies on paradigmatic assumptions and principles. By RAP principles and assumptions, such criteria are to be determined and assessed by research participants in reflective dialogue with researchers.

References

American Educational Research Association. (2006). Standards for reporting empirical social science research in AERA publications. *Educational Researcher, 35*(6), 33–40.

American Educational Research Association. (2009). Standards for reporting in humanities-oriented research in AERA publications. *Educational Researcher, 38*(6), 481–486.

Apple, M. (2004). *Ideology and Curriculum* (Third ed.). New York: Routledge Falmer.

Apple, M. (2006). *Educating the "Right" way* (Second ed.). New York, NY: Routledge.

Armstrong, P. F. (2004). Praxis in adult education: a synthesis of theory and practice: An account of the Praxis Study Group. Retrieved from www. dissidentvoice.org/

Ayers, B. (2008, November 7). What a long, strange trip it's been: Looking back on a surreal campaign season. *In These Times*. Retrieved from http://www.inthesetimes.com/article/4028/

Ayers, W. (2006). Trudge toward freedom: Educational research in the public interest. In G. Ladson-Billings & W. F. Tate (Eds.), *Education research in the public interest*. New York, NY: Teachers College Press.

Bajtin, M. M. (1982). *Estética de la creación verbal [The aesthetic of verbal creation]*. T. Bubnova (trans.). *Hacia una metodología de las ciencias humanas [Toward a methodology of Human Sciences]: First published in Russian, 1979*. Mexico, D. F.: Siglo XXI Editores.

Bakhtin, M. M. (1986a). The problem of speech genres. (V. McGee, Trans.). In C. Emerson and M. Holquist (Eds.), *Speech genres and other late essays* (pp. 60–102). Austin, TX: University of Texas Press. .

Bakhtin, M. M. (1986b). The problem of text in linguistics, philology, and the human sciences: An experiment in philosophical analysis. (V. McGee, Trans.). In C. Emerson and M. Holquist (Eds.), *Speech genres and other late essays*. (pp. 158–172). Austin, TX: University of Texas Press.

Bakhtin, M. M. (1986c). Toward a methodology for the human sciences. (V. McGee, Trans.). In C. Emerson and M. Holquist (Eds.), *Speech genres and other late essays*. (pp. 132–158). Austin, TX: University of Texas Press.

Bernstein, R. (1971). *Praxis and action: Contemporary philosophies of human activity*. Philadelphia, PA: University of Pennsylvania Press.

Bishop, R. (2005). Freeing ourselves from neocolonial domination in research: A Kaupapa Maori approach to creating knowledge. In N. K. Denzin & Y. S. Lincoln (Eds.), *Handbook of qualitative research* (pp. 109-138). Thousand Oaks, CA: Sage.

Brown, L. D., & Tandon, R. (1983). Ideology and political economy in inquiry: Action Research and Participatory Research. *The Journal of Applied Behavioral Science, 19*(3), 277-294.

Buber, M. (1970). *I and thou.* New York, NY: Touchstone.

Cardoso, H. H. (1998). Knowledge and political practice. In O. Fals-Borda (Ed.), *People's participation: Challenges ahead* (pp. 11–18). New York, NY: The Apex Press.

Cendales, L., Torres, F., & Torres, A. (2005). "One sows the seed, but it has its own dynamics": An interview with Orlando Fals-Borda. *International Journal of Action Research 1*(1), 9–42.

Chambers, R. (1998). Beyond "whose reality counts": New methods we now need. In O. Fals-Borda (Ed.), *People's participation: Challenges ahead* (pp. vi-xv). New York, NY: The Apex Press.

Chomsky, N. (2000, May 12). Assaulting solidarity—Privatizing education. *ZNet.*

Chomsky, N. (2003). *Hegemony or survival: America's quest for global dominance.* New York, NY: Metropolitan Book.

Contreras, R. (2000). *La Investigación Acción Participativa (IAP): Revisando sus metodologías y sus potenticialidades [Participatory Action Research (PAR): Revising its methodologies and potentials.* Paper presented at the Experiencias y metodología de la investigación participativa [Experiences and methodology of participatory research],, Santiago de Chile.

Denzin, N., & Lincoln, Y. (Eds.) (2005). *The Sage handbook of qualitative research.* Thousand Oaks, CA: Sage.

De-Souza, J. F. (1990). Ponencia de apertura del III Encuentro Mundial de Investigación Participativa [Keynote at III Worldwide Encounter on Participatory Research] Vol. 20. (pp. 79–91). *Investigación Acción Participativa.* Bogotá, Colombia, Dimensión Educativa.

Dorston, J., & Miranda, f. (2000). Introducción. Experiencias and metodología de investigación participativa [Experiences and methodology of participatory research]. Santiago de Chile, United Nations: Division of Social Development.

Eikeland, O. (2006). Phronesis, Aristotle, and action research. *International Journal of Action Research, 2*(1), 5–53.

Epstein, S. S. (1998). *The politics of cancer revisited.* New York, NY: East Ridge Press.

Falabella, G. (2000). *Investigación participativa: Nacimiento y relevancia de un nuevo encuentro ciencia-sociedad [Participatory research: Birth and relevance of a new science-society encounter].* Paper presented at the Experiencias y metodologia de la investigación participativa [Experiences and methodology of participatory research], Santiago de Chile, Chile.

Fals-Borda, O. (1970). *Ciencia propia y colonialismo intelectual [Endogenous science and intellectual colonialism].* Mexico, D. F.: Editorial Nuestro Tiempo.

Fals-Borda, O. (1976). El problema de cómo investigar la realidad para transformarla [The problem of how to investigate reality to transform it]. *Fundación para el Análisis de la Realidad Colombiana—FUNDARCO.* Bogotá, Colombia.

Fals-Borda, O. (1985). *Knowledge and people's power: Lessons with peasants in Nicaragua, Mexico, and Colombia* (B. Maller, Trans.). New Delhi, India: Indian Social Institute.

Fals-Borda, O. (1990). La investigación: Obra de los trabajadores [Research: Labor of workers]. *Dimension-Educativa* Aportes, *20*, 11–16.

Fals-Borda, O. (1991). Some basic ingredients. In O. Fals-Borda & M. A. Rahman (Eds.), *Action and knowledge: Breaking the monopoly with participatory action research* (pp. 3–12). New York, NY: The Apex Press.

Fals-Borda, O. (1995, April 8). *Research for social justice: Some North-South Convergences.* Paper presented at the Plenary Address at the Southern Sociological Society Meeting, Atlanta, GA.

Fals-Borda, O. (1998a). Introduction. In O. Fals-Borda (Ed.), *People's participation: Challenges ahead* (pp. vi-xv). New York, NY: The Apex Press.

Fals-Borda, O. (1998b). Part III: Theoretical and practical experiences. In O. Fals-Borda (Ed.), *People's participation: Challenges ahead.* (pp. 155–220). New York, NY: The Apex Press.

Fals-Borda, O. (2002). *Participatory action research and participation in development.* Seminar on Participation and Development, Uppsala, Sweden, Uppsala University.

Fals-Borda, O. (Ed.). (1998). *People's participation: Challenges ahead.* New York, NY: The Apex Press.

Fals-Borda, O., & Rahman, M. A. (Eds.). (1991). *Action and knowledge: Breaking the monopoly with participatory action research.* New York, NY: The Apex Press.

Freire, P. (1992). *Pedagogy of the oppressed.* New York, NY: Continuum.

Freire, P. (1994). *Pedagogy of hope.* New York, NY: Continuum.

Freire, P. (1998). *Pedagogy of heart* (D. Macedo & A. Oliveira, Trans.). New York, NY: Continuum.

Freire, P. (2003). *El grito manso [The gentle shout].* Buenos Aires, Argentina: Siglo XXI Editores.

Freire, P. (2005). *Pedagogy of indignation.* Boulder, CO: Paradigm Publishers.

Freire, P. (2007). *Daring to dream: Toward a pedagogy of the unfinished.* Boulder, CO: Paradigm Publisher.

Fricke, W. (2006). General reflections on how to practice and train for action research. *International Journal of Action Research, 2*(3), 269–282.

Fromm, E. (1968). *The revolution of hope: Toward a humanized society.* New York, NY: Harper and Row.

Generation Five. (2008, Sept-October). Towards transformative justice: Why a liberatory response to violence is necessary for a just world. *Resist, 17,* 4, and 10–11.

George, S. (1999, March 24–26). *A short history of neoliberalism.* Paper presented at the Conference on Economic Sovereignty in a Globalising World.

Giroux, H. (2008). *Against the terror of neoliberalism: Politics beyond the age of greed.* Boulder, CO: Paradigm Publishers.

Giroux, H. (2004a). Neoliberalism and the demise of democracy: Resurrecting hope in dark times. *Dissident Voice.* Retrieved from www.dissidentvoice.org/

Aug04/Giroux0807.htm.

Giroux, H. A. (2004b). *The terror of neoliberalism: Authoritarianism and the eclipse of democracy.* Boulder, CO: Paradigm Publishers.

Gonzalves, S. (2008, November 5). Anything is possible. Retrieved from www. commondreams.org.

Gramsci, A. (1971/1950). *Selections from the Prison Notebooks.* Edited by Q. Hoare and G. Nowell Smith. (J. A. Buttigieg, Trans.). New York, NY: International Publishers.

Greer, C. (2008, May-June). Philanthropy as solidarity: When social change becomes dependent on private wealth, how do we work for justice? *Resist, 17 (3),* 6–7.

Guba, E., & Lincoln, Y. (1989). *Fourth generation evaluation.* Newbury Park, CA: Sage Publications.

Habermas, J. (1987). *The theory of communicative action—Lifeworld and system: A critique of functionalist reason.* Boston, MA: Beacon Press.

Hall, B., Gillete, A., & Tandon, R. (Eds.). (1982). *Creating knowledge: A monopoly? Participatory research in development.* New Delhi: Participatory Research Network.

Hoffman, J. (1975). *Marxism and the theory of praxis.* New York: International Publishers.

Kemmis, S., & McTaggart, R. (2005). Participatory action research: Communicative action and the public sphere. In N. K. Denzin & Y. S. Lincoln (Eds.), *Handbook of qualitative research* (pp. 559–603). Thousand Oaks: Sage.

Klein, N. (2007). *The shock doctrine: The rise of disaster capitalism.* New York, NY: Metropolitan Books.

Kohl, H. (1998). *The discipline of hope: Learning from a lifetime of teaching.* New York, NY: The New Press.

Kuhn, T. (1962). *The structure of scientific revolutions.* Chicago, IL: University of Chicago Press.

Lather, P. (1986). Research as praxis. *Harvard Educational Review, 56*(3), 257–277.

Maccani, R. J. (2008, May-June). "Be a Zapatista wherever you are": Learning solidarity in the fourth world war. *Resist, 17* (3), 1–4, 11.

Mariño, G. (1990). "La investigacion participativa pa' semianafalbetas y positivistas arrepentidos" [Participatory research for semiliterates and repented positivists]. *Dimensión-Educativa Aportes, 20,* 35–57.

Marx, K., & Engels, F. (1970/1845). *The German Ideology* (International Publishers, Trans.). New York, NY: International Publishers.

Masters, J. (1995). The history of action research. *Action Research Electronic Reader.* I. Hughes. Sidney, Australia: University of Sidney.

Max-Neef, M. (1998). Economy, humanism and neoliberalism. In O. Fals-Borda (Ed.), (pp. 63-80). *People's participation: Challenges ahead.* London, UK: The Apex Press-Intermedia Technology Communications.

Mercalfe, A., & Game, A. (2008). Significance and dialogue in learning and teaching *Educational Theory, 58*(3), 343–356.

Mihm, S. (2009, September 14). Why capitalism fails: The man who saw the meltdown coming had another troubling insight: It will happen again. *Boston Globe.* Retrieved from http://www.commondreams.org/view/2009/09/14-6

Minsky, H. (1992). *The financial instability hypothesis.* Unpublished manuscript.

Molnar, A. (2006). Public intellectuals and the university. In G. Ladson-Billings & W. F. Tate (Eds.), *Education research in the public interest: Social justice, action, and policy* (pp. 64–80). New York, NY: Teachers College Press.

National Research Council. (2002). *Scientific research in education.* Washington, DC: National Academic Press.

Niño-Díez, J. (1998). Education and participatory research. In O. Fals-Borda (Ed.), *People's participation: Challenges ahead* (pp. 19–22). New York, NY: The Apex Press.

Perkins, J. (2004). *Confessions of an economic hit man.* San Francisco, CA: Berrett Koehler.

Perkins, J. (2007). *The secret history of the American empire.* New York, NY: Dutton.

Peters, M. A., & Burbules, N. C. (2004). *Poststructuralism and educational research.* Lanham, MD: Rowman and Littlefield.

Pilger, J. (Writer). (2007), and Goodman, A. (Director). Freedom next time: filmmaker & journalist John Pilger on propaganda, the press, censorship and resisting the American empire [Democracy Now]. In S. A. Kouddous (Producer). Retrieved from http://www.democracynow.org/2007/8/7/ freedom_ next_ time/filmmaker_journalist_john.

Rahman, M. A. (1991a). The theoretical standpoint of PAR. In O. Fals-Borda & M. A. Rahman (Eds.), *Action and knowledge: Breaking the monopoly with participatory action research* (pp 13-23). New York, NY: The Apex Press.

Rahman, M. A. (1991b). Glimpses of the "other Africa." In O. Fals-Borda & M. A. Rahman (Eds.), *Action and knowledge: Breaking the monopoly with participatory action research* (pp. 84–108). New York, NY: The Apex Press.

Rahman, M. A. (1994). *People's self development: Perspectives on participatory action research: A journey through experience.* Dhaka, Bangladesh: University Press Limited.

Rodriguez-Brandão, C. (2005). Participatory research and participation in research: A look between times and spaces from Latin America. *International Journal of Action Research, 1*(1), 43–68.

Sánchez-Vázquez, A. (1977). *The philosophy of praxis.* London: Merlin Press.

Schachet, C. (2008, May-June). Which side are you on? The relationship between resistance and solidarity. *Resist, 17*(3), 7.

Schaick, A. V., Friedman-Rudovsky, J., & Dangl, B. (Writers) & Goodman, A. (Director), (2008). US Embassy in Bolivia tells Fulbright Scholar and Peace Corps Volunteers to spy on Venezuelans and Cubans in Bolivia [Democracy Now]. In S. A. Kouddous (Producer). Retrieved from http://www.democracy now.org /2008/2/11/us_embassy_in_bolivia_tells_fulbright

Schön, D. (1983). *The reflective practitioner: How professionals think in action.* New York, NY: Basic Books.

Shor, I., & Freire, P. (1987). *A pedagogy for liberation: Dialogues on transforming education.* South Hadley, MA: Bergin & Garvey Publishers.

Streck, D. (2007). Research and social transformation: Notes about method and methodology in participatory research. *International Journal of Action Research, 3*(1& 2), 112–130.

Sweeney, M. (1999). Critical literacy in a fourth-grade classroom. In C. Edelsky (Ed.), *Making justice our project: Teachers working toward critical whole language practice* (pp. 97–114). Urbana, IL: National Council of Teachers of English.

U.S. Food Crisis Working Group. (2009). *"Business as usual" will not solve the global hunger crisis: The "top-down" approach has failed before* (Humanitarian Progress Report). Washington, D.C.: Grassroots International. Retrieved from http://www.grassrootsonline.org/news/press-releases/%E2%80%business

Vio-Grossi, F. (1983). *La investigación participativa and la educación de adultos en América Latina: Algunos problemas relevantes* [Participatory research and adult education in Latin America: Some relevant problems] (Vol. 10). Pátzcuaro, Mexico. CREFAL.

Vio-Grossi, F., Gianotten, V., & Witt, T. D. (Eds.). (1978). *La Investigación Participativa in América Latina [Participatory Research in Latin America]*. Pátzcuaro, México: CREFAL.

Wallerstein, E. (1998). Spacetime as the basis for knowledge. In O. Fals-Borda (Ed.), *People's participation: Challenges ahead* (pp. 43–62). New York, NY: The Apex Press.

Yatvin, J. (2002). Babes in the woods: The wanderings of the National Reading Panel. *Phi Delta Kappan, 83*(5), 364–369.

Zinn, H., & Macedo, D. (2005). *Howard Zinn on democratic education.* Boulder, CO: Paradigm.

Chapter 3

Circumventing the Rigor Shibboleth with Democratic Epistemologies and Social Responsiveness of RAP

Myriam N. Torres

We are witnessing today in the U.S. education system the resurgence of the positivist research hegemony. The principles of *Scientific Research in Education* (SRE) in the National Research Council (National Research Council, 2002) report are considered as "underlying all scientific inquiry" (p. 2). This report has been followed by the creation of task forces for establishing *Standards for Reporting Empirical Social Science Research* (American Educational Research Association, 2006) and *Standards for Reporting in Humanities Oriented Research* (American Educational Research Association, 2009) for publishing in AERA journals. The bottom line is the privileging of experimental research, especially randomized experiments, as the gold standard of scientific research, implied but not always acknowledged by promoters and advocates of this "repositivization" of education research as referred to by Lather (2008).

Examining the process of repositivization of education research in the name of rigor in the United States and elsewhere is of great importance for RAP inquirers for the following reasons:

1. the expansion and institutionalization of positivist research increases the marginalization of research approaches such as RAP;
2. understanding the positivist logic and its disguising language will help us deepen the principles of RAP as an alternative paradigm; and
3. being aware of hegemonic strategies helps us evaluate realistically our plans and projects

Consequently, the first part of this chapter is devoted to the exposé of that repositivization and the second part to "goodness" and "social responsiveness" of RAP.

Education Research Repositivization Under the Rigor Drive

Too many researchers and educators have fallen under the enchantment of "rigorous research." Indeed, this expression brings up a halo of scientific, truthful, prestigious, and objective knowledge—the type of words that Hacking (1999) calls "elevator words." *Scientific Research in Education* (SRE) and *Scientifically Based Research* (SBR) are titles with "elevator words" that captivate many by preventing them from raising questions and refuting their real meaning, validity, or social responsiveness. Eisenhart (2005), one of the writers of the SRE report, acknowledges that using such words/expressions has "political resonance" (p. 52) with the U.S. Congress and others. As the enchantment spreads out, too many researchers fail to step back and find out more about the meaning, connotations, and implications of this positivist notion of rigor.

The enchantment is certainly broken when we simply look up the dictionary definition of "rigor." I did look and found that "rigor" is defined (*The American Heritage Dictionary of English Language,* 2000) as follows:

> *Rigor*: strictness or severity, as in temperament or judgment, hardship, a harsh and cruel act.

Syn: Stiffness, rigidness, inflexibility, severity, harshness, strictness, exactness.

This definition of rigor hardly includes elevator words. It is true that meanings change as we reconstruct them. However, words such "stiffness, rigidness, inflexibility, strictness" are strong words that indeed do characterize the *iron cage* that SRE represents for researchers whose inquiries are framed within other paradigmatic assumptions.

The Resurgent Positivist Hegemony Takes over the Research Establishment

The positivist orthodoxy is taking over the research establishment in this country by creating and taking control of the Institute of Education Sciences (IES). Its director (Whitehurst, 2008) assures us that there were no valid education research studies before the creation of IES in 2002. Hence, the statutory mission of the IES is "to conduct scientifically valid research" (p. 5). He claims that IES is politically independent. However, the director is appointed by the president and approved by Congress. Actually, the role of the IES in promoting the positivist agenda has to do more with developing "policy entrepreneurs" rather than searching for replicable and cumulative knowledge that justifies its creation in the first place, as Lather (2008) contends.

The SRE report suggests that the American Educational Research Association (AERA) be the leader in the effort to improve education research. The results are not unexpected: development of standards for research reporting; ongoing elitization by increasing fees and decreasing presentation opportunities, making reviewing a competitive privilege rather than a service with pre-approved reviewers; and weakening of democratic bottom-up decision making. Every change is claimed to be aimed at improving the "awful reputation" of education research. However, the price for this improvement is a significant reduction in democracy at all levels and dimensions of the organization such as real bottom-up participation in governance, diversity of epistemologies, diversity of approaches, and above all, social, cultural, and environmental responsiveness as priorities. Consequently, diverse and divergent ways of doing research and thinking about research are squeezed and sterilized until they disappear.

The mindset of this positivist "orthodoxy" is to seek standardization of principles, procedures, and mechanisms of control of quality of education research. The National Research Council report (NRC, 2002) *Scientific Research in Education* provided the following principles "underlying all scientific inquiry" (p. 2):

1. Scientific inquiry must pose significant questions that can be investigated empirically (p. 3);
2. Scientific inquiry must link research to relevant theory (p. 3);
3. Scientific inquiry must use methods that permit direct investigation of the question" (p. 3);
4. Scientific inquiry must provide a coherent and explicit chain of reasoning (p. 4);
5. Scientific inquiry claims that can be replicated and generalized across studies (p. 4);
6. Scientific inquiry must disclose research to encourage professional scrutiny and critique (p. 5).

What clearly underlies these principles is the premise "unity of science" under the rules of empiricism, experimentation, and the "natural science model for social science" (Erickson in Moss et al., 2009, p. 508).

"Repositivization" of education research (Lather, 2008) is a process that became fully operational with the NCLB and the infamous phrase Scientifically Based Research, which gave prestige and "political resonance" (Eisenhart, 2005) to this education policy. Nonetheless, SRE is the same emperor in new clothes. It has been heavily used to legitimize the resurgent hegemony of positivist research under the flags of *rigor* and *evidence-based* assessments. The promoters of this agenda (Eisenhart, 2005; Feuer et al., 2002; Levine, 2007; National Research Council, 2002; Whitehurst, 2008; Schneider in Moss et al., 2009), among many others visible and invisible but not less effective, are in concert in discrediting education research while pushing the "positivist orthodoxy" (Howe, 2009).

Discrediting Campaign to Facilitate the Public Acceptance of Positivist Research Principles

In parallel with the institutionalization of positivist epistemology and methodology, the campaign for discrediting education research advances. The grim picture that is being painted includes, among others: "awful reputation of education research" (Kaestke, 1993; Sroufe, 1997); too many weak programs of preparation of researchers because of the "...lack of an agreed-upon focus, inconsistent methods of inquiry and standards and little or no utility for various audiences" (Levine, 2007, p. 27); the absence of significant education research until the creation of the Institute of Education Sciences (IES) (Whitehurst, 2008); the large number of educational researchers: "How can so many people all be engaged in high quality work?" (Schneider in Moss et al., p. 507).

In attempting to explain the "poor quality" of education research, Levine (2007) blames the "lack of agreement on methods and standards" (p. 29) and summarizes the critique of the National Research Council report on SRE:

> Educational researchers themselves are often their own harshest critics (e.g., Kaestke, 1993). They are often joined by a chorus of social scientists, engineers and business leaders who lament weak or absent theory, accumulations of anecdotes masquerading as evidence, studies with little obvious policy relevance, seemingly endless disputes over the desired outcomes of schooling, low levels of replicability, large error margins, opaqueness of data and sources, unwillingness or inability to agree on a common set of metrics and the inevitable intrusion of ideology at the ground level. (p. 30)

What a great preamble to justify the repositivization of education research: Production of "hard data," high replicability, and generalizability, transparency of data and sources, standards, and neutrality are all qualities of positivist research as alleged by its advocates.

Continuing with the bashing of education research, Whitehurst (2008) puts the blame on postmodernist research and weak quantitative studies for its poor quality:

In the context of declining interest in studies of the effectiveness of education programs, the ascendance of postmodern approaches to education
research, and the frequent use of weak methods to support strong causal
conclusions, IES took a clear stand that education researchers needed to
develop interventions that were effective in raising student achievement
and to validate the effectiveness of those interventions using *rigorous
methods* (as defined and accepted within the quantitative social, behavioral, cognitive, and health sciences). (p. 6, emphasis added).

Clearly Whitehurst is justifying the use of randomized experiments as "rigorous methods" are required.

Levine (2007) goes on to blame the field of education itself for
the lack of good programs for preparing "world-class researchers":
"...the greatest challenge to preparing world-class education
researchers is the state of education research itself...an amorph-
ous field, lacking focus and boundaries, which seemingly embraces
all subjects. Beyond this, there is also little agreement on the
appropriate methods and standards for research in the field"
(Levine, 2007, p. 30).

The discrediting campaign also targets the American Educational Research Association (AERA), the nominal leader of education research in the country. Concerning the research quality of
presentations, Levine (2007) concludes:

The deans of many of the highest ranked graduate schools of education
expressed to the authors of this report dissatisfaction...[and] commented
that there is far too much low-quality work on the program. This is em-
barrassing for the profession, sends an unfortunate message about what
the profession values and provides a poor example for graduate students
who attend the event (p. 30).

He also critiques the AERA because it is too diverse. His in-
terviewees (deans in colleges of education and other education
administrators) consider that AERA is not so much a "close-knit
research community as a research holding company in which
differences among members loom larger than commonalities"
(Levine, 2007, pp. 30–31).

Obviously, these critics echo very similar messages: the quality
and reputation of education research are so "awful" that radical
reform is needed. The positivist epistemology and methodology are

the way. Therefore, we need unity of science, homogeneity with standards for everything, a cadre of highly qualified education researchers, methods for establishing strong causation studies, replicability, generalizability, and so on. Discrediting the opposition for advancing a specific political agenda is a well-known strategy. Indeed, this is also happening in public education. Of course, we need improvement of education research. The problem with the positivist solution is its exclusive character, even though its proponents claim that they are inclusive. The shutting down of diverse ways of knowing and conducting research is hegemonic thinking.

Inclusive and Other Disguising Language in and About SRE

Given the disguising language that its proponents use to characterize SRE, who will dare to challenge plans for improving education research? The report is charged with elevator words and phrases such as "rigorous methods," "scientifically based," "high quality research," "replicable," and "objective." Furthermore, the report also uses emotionally charged rationales to improve education research programs in order to prevent "an endless carousel of untested and unproven school reform efforts, dominated by the fad du jour. Ideology trumps evidence in formulating educational policy. And *our children are denied the quality of education they need and deserve*" (Levine, 2007, p. 71, emphasis added). What Levine does not say is that the policies based on this positivist orthodoxy such as NCLB—Reading First Initiative (Coles, 2003; Cummins, 2007; Yatvin, 2002), and Teacher Education alternative certification programs (Darling-Hammond & Youngs, 2002) ended up having precisely the problems he points out and becoming a causal factor in the crisis of education (Hursh, 2004, 2008).

Schneider (in Moss et al., 2009) uses inclusive language such as "high quality research *can take multiple approaches*" (p. 507, emphasis added), while in few sentences later she situates quality of research in studies "estimating causal effects and those that seek generalization," specifically "randomized clinical trials" (p.

507). Likewise, Eisenhart (2005) assures us that the SRE report is framed as "postpositivism," which is "a conceptual advance over either positivism or intrepretivism alone" (p. 53) and is "relatively inclusive and relatively accessible" (p. 53). Postpositivism may mean different things to different researchers, but a lack of inclusiveness can be identified easily when our research does not fit the "iron cage" of SRE principles and premises.

Despite the extended lip self-service of its promoters, the SRE approach is no more than explicit or implicit "orthodox positivism." The chain of reasoning and justification goes on: In the search for scientific knowledge we need to use designs that allow for causation, objective knowledge and predictable relationships between variables, and which can be generalized to other similar populations. Descriptive, exploratory studies may shed light on the contextual factors to be submitted later to causation studies. Indeed, the typical qualitative studies have no room in this mindset. Eisenhart (2005), co-author of the SRE report, acknowledges the minimal role of interpretive qualitative studies in this view of education research.

Calls for Unity of Science

Calls for "unity of science" in terms of generic principles, purpose, standards, and preparation of researchers, under the rules of the positivist power game, are both strategic and naïve. Lather (in Moss et al., 2009) fears the imperial "one best way of thinking" and "one size-fits-all" attitude concerning quality of research; standardization in the name of rigor, especially in qualitative research while missing "the opportunity to move from an imperialist science and toward a science capacious and democratic..." (p. 507).

In a broader context, similar concerns about the imperialist and Eurocentric conception of science dominant in the west are expressed by Linda T. Smith (1999) and Sandra Harding (2006). Smith questions the "western thought": science, knowledge, and research as homogeneous and superior. She considers this as an imperial way to dismiss indigenous ways of knowing, being, and relating as inconsistent with of the enlightened civilization, democracy, development, culture, and science, which are poles upon which the superiority of so-called "developed" nations over other people is built. These other countries hence fall into the categories of "underdeveloped" (or euphemistically, "developing"), uncivilized, believing in mythical/non-scientific knowledge, being different (meaning lower than westerners). For her, the imperial perception of research is a cultural formation that overvalues empiricism and its relative positivism and which reduces phenomena, whether natural or social, to what is measurable, observable and operationally defined. Furthermore, this approach compartmentalizes both knowledge and human beings. Smith points to the interdependence among knowledge, research, and imperialist ideology as a colonization of the mind; other types of knowledge and ways of knowing, as those of indigenous people, are undermined or excluded. Even when people from these excluded communities have the chance to articulate and document the value, history and social benefits of types of knowledge and research outside the ring of the "West's cultural archive" (Smith, 1999, p. 48), they are not taken seriously by academics, not even by those who call themselves critical educators.

Harding (2006) contends that value-free scientific assumptions, frames, and methods constitute unquestionable assumptions. Eurocentrism is at the core of the dominant beliefs and practices of science: e.g., unity of science and universalism. It makes other studies and knowledge appear magical, superstitious, and unreliable. Tolerant pluralism does not challenge the Eurocentric hegemony. In contrast, multicultural and postcolonial feminist studies validate other types of sciences under the belief that democratic values and goals can also construct the results of scientific research. Harding, like many other feminists and postcolonial authors, re-conceptualized science as systematic practices rather than a coherent representation of nature and social relations. One major reason, she argues, is that this representation of the phenomenon under study absolves scientists of responsibility for the politics behind the science represented.

Standards and Standardization in the Name of Rigor in Education Research

The standards movement has invaded practically all areas of education, claiming more rigorous standards and testing. Michael Apple (2006) identifies its advocates as middle-class managerial professionals, one of four right-wing groups, who have taken over education as part of their agendas. Of course, education research cannot escape this imperial idea, but we can counteract these agendas by asking: Whose standards? Who are the persons being served with those standards? Whose knowledge and ways of seeking and using knowledge are privileged?

The development of standards for publishing in AERA journals (AERA, 2006, 2009) was given to task forces composed of quantitative– and qualitative–oriented members), who were in effect bounded by pre-established principles of scientific research included in the SRE report (NRC, 2002). The final result was the "triumph of standardization in the name of rigor" (Lather, in Moss et al., 2009). One can only imagine the hard work that participants in those task forces needed to do in order to negotiate standards that somewhat acknowledge the significance and relevance of other types of education research distinct from the experimental-randomized trial and narrow scientism. I am sure that without their help we would have today just one set of standards, ruling out any other type of study that does not fully fall into the positivist epistemology and methodology. Despite the avoidance of more disastrous standards for education research at the leading organization on this matter, these standards constitute an *iron cage* for many of us—those doing research whose main role is precisely the democratization of research and knowledge and the empowerment of people to act on their own behalf—the goals of RAP.

Empirically based evidence became the principle on which natural science and social sciences collide, as in effect happened with AERA "Standards for Reporting Empirical Social Science Research". This controversy is a major issue because it is a direct path to homogenize not just the ways of reporting research, but how to conceive and conduct studies aimed at presenting or publishing. This reductionism forces us to twist and squeeze our research to fit into the iron cage of standards, which reflects the principles of the positivist epistemology more than any other. Hence, we are forced to accept the natural science model of research for studying social and human phenomena, which results in what Erickson (2005) calls a "social engineering." He goes on to state his fears about the SRE's "extreme form of naïve scientism" (p. 4) and raw empiricism: "I believe that this agenda is not simply an intellectually neutral search for better knowledge, but it is about knowledge production for social engineering—and we should be aware that this is social engineering toward extreme right-wing ends. Make no mistake; these are dangerous times" (p. 9).

The title "Standards for Reporting in Humanities-Oriented Research" is an oxymoron in the first place. Nonetheless, it is worth noting that there are many what one might call "if" conditions that leave some windows open for adjustment. However, there are included many ways to set the boundaries of humanities, to define the subject matter, despite the explicit negating statement. We know that the mandated homogenization in reporting influences, retrospectively, the conception and the implementation of a research project, which in turn affects the unique open nature of the subject matter and creativity. The mandate to subordinate subject matter to method and procedures will destroy the distinctiveness of the subject matters (humanities/arts) and even presage its extinction. Mackenzie (1977, cited by Smith, 1986) illustrates how this subordination of subject matter to method is the reason for the downsizing of behaviorism in America. Whether or not this decrement is true, letting methods determine the subject matter is really problematic. This dynamic reflects a slippery slope toward transforming education research into a methodologization or into social engineering, as Erickson (2005) warns us. Both transformations are happening already, and we are witnessing their devastating impact in education research, in particular, and education and society in general.

The following is an illustration of how a clearly identified conceptual paper submitted to an AERA journal was judged by a blind peer reviewers as not meeting the "reporting criteria": "Authors should be mindful of reporting criteria as described in the document "Standards for Reporting on Empirical Social Science Research in AERA Publications" (AERA, 2006)...These standards have applicability to *all sections* of ER with respect to synthesizing and reporting on qualitative, quantitative, and mixed or multimethod traditions." (Blind peer-reviewer's comment, italics added).

Referring to the SRE principles of research, Gee (2005) considers them vague and dangerous because "they can be applied in so many different ways based on the political interest of the person or agency applying them" (p. 17). The standards derived from such principles fall into the same tray. I myself have experienced the effect of mindless application of those standards.

Hegemony of Positivist Education Research nder the Mantra of Improving Quality

Principles and standards have been used as excuse and vehicle for promoting the positivist education research approach as the dominant paradigm. The exclusionary character of education research as outlined in the SRE report (NRC, 2002) is clear despite its authors' and supporters' claims to include multiple approaches, methods, and epistemologies. Yes, each paradigm involves multiple methods and designs, but under unique rules, beliefs, assumptions, and criteria of quality. To accept multiple research paradigms, each with its own game rules, is unthinkable for positivist researchers. That would declare untenable their systemic denial of beliefs and values, political agendas, such as universalism of principles, universalism of the nature of phenomena to be studied, universalism of rules (their rules) and universalism of ways of knowing and making meaning of the results of research. By denying, rather than examining and questioning their own values and premises when they talk about research, they leave unquestioned their imperialist, Eurocentric, elitist, and blatantly anti-democratic views of research. The problem here is the hegemony of this type of thinking about education research by self-appointed "scientist mandarins" (Erickson's expression), whose political agendas are shielded behind their alleged neutrality.

Example of Failing Education Policies Grounded on Positivist Research

The resurgence of positivist education research has manifested itself in a key policy for public education: "Reading First Initiative" concerning the teaching of literacy part of the NCLB Act. The implementation of this policy shows that the trumpeted "scientifically based research" has been neither effective nor served to improve public education as has been announced with great fanfare by its fans. The National Reading Panel report, on which this policy was based, was anything but scientific and empirically-based (Coles, 2003; Yatvin, 2002). The decision of selecting and imposing the teaching of literacy based on the skill-based approach with high saturation of phonics only served the political and economic interests of parties involved and resulted in the institutionalization of "pedagogies for the poor" (Cummins, 2007) and many other maladies. Schools serving poor and minority children, under the pressure of increasing scores at any cost, are too often teaching to the test, drilling students, and buying at high cost narrow, unappealing, and irrelevant curricula and materials.

Teachers and lower-range administrators have also been harmed in terms of academic autonomy and professionalism; even their dignity has been under siege. Some may say "but children are learning and improving their scores." Yes, children are intelligent and learn many things, many of them not really for their own benefit. Too many of them are learning to hate reading, writing, and school among other things. Too many good teachers have left teaching because they cannot accept disrespect to their profession and dignity (Darling-Hammond, 2004; Meier, 2004; Valenzuela, 2005; Wood, 2004). Worst of all, according to the 2009 report of the National Assessment of Educational Progress (NAEP, 2009), there were no gains in the average national reading scores for 8th graders during the 2003–2009 period, whereas during the previous period—1998–2002, before NCLB, there were some minimal gains (4 points). Actually, as Krashen (2008) puts it "'No improvement' really means failure" (p. 32), because Reading First demands 100 minutes of extra reading instruction per week. With this came a significant increase in homework (Kohn, 2006; Wallis, 2006), and intensity and frequency of testing (McMahon, 2009/2010; Ravitch, 2010), the establishment of the "pedagogy of the absurd" (Goodman, 2006), among other nonsense practices. All in all, the absence of improvement under the NCLB-Reading First Initiative is an undeniable failure of this policy and the approaches to research, teaching and learning of reading on which it is based.

A case in point: Rachel Cloues (2008), an experienced elementary teacher, points to grave problems plaguing the implementation of the Reading First Initiative. For her "scripted programs undermine teaching and children's love of books" (p. 25). She also denounces the problems of scripted training for teachers: "My Houghton Mifflin trainer told me she was not allowed to answer questions that deviated from her training script" (p. 25). Make no mistake: experiences like these are found in every public school in this country, and especially those serving poor and minority students.

One may say that the Bush era is gone, and we have a new policy, Obama's Race to the Top (RTTT). The problem is that Obama built his education reform upon Bush's NCLB (Ravitch, 2010). It is still too early to have studied its impact, but it can easily be predicted, since standardized testing continues to be the sole indicator of improvement and generator of punishments and rewards in public schools. In addition, standardized testing has been extended to the preschool ages, from birth to kindergarten. To his credit, Obama does not believe in punishing schools that perform poorly by cutting funding, but he is willing to have them compete for funding by presenting proposals. Will poor districts with reduced personnel and resources have the same chances to get needed funding as larger, wealthier districts? Probably not. Ravitch (Ravitch & Flanders, 2010, July 20) points to this issue, which she refers to as "Skim off the Top" race rather than a RTTT.

Concerning literacy, the main change has been in the name: Literacy Education for All, Results for the Nation (LEARN) Act has replaced the Reading First Initiative. To its credit, we now talk about literacy, not just reading. However, the conception and approach to literacy are the same: centered in phonics, with the pedagogy centered in direct instruction. Krashen (2010) does not support the LEARN Act because it is

> Reading First expanded to all levels. It is Reading First on steroids. LEARN for K-3 is identical to the five 'essential components' of the National Reading Panel....[It is] systematic, and explicit instruction in phonological awareness, phonic decoding, vocabulary, reading fluency, and reading comprehension. The conclusions of the panel were thoroughly criticized by some of the most respected scholars in the field...To make matters worse, LEARN presents the same philosophy of literacy development for grades 4–12...[which is direct and explicit instruction that builds academic vocabulary and strategies and knowledge of text structure for reading different kinds of texts within and across core academic subjects.

Of course, literacy is only one dimension of the entire policy. By and large, school reform keeps getting worse, or more impoverished as Berliner (2006) notes. The problem is even larger and more dramatic; it is one of inequality and inequity, not lack of good research. What we see is a state of disarray of the educational system and the political, social, and economics systems corrupted by big money. Actually, there is abundance of research done by academics and also practitioners documenting the devastating impact of, for example, the NCLB (Bracey, 2003; Chenfeld, 2007; Cummins, 2007; Darling-Hammond, 2004; Hursh, 2004, 2008; Kohn, 2007; Krashen, 2008; Lipman, 2006; Macedo, 2006; Meier, 2004; Wood, 2004). There are as well creative and humane practices—pedagogies not only of learning but of human fulfillment and liberation (Christensen, 1998, 1999, 2000, 2009; Edelsky, 1996, 1999; Flecha, 2000; Freire, 1992, 1994, 1998; Freire & Macedo, 1987; Reyes & Alcón, 2001).

Paradigmatic Differences

Phillips (Moss et al., 2009), talking about quality in education research, points out to the deep differences concerning "nature," "purpose," "methodologies," "standards of rigor and relevance" among paradigms in education research. He uses Kuhn's (1962) ideas but critiques his notion of incommensurability among different paradigms because, he argues, communication across paradigm adepts is possible. Phillips uses the notion of "language games" to explain how from within a paradigm "there is no non-paradigmatic standpoint to judge that paradigm 1 is right and paradigm 2 is wrong" (p. 503). Hence, each game has its own rules. I will use the expression "power games" to refer to the resurgence of the positivist hegemony, through this official document SRE (NRC, 2002), by which we are enclosed in an iron cage of "underlying principles of all scientific inquiry" (p. 2) and the standards that followed them. The metaphor of the iron cage fits quite well the synonyms of rigor: "stiffness," "rigidity," and "inflexibility."

The power game of the iron cage demands that research approaches that are distinct from the positivist fit into it to be considered valid, publishable, and relevant to policy and practice. Differences in research approaches are not just different methods or even methodologies, as Erickson (Moss et al., 2009) argues: Research paradigms are not just qualitative-quantitative or right-left, their differences are in the assumptions about the goals and meaning of education, knowledge, research, method, values, beliefs, diversity, democracy, and so on. He uses the intellectual history of researching social and human phenomena to remark on the irreducible differences between the nature of social life and that of natural sciences. It is given that humans as social beings are unpredictably responsive to the situation they are in, even in lab-like contexts. Furthermore, meaning is historical and context bounded, and there is inherent "non-uniformity in nature of social life" (p. 508). Erickson goes back to the nineteenth century to indicate how Dilthey defended this deep difference between natural and human sciences and developed the hermeneutics approach to validate the differences in meaning of each setting and worldview. Therefore, we cannot expect uniformity in human and social phenomena, nor are they static over time. Erickson maintains that a hermeneutics approach—interpretive and qualitative research—is a "serious, respectable alternative to the natural sciences model for social science" (p. 508). Therefore, for him, the notion of "best practices" does not make sense: "Best practices as specific behaviors don't travel intact across the hall in one school building, let alone across the country" (pp. 508–509). In brief, reducing social and human phenomena, education included, so that they can be studied in the same manner as natural phenomena, is not only against human social nature, but it misses the point of what knowledge is about and what it is for.

Disclaimer: To be consistent with the position stated in this chapter, that each paradigm (game) has its own rules to conduct and validate the knowledge achieved, I consider it fair that positivist research be part of the spectrum of paradigmatic possibilities of education epistemologies. What I really have a problem with, based on the current trend, is accepting the fact, that the more our research resembles positivist principles and standards, the more chances it has to fit the standards and to be considered scientific and cognitively significant. Such an *iron cage* is not only unfair, but hegemonic, and openly antidemocratic.

Assessing Goodness and Relevance in RAP: A Paradigmatic Affair

The prior exposé of the resurgence of the hegemony of positivist research helps us to deepen our understanding and develop sharper arguments against its alleged neutrality, objectivity, rigor, generalizability, and relevance to policy and educational practice. Above all, though, we need to question its excluding and elitist character.

Relative Incommensurability of Paradigms

Kuhn's (1962) notion of incommensurability of paradigms concerning philosophical assumptions and assessment criteria is very
useful here. As indicated in Chapter 2, RAP is a distinctive
paradigm of research given its principles and assumptions of
radical participatory democratic research and transformative
collective action. RAP projects are aimed at benefiting research
participants and their communities of origin. Its openly political
goal of social transformation for the benefit of the most economically and politically marginalized makes this research paradigm
very distinctive. Given these principles and assumptions about
research, knowledge, and use of knowledge, we consider that RAP
is incommensurable with positivist research but commensurable
with qualitative approaches at least along some dimensions, in
particular those approaches that embrace action as a *sine qua non*
part of research and have a critical emancipatory approach to
research.

Following the notion of "language games" used by Phillips
(Moss et al., 2009) to refer to paradigmatic differences of philosophical underpinning and criteria of quality, the point to make is
that the criteria of validity, rigor, and relevance should fit paradigmatic assumptions. Indeed, this concept presents a challenge of
standardization (Harding, 2006; Smith, 1999; Lather, in Moss et
al., 2009; Schön, 1983). Thus, RAP, as a distinctive paradigm of
research, somewhat different from qualitative interpretive approaches and diametrically different from positivist research, is
entitled to have its rules of goodness and relevance based on its
own principles and assumptions. First, I want to elaborate why
"goodness" is a better term than validity when applied to quality of
a RAP *vivencia*. Then, I will revise some criteria of validity used in
qualitative research approaches and in practitioner research,
which will help set a distinctive understanding of RAP criteria of
goodness and relevance.

Abandoning Rigor and Validity in Judging the Quality of RAP Vivencias

Rigor and validity are theoretical constructs belonging to the framework that proclaims the possibility of objective representation of the world as it *is*, not as it is interpreted by the researcher or observer. Rigor and validity are deeply associated with positivist research, which cannot admit or explain democratic values or any other kind of values as part of research. The politics of "conscious purposes and unconscious interests" of positivist research, as pointed out by Harding (2006), is an opportunity for power to work its way without being recognized. Validity depends on power relations and politics of institutions (Lather, in Moss et al., 2009, Smith & Hodkinson, 2005), as do knowledge, curricula and teaching (Apple, 2010). In evaluating an account of the state of the world in terms of injustice, inequity, degradation, poverty, suffering, and corruption, we need to advance a description of the world as it ought to be. This dynamic implies that we must include not only the empirical studies that give us the reasons and justification but also the moral values, beliefs, and goals of a better world for the people struggling to improve their life conditions (Freire, 2005, 2007; Hostetler, 2005). The notion of "goodness" in research connotes values and judgment directly and openly. This articulation does not reflect new language, since qualitative researchers began using 'goodness of inquiry' in the early 1980s (Guba & Lincoln, 1982, 1989; Kvale, 1989; Lincoln & Guba, 1985; Wolcott, 1990).

Hostetler (2005) talks about "good" education research as that which addresses people's well-being and democratic values as inherent to the process and product of research. In this regard, Lynd (1939) considers that having democratic values as our frame, we inherently recognize the dignity and worth of an individual's actions. Actually, for him the ultimate goal of social science research is the well-being of the masses, which in turn depends on the survival of a strong democracy. He refuses the past and present generalized assumption that human welfare comes automatically from making money. Therefore, as Harding (2006) argues, researchers should be accountable for orienting their research to be socially responsible. In other words, scientific research should be politically engaged, so that democratic values can also construct the results of scientific research.

Validity in Qualitative Research Approaches

What is loosely called the qualitative research paradigm is far from monolithic. It may vary in purpose, methodologies, methods, and political and philosophical leanings such as constructivist, narrative, feminist research, critical ethnography, and discourse analysis. Given those differences, many criteria have emerged in the last four decades for evaluating the quality of process and outcomes in naturalistic and interpretive research, among other types of qualitative research. A comprehensive account of all these criteria is outside the purpose of this chapter; I will include only those that are most illustrative and closest to RAP characteristics as a paradigm.

In qualitative research and evaluation, Lincoln and Guba (Guba & Lincoln, 1982, 1989, 2005; Lincoln, 1995, 1997; Lincoln & Guba, 1985, 2003), as pioneers of the constructivist research paradigm in education research, worked on criteria of validity in terms of "authenticity," grounded in the assumptions of the constructivist and phenomenological view of research, which applies to both process and outcomes. Lincoln and Guba (2003) describe the criteria of authenticity as including: *fairness*—inclusiveness of perspectives, claims and voices of stakeholders; *ontological and educative authenticity*—existence of a "raised level of awareness" (p. 278) of the moral and ethical character of the implications of research; and *catalytic and tactical authentici-ties*—relevance of a given research project for social and political action involving research participants. The authors acknowledge that these criteria are most pertinent to types of research such as critical inquiry, action research, and participatory/collaborative inquiry, especially those projects that have emancipatory goals.

Certainly, Lincoln and Guba have provided leadership in the direction of outlining some criteria of goodness for RAP.

Another emergent criterion has been *transgressive validity,* developed especially by critical feminists as ways of resisting and transgressing rules and standards of established paradigms. Patti Lather (1986, 1993) came up with quite imaginative types of validity to disrupt and transform the status quo in research practices. She includes: *catalytic validity* (prompt to action) *ironic validity* (simulacra), *neo-pragmatic validity* (heterogeneity), *rhizomatic validity* (multiple openings), and *voluptuous/situated validity* (bridges ethics and epistemology). Lincoln (1995) engaged in bridging the various dimensions of quality of research and identified seven standards:

1. positionality or standpoint;
2. arbiters of quality left to discourse communities and research sites;
3. polyvocality in the text;
4. critical subjectivity / self-reflexivity;
5. reciprocity or symmetrical relationships;
6. sacredness of human "flourishing" as a goal of research and science;
7. sharing privileges as academics.

Of course, these standards, as Lincoln calls them, are subject to the specific socio-cultural, political, and historical conditions of the community engaged in a given project. At any rate, the interconnection among epistemology, ethics, and the interpersonal dimensions in the research activity are highly relevant to the definition of criteria of goodness and relevance for RAP.

The notion of multiplicity of dimensions and views of quality in research is defended by Scheurich (1997) as he critiques the emulation of conventional (univocal) criteria of validity and advocates for the radical heterogeneity of the "other" (manyness and polivoiceness), the role of context and history in meaning making, the ever-changing dynamic of human phenomena, the bottom-up process of understanding local realities, and the interdependence of ethics and epistemology.

A critical synthesis of the various conceptualizations of the emergent needs and drives to identify criteria of validity in qualitative research is made by Cho and Trent (2006). They identify two major categories of validity that have been developed in this field to replace the traditional (positivist) view of validity as an accurate representation of reality. They are *transactional validity* and *transformational validity*. *Transactional validity* has to do basically with the account/text of the study in terms of "thickness" and "accuracy" by using member-and peer-checks. The authors propose a holistic approach to validity that includes, e.g., transactional validity, transformational validity and other traditional criteria to be applied to the same study.

Cho and Trent (2006) advance the notion of "validity as a process," which implies that there is an ongoing checking of validity and unveiling of the subjective meanings of the researcher. In sum, they propose an inclusive, holistic view of validity as "ever present and recursive as opposed to either a 'step' in a linear sequence or an over-reliance of subjectivity in the 'a priori' assumption" (p. 322). Echoing Maxwell (1996), Cho and Trent propose moving beyond magic ways of ensuring validity that lie in generic and abstract concepts and procedures such as "members check," "triangulation," and "bracketing." Their proposal calls on qualitative researchers to reconfigure concerns of validity with each major overarching purpose underlying their research, as categorized by Donmoyer (2001): "truth" seeking, thick description, developmental, personal essay, social/praxis. The authors include within *transformational validity* those referred to as *transgressive validity*, as, for example, Beverley's (2005) proposal of "testimony" as a qualitative research strategy. These first-person narratives find their validity in their ability to raise consciousness and thus provoke political action to remedy problems of oppressed peoples (e.g., poverty, marginality, exploitation).

In response to the report on Scientific Research in Education principles and standards (AERA, 2006, 2009), several qualitative researchers critiqued its narrow view of research while widening the horizon of alternative approaches, methods and understanding of validity. Erickson (Moss et al., 2009) defines quality of research in terms of technical soundness and "educational imagination." By technically sound, he means a prolonged time in fieldwork, continual and recurrent examination and identification of patterns, clear and substantive report writing, details, and the big picture, in brief, "tree wise and forest wise" (p. 504). By "educational imagination," he means going beyond the business model of efficiency and effectiveness, the researchers' tours to the research sites, and the top-down models, theories, and practices. On the contrary, research should be insightful to curriculum, pedagogy, and school mission, instead of testing hypotheses and interventions. Erickson points out the inappropriateness of using the model of natural sciences to study the social sciences, which is a major assumption in the NRC (2002) report on SRE.

Lather (Moss et al., 2009) contends that she does research that questions and disrupts orthodox ideas of rigor, standards, homogenization, "one-best-way of thinking" (p. 506), narrow scientism, and imperialist science. For her, validity has to do with "credibility" and the criteria of quality of research are "situated, relational, temporal, historical" (p. 506). Moreover, she considers that research and the researcher should be accountable to *complexity* of social and educational problems. Her critique of the SRE report is loud and clear: "After almost a decade of overblown rhetoric of how science rigor will heal our schools, how do we make productive use of being left to work within, against, and across traditions that are all positioned within a crisis of authority and legitimization that goes well beyond the academe?" (p. 510).

In the same critical tone with reference to SRE, Berliner (2002) calls our attention to how fast research findings become outdated in an ever-changing world at macro, micro, and individual levels. He points out that this SRE policy betrays the focus on children's well-being by forgetting that they and their teachers are conscious and purposive human beings and cannot live and learn merely for the purpose of raising scores.

Validity in Practitioner Research

Whether practitioner research falls into the qualitative paradigm or is considered an independent paradigm, its promoters have identified some unique characteristics and hence pertinent criteria of validity. Schön (1983) highlights the uniqueness of the reflective practitioner type of scholarship, which differs from research framed within the positivist epistemology of practice grounded in technical rationality. The advantageous role of insider, the involvement in action, and the complex and dynamic nature of professional practice are unique characteristics of practitioner research. Anderson and Herr (1999) further elaborate on Schön's ideas and come up with five types of validity, specifically concerning practitioner (teacher) research:

1. *Outcome validity*—actions undertaken to address the problem that motivated the study. They warn us to find out who benefits from this solution.
2. *Process validity*—the process of research includes multiple perspectives, embraces the complexity of the events, and serves the public good.
3. *Democratic validity*—the research is done with other stakeholders (e.g., students, parents), not just as a courtesy but as a moral and social justice endeavor. Also included are "local" validity and "relevance" of the research results to the situation in which the study is carried out.
4. *Catalytic validity*—the research activities generate enthusiastic involvement by participants for studying their own social situation and moving toward transforming it for the better.
5. *Dialogic validity*— "critical friends" or collaborative inquiry establish a reflective dialogue. The authors alert us that these criteria are tentative and malleable.

The epistemology of reflective professional practice advanced by Schön (1983), in his seminal book *The Reflective Practitioner* is certainly an alternative to the positivist epistemology of practice by which research, education, and practice are just "instrumental problem-solving" matters. The latter requires that we use positivist scientific principles, methods, and techniques. The role of professions, including that of education, is basically to apply accumulated scientific knowledge to solve the problems pertaining to a given discipline. Schön calls "technical rationality" the basic knowledge of a profession which should be "specialized, firmly bounded, scientific, and standardized" (p. 23). He elaborates on how the positivist epistemology of practice cannot deal with the complexity, uniqueness, uncertainty, and unpredictability of actual professional practice. Professionals face the dilemma of "rigor or relevance." Situations that are complex, unique, and messy do not allow rigorous technical expert knowledge production or application, but rather they are engaging with crucially important problems. A laboratory type of environment for conducting research and testing practices indeed facilitates rigorous studies, but the solutions will be artificial, simple, and unable to cope with the messiness of the real situations of professional practice. This dilemma shows the limitations of technical rationality and the dilemma generated: rigor and relevance as criteria of quality in research in professional practice. Schön urges professionals to rethink science "as a process in which scientists grapple with uncertainties and display *arts of inquiry* akin to the uncertainties and arts of practice" (p. 49, italics added). He maintains that the technical rationality concept of practice cannot compete with "practical competence in 'divergent' situations" (p. 49).

The frame of epistemology of practice developed by Schön departs from the view of theory-practice relationship framed by technical rationality. It also gives value to the artistic and intuitive process that practitioners embrace to deal with uncertainty and complexity by using reflection-in-action and reflection-on-action: "When someone reflects-in-action, he [she] becomes a researcher in the practice context. He [she] is not dependent on the categories of established theory and technique, but constructs a new theory of the unique case" (p. 68). In so doing, this practitioner integrates means and ends by defining them within the frame of the problematic situation and integrates thinking and doing, even in uncertain situations.

Given the entrenchment of technical rationality in the way people understand professional knowledge and practice, many undervalue reflection-in-action as legitimate professional knowledge. Even those who embrace this epistemology of practice feel uneasy because they cannot present their knowledge in the conventional ways with rigor (Schön, 1983). In sum, the dilemma of "rigor or relevance" generated by the conception of knowledge and research under the "technical rationality" way of thinking about them disappears when we turn to the epistemology of practice grounded in *reflection-in-action* type of inquiry in the real complex, uncertain, and unpredictable world of practice. Schön accomplishes this goal by reframing technical problem solving:

> The dilemma of rigor or relevance may be dissolved if we can develop an epistemology of practice which places technical problem solving within a broader context of reflective inquiry, shows how reflection-in action-may be rigorous in its own right, and links the art of practice in uncertainty and uniqueness to the scientific art of research. We may thereby increase the legitimacy of reflection-in-action and encourage its broader, deeper, and more rigorous use. (1983, p. 69)

Schön's ideas for facing the complexity of the real world of practice serve as an introduction to the next section about complexity of the human, social, and educational phenomena as preamble to developing the criteria of goodness and relevance of RAP.

Addressing Complexity in Human, Social, Cultural and Educational Research

As researchers in human, social, and educational phenomena, we need to be accountable to their complexity (Lather, in Moss et al., 2009). Berliner (2002) challenges the widely asserted dichotomy between hard sciences that rely heavily on experiments and statistical tests and procedures, and soft sciences based on descriptions, texts, and other qualitative approaches. Education research is for the most part placed into the soft sciences category. He asserts that education research is the "hardest science of all," as opposed to the "easy sciences" that focus on subjects that are not as complex as the educational phenomena. This redefinition would do justice to what really matters when we do research directly in the complexity of human phenomena. However, nowadays the move in education is to reduce everything in teaching to an input into a black box (inside children) with high scores as output. This approach reflects an outrageous oversimplification of education and research in teaching and learning. It is reminiscent of the behaviorist Skinner's box for conditioning rats, pigeons, monkeys—and kids too! Reductionism on the one hand and parsimony on the other explain the incapability of positivist research to address complexity in the world as it *is,* while paying no attention to what the world *should be.*

Kincheloe and Berry (2004) conceptualize *bricolage* as a venue to prepare ourselves in the *literacy of complexity* in human, social, and education research. The pursuit of complexity by the *bricoleur* in an ever-changing world requires multi-logistics, interdisciplinarity, radical pluralism, and emancipatory goals. All these concepts contrast with the current wave of reductionism and scientism with the excuse of improving rigor in research. The *bricoleur* is vested with more creative roles than those of conventional researchers. Denzin and Lincoln (2005) defined some of these creative roles by looking at the historical development of the notion of *bricoleur*. The *interpretive bricoleur* creates *bricolages* as emergent montages by piecing together multiple but connected representations of the situation at hand. The *political bricoleur* understands that knowledge and power are interconnected and have tremendous implications in supporting, or not, a "civic social science" (p. 6) rooted in hope. The *gendered narrative bricoleur* knows that researchers tell accounts framed within the traditional story telling of the paradigm to which they subscribe. The *theoretical bricoleur* reads extensively about the philosophical underpinnings of research such as the set of premises and assumptions distinctive to each research paradigm. The *methodological bricoleur* adapts continuously to a wide range of tasks and embraces many methodologies.

How does the researcher-as-*bricoleur* play these creative roles in order to embrace complexity of the human, social, psychological, cultural, discursive, and educational world? Kincheloe and Berry (2004) believe that the need for *bricolage* and *bricoleurs* lies in the necessity for understanding the complexity of these interconnected worlds of humans. Thus, research that dismisses emotional, affective, and value-laden dimensions of the social, psychological, discursive, cultural and educational worlds cannot understand the complexity of these worlds in their interconnectedness and inter-dependency. Diverse ways of knowing are predictably unpredicta-ble and uncertain at the task of making meaning of a given research subject. Within this conceptual framework, rigor in research actually means "the pursuit of complexity" (p. 44).

The researcher-as-*bricoleur* knows that there are multiple forces that shape the production and legitimization of knowledge about the world. When researchers engage in producing interpre-tive knowledge without understanding the power dynamics, their interpretations are not rigorous or even worth doing. Knowledge and power are related in a multilogical and constantly shifting manner. Their relationship has different configurations depending on the social, cultural, and historical context. Power is always at work in the production and legitimization of knowledge, and its impact is larger when its presence is denied or left unquestioned. Therefore, literacy of power dynamics should be part of the *brico-leur's* repertoire (Kincheloe & Berry, 2004).

The *bricoleur* studies the complex relationships between hu-man perception and the natural world. No single interaction or dialogue accounts for that complex relationship but rather the dynamic relationship between nature and culture (complex and unpredictable cultural domain) in a given historical, social, politi-cal context (Lévi-Strauss, 1966). Kincheloe and Berry (2004) assert that being accountable to complexity implies that we need to focus on the patterns of change in the "impermanence of the lived world" (p. 23). Actually, the positivist epistemology and its empiricism promote the illusion that human problems are easily defined, predicted, and conceptualized, and solutions to them can be clear-cut packaged responses and devices, as well as valid indefinitely over time and across contexts.

Bricoleurs work in vexing circumstances of multiple understandings and perceptions and emergent issues. They integrate diverse knowledge and perspectives, and ask hard questions. Given these demanding roles, *bricoleurs* cannot let themselves be overwhelmed by the complexity of the issues at hand but rather need to address the long-ignored and repressed complexity of the world. To face these challenges, *bricoleurs* need to understand the ethical, moral, epistemological, ontological, and political interdependent dimensions of the research activity. Indeed, the knowledge produced by the *bricoleur* is provisional and historical and needs to be seen in multiple layers of complexity. Interpretations should be descriptive (as things appear to be) as well as normative (things as they should be). In this regard, ethics and epistemology go together. Performing these multiple tasks and roles, the researcher-as-*bricoleur* does not suppress subjectivity but becomes aware of how this subjectivity makes its way into research and exposes it (Kincheloe & Berry, 2004).

Bricoleurs act on their understanding of the complexity of the world. The *bricoleur* examines newfound patterns of knowledge, understanding, and ethical imperatives that lead to action. Thus, interpretations and understanding need to pave the way to action. One important move is to democratize the production of knowledge by bringing marginalized knowledge and experiences to participate in the dialogue toward taking action. "Once research is viewed as a humanly constructed process and not a transcultural and transhistorical universal enterprise, *bricoleurs* contend that diverse and conflicting perspectives can be viewed as a resource" (pp. 47–48). Indeed, divergent positions about the issue at hand help to go beyond local perspectives. Thus, the *bricoleur* reinserts academic research into the lived world (Kincheloe & Berry, 2004).

The notion of the *bricoleur* and the distinctive interconnected roles, as characterized by Kincheloe and Berry (204) and described in the previous paragraphs, set the path for expanding understanding of the roles of the RAP inquirer and the complexity of situations where RAP is taking place. These are some ideas especially relevant to the RAP endeavor: the inevitable and un-reducible complexity of the human, social, and educational worlds; the understanding that complexity is a challenge faced by re-searchers but not an obstacle to rigorous research; and the in-sightful idea that rigor is actually the "pursuit of complexity." As described in chapter 2, the outside RAP inquirer is in principle a co-researcher along with research participants (group or communi-ty). Actually, the outside RAP inquirer is a co-actor, co-interpreter, and co-decision maker on an equal footing with the inside co-researchers. In this respect, the power and functions of decision-making by the outside RAP inquirer are more shared than those of the *bricoleur.*

Criteria of Goodness and Relevance of RAP vivencias

The second part of this chapter starts with the assertion that goodness and relevance of RAP work are a paradigmatic affair. Using the language of games, RAP work is a game with its own rules: principles and criteria of goodness and relevance. The principles of RAP, extensively elaborated in chapter 2, frame this type of research as radically democratic and transformative of researchers' and participants/co-researchers' life conditions, and RAP itself comes across as a philosophy of life and work for the public good. RAP practitioners often work *with* the most margina-lized and exploited people, whether school children, their parents, teachers, and communities. Thus, RAP work is openly political and moral. I will refer to the various dimensions of these principles as needed while defining RAP's criteria of goodness and relevance.

"What is good education research?" Karl Hostetler (2005) asks. The response depends on the researcher's individual paradigmatic allegiance. This allegiance could be conscious or unconscious. It is not difficult to guess what will be the response from the positivist orthodoxy: the published principles of scientific research (NRC, 2002) and the like. Hostetler's response is pretty much the re-sponse of a RAP inquirer. The ultimate goal of research is to serve the public good: human well-being. Researchers should explicitly demonstrate the links between their research and such a moral goal. Bringing human basic needs to the forefront as the purpose of the research endeavor is central to RAP inquirers. Who defines such human needs is critical to clarify. Max-Neef (1991, 1998) and Rahman (1994) define development in terms of meeting real human needs beyond economic indicators. Justification for any research project is based on the belief that people have a prime role in identifying their needs and the direction of their own self-development as a community.

Open-Endedness Criteria. Self-study and self-determination are possible under the frame of "radical participatory democracy," which is the central principle of RAP work. By adhering to this principle we avoid the common problem of external questionnaire-based need assessment, which more often than not fails to grasp the felt needs of people. Furthermore, the patronizing action of top-down models of improvement/development has little chance to succeed in advancing people's well-being. In other words, based on the principle of *radical participatory democracy*, RAP means research done *by* the people, *with* the people, *and for* the people. To be in accordance with this principle, we need to have *open-ended* criteria of goodness and relevance of RAP. Whereas most criteria limit diversity of perspectives of what is good research, radical participatory democracy opens possibilities to define what is meaningful research and its relevance to people's well-being *by* and *with* the people themselves.

Connecting to the criteria of validity of qualitative research, Guba and Lincoln (1989, 2005) advance the overarching criterion of *authenticity,* in which *fairness* refers to inclusion of all perspectives and claims. This dynamic engenders the value of democracy in research. Is it radical democracy? It is not clear as to who determines if all perspectives and claims are included. Lincoln (1995) goes a step forward by including the standard that discourse communities and research sites are important "arbiters of research quality." Concerning practitioner research, Anderson and Herr's (1999) *process validity* and *democratic validity* are definitely on the same page with the RAP notion of *open-ended criteria.* By *process validity* they mean involving all stakeholders in the research and including their perspective. *Democratic validity* refers to this inclusive character and also to the recognition of stakeholders' right to be part of the research and benefit from it.

In the human, social, and educational world, the process of reaching a consensus on what is good research, and whether or not it is worthwhile to act on that knowledge, is very complex. Power struggles and hegemonic practices of social interaction are always at work, even in marginalized communities. As discussed in chapter 2, the outside researcher and the team of inside co-researchers need to work hand in hand permanently for radical participatory democracy to take place. They become the midwives of bottom-up democracy. Through engagement in dialogic encounters among co-researchers and the community they are working with, the ideal is that public interest and common good will eventually prevail over special interests coming from inside and/or outside the group or community. Certainly, this is difficult, but it is possible. RAP inquirers and public intellectuals (e.g., Chambers, 2002; Fals-Borda, 1976, 1985, 1998; Freire, 1992; Gaventa, 1991; Hall, Gillete, & Tandon, 1982; Horton & Freire, 1990; Rahman, 1994; Streck, 2006; Stringer, 1996), among many others, have devoted their lives to working with people with this RAP philosophy, and they have given varied and extended testimonies that this alternative paradigm of research is possible. In addition, when conditions of oppression and exploitation are so overwhelming, people stop adapting and start looking for alternatives: dialogic encounters (as Freire, 1992, calls them) for sharing their pains and their visions of a better world, building solidarity and countervailing power through their collective actions. By engaging in the democratic process of RAP *vivencia*, people's understandings, fears, dreams of their worlds are not only acknowledged and valued but also enriched through dialogue, collective research, and mutual education between the outside researchers and/or people inside the community who have become public intellectuals.

In sum, the *open-ended* criteria of goodness and relevance of RAP inquiries are the main spring of radical participatory democracy. For Fals-Borda (1985) the most significant validation of RAP vivencias is done by participants in the research activities on their own, especially when they move into praxis. The social public assessment (community, base groups, or research participants) of the goodness and relevance of research is an endogenous process within the RAP work. The social validation proceeds alongside the research process to determine the implications and relevance for their causes.   Fals-Borda (1991) points out the importance of encouraging people's realization of the worth of their knowledge and wisdom.   In this regard, Freire (1994) purposely demonstrated to illiterate peasants, by means of engaging them in games, that nobody is fully literate and nobody is really illiterate, and that so-called illiterate people have many areas of expertise.

The indigenous intellectual and activist Linda T. Smith (1999) talks about "decolonizing methodologies" for the Maori people in New Zealand, aligned in full with RAP philosophy and criteria of goodness. She notes that, traditionally, indigenous people have been the "objects" of research done by scholars who have consciously or unconsciously adopted colonizing attitudes and practices. She considers that intersubjective lived experiences of indigenous people who are undertaking research for the benefit of their own communities are the best arbiters of what is good research. Thus, engaging in inquiry should give indigenous people the chance to articulate and document the historical value and social benefits of this type of decolonizing research, outside the western knowledge archive and practices.

Bishop (2005) unites with Smith (1999) in rejecting western research practices as intellectually colonizing. His own community—the Maori indigenous people from Aotearoa, New Zealand, give testimony of such colonization. Bishop presents a "participatory as well as participant-driven approach to research" (p.120) as a decolonizing alternative, which is part of the Maori people's philosophy (Kaupapa). Participant-driven research implies that rules and procedures are established inside any research project. Therefore, participants are the active agents in constructing, representing, validating, and legitimizing knowledge. Who better can judge this research than inside researchers, he asks. According to the Kaupapa framework, knowledge produced belongs to every Maori member. Everyone should be able to access such knowledge and articulate it: "Just as Maori practices are epistemologically validated within Maori cultural contexts, so are Kaupapa research practices and texts" (p. 128). Citing Davies and Harré (1990), Bishop indicates that the colonizing discourse of the "other" is also used by several qualitative researchers. This discourse is hidden not only under the mantle of objectivity and neutrality but under subjectivity: Whose voices are represented? Whose interpretations are conveyed in the text? Whose power of decision is at work?

Social Responsiveness Criteria. In the literature on qualitative research and practitioner research noted above, there have been elaborated some validity criteria somewhat in tune with the social responsiveness criteria of RAP. Cho and Trent (2006) identify *transformative validity,* which refers to achieving an ideal such as liberation and social justice.

In building the movement of Participatory Action Research in Latin America as a true social praxis, Fals-Borda (Cendales, Torres, & Torres, 2005) and his research group worked with this scheme: "Research, what for? Well, to transform. Why?" (p. 28). These questions point to the social responsiveness of research. The second principle of RAP is precisely about "transformation toward a better world." What is transformed? In general we can say those life conditions of the people participating in the research, and by extension those of their communities, can be transformed in the direction they are dreaming a better world. As research participants act on the understanding of their own problems and needs and the possibilities for betterment, participants need to engage in collective action in solidarity to build countervailing power. Often these are major, long struggles. Persistence and flexibility could be good indicators of progress. As noted above, the ultimate goal of RAP has to do with human fulfillment and well-being. To make the research process and results socially responsive, radical participatory democracy and hence the primacy of common good should be permanently at work.

In brief, social responsiveness criteria are related to relevance or significance of research first for people who are participating: Are they improving their understanding of their own situations as individuals and as a collective? Are they acting in that under-standing to improve their conditions? Are they building counter-vailing power as a group or community to solve the shared problems and situations? These and others are questions research participants and co-researchers could be reflecting upon. At any rate, the specifics of the social responsiveness criteria should be built through dialogue with people, and, like the open-endedness criteria, the assessment is ongoing both in the research process and in the results. We need to remember that RAP involves "systematic devolution of results to the community." The evalua-tion of each step, action or activity is the normal process of RAP.

Some RAP practitioners have shared ideas on the meaning of rigor or validity of research as opposed to the positivist dogmas of rigor and objectivity. Rodriguez-Brandão (2005) questions these dogmas and argues that participatory research has other social and moral values. For him the "reliability of a science lies not so much in the positive rigor of its thinking but in the contribution made by its practice in the collective search for knowledge that will make human beings not only more educated and wise, but also more fair, free, critical, creative, participatory, co-responsible and expressing solidarity" (p. 45). He actually gives a good definition of what it may imply when we say that the ultimate goal of research should be "improving human well-being." Again, specific meanings depend on the people participating in the research; hence, they are specific to each community engaged in a RAP vivencia.

Streck (2007) concurs with Rodriguez-Brandão with respect to the importance of research participation in popular movements, beyond popular participation in research. The goodness of research can also be seen in how researchers integrate scientific (academic) knowledge and popular knowledge as well as contribute to the constitution of the public sphere (where the public sees and listens to itself).

Rahman (1994) looks at research results and the procedures to reach them as the locus of the goodness of research: achieving people's self-development and self-understanding grounded in indigenous knowledge, culture and skills. The ultimate goal is to achieve people's self-reliance. Only under radical participatory democracy are these goals invoked and participants enabled to reach them. Calls for self-determination as part of and a conse-quence of research studies come from the realization by poor people in the Third World (in Asia, Africa, and Latin America) of the negative impact of what Rahman calls "elitist developmental-ism" that creates deficit thinking and dependence. Thus, the assessment of the goodness and relevance of RAP vivencias is the right of participants, Rahman argues. Bishop (2005) echoes Rah-man on affirming the Maori people's right to enact their own cultural values and philosophy in their research practices and knowledge legitimization.

Embracing social responsiveness of research also implies mak-ing RAP vivencias available and accessible to anyone interested in them. That includes, at the very least, research participants, practitioners, the general public, media agents, and scholars. Fals-Borda (1985) emphasizes in this respect two important issues: first, systematic devolution of partial research results to partici-pants to substantiate their reflective evaluation of their participa-tion in the research process; and, second, systematizing the vivencias of participatory action research (meaning writing and publishing them) and democratizing availability and access to them.

Making these texts and materials of experiences democratical-ly available implies that we should have multiple versions of them depending on the audience or readership. Fals-Borda (1985) has identified four levels of communication to report these vivencias:

1. visual (based on pictures and symbols);
2. visuals and written words in the form of pamphlets;
3. as illustrative examples with some general conceptualization for training community leaders;
4. scholarly written texts with deeper conceptual analysis.

Again, the levels of communication depend on the specific characteristics and dynamics of a given group/community as well as the
identified relevance of the texts to a wider audience.

In addition to making RAP vivencias available in the language
and format that the various types of audiences and readers can
fully understand and use, the issue of access to those vivencias is
very important in terms of making this specific project socially
responsive beyond research participants and their communities.
In the context of RAP philosophy, knowledge generated through
the vivencias is undoubtedly a public good. This idea is further
developed by Hess and Ostrom (2007); they called it a "knowledge
commons." To counteract the commodification of knowledge, they
advance the idea of "open access," by means of using the current
technological advances, at no or very low cost. Along the same line
of thinking, Willinsky (2002) directs the "Public Knowledge
Project" to enforce the public role of research. At the time of his
publication, thirty thousand scientists from 177 countries had
signed up to participate in his project. Willinsky (2005) also
responded to the SRE report (NRC, 2002), specifically to the sixth
scientific principle ("Scientific inquiry must disclose research to
encourage professional scrutiny and critique," p. 5). He takes issue
with "disclosure" as the form of research dissemination, which he
says fails to include democracy in research in terms of our responsibility to maximize access to research as an "open flow and
exchange of knowledge" (p. 42). Disclosing research to professionals primarily is publication for just "ensuring that educational
research falls within long established norms for the republic of
science...[it] is unduly constrained in ways that neither serve
science nor society" (p. 39).

Commitment Criteria of Goodness and Relevance of RAP. Commitment on the part of outside researchers and inside co-
researchers in the research team is crucial for a RAP project to
succeed as a radically democratic and socially responsive endeavor. Therefore, commitment is a principle in itself with derived
criteria of goodness and relevance. The overarching role of external researchers should be precisely, at least at the very beginning,

that of "animators," "bricoleurs," or "catalyzers" of radical participatory democracy as the necessary condition for other good dynamic dialogue to occur in the RAP vivencia. Since all responsibilities in the research process are shared with participants, roles and commitments should be self-assessed and collectively discussed based on the criteria developed, *with* research participants. Periodical renewal of this commitment is part of the RAP process, especially regarding the systematic devolution of results to research participants.

In chapter 2 section on commitment is included a relatively extensive description of the roles and values of a commitment to RAP work. Hence, I will focus on the criteria derived from such roles and values. First of all, outside (of the group or community) researchers have a major responsibility in devising and maintaining the conditions that make possible radical participatory democracy. Thus, all participants stand on an equal footing as contributing dialoguers. To do so, the outside researcher, if necessary, facilitates the preparation of leaders of the participant community to help coordinate the different research activities and collective actions to be undertaken.

The second major task for the research team is to act as "organic intellectuals," using Gramsci's (1985) notion in order to animate the involvement of the community members in participating in studying their realities to find common ground as well as to catalyze their understandings, consciousness raising, and actions taken. The assessment of goodness and relevance of commitment can be guided by the social responsiveness of these research activities and processes, first to participants themselves and their communities, and then to society at large. In brief, commitment is, first, to the people with whom we are working. Fals-Borda (1985) indicates that the success of organic intellectuals depends on preparing the community for self-agency and transformative dynamics and on deepening and widening horizons at micro and macro levels. The commitment criteria referred to here seem similar to what Anderson and Herr (1999) and Guba and Lincoln (2005) refer to as *catalytic validity*.

Concluding Remarks

Defining "rigorous," "valid," or "good" research is a paradigmatic affair. Each paradigm (game) has its own rules about the nature and unique characteristics of the phenomena of the subject matter, the ways to approach its study, the purpose, and the criteria of quality. However, it all depends on how we define what a research paradigm is. In terms of philosophical principles, worldviews, assumptions, and beliefs concerning search for knowledge, RAP rules of quality in research are in many ways different from the positivist paradigm's rules of rigor, but they overlap in different degrees with several approaches of the qualitative research paradigm, including practitioner research.

In the specific case of RAP, criteria of goodness and relevance come from its core principles, which precisely demand that these criteria should be democratically identified and performed by research participants working with inside and outside RAP inquirers. Due to these open-ended criteria, the research undertaken can be socially responsive, first to participants and their communities and by extension to other communities and social movements.

There are several indicators of the resurgent hegemony of positivist research and the subsequent elitization of education research. As critical educators and RAP practitioners, we need to be aware of the repositivization of education research—advances and strategies—in order to expose them, talk back, and educate others and the public about the misguided discourses (e.g., scientifically based research," "standards for rigorous research"), and disseminate alternative proposals and studies. RAP is an alternative paradigm of education/social research aimed at democratizing research activities, knowledge, and epistemology, and serving the public good, thus circumventing the rigor shibboleth.

References

American Educational Research Association. (2006). Standards for reporting empirical social science research in AERA publications. *Educational Researcher, 35*(6), 33–40.

American Educational Research Association. (2009). Standards for reporting in humanities-oriented research in AERA publications. *Educational Researcher, 38*(6), 481–486.

The American Heritage Dictionary of the English Language. (2000). (4th ed.). Boston, MA: Houghton Mifflin.

Anderson, G. L., & Herr, K. (1999). The new paradigm wars: Is there room for rigorous practitioner knowledge in school and universities? *Educational Researcher, 28*(5), 12–21.

Apple, M. (2006). *Educating the "right" way* (2nd ed.). New York, NY: Routledge.

Apple, M. W. (2010). Putting "critical" back into education research: Theory, research, and the critical scholar/activist. *Educational Researcher, 39*(2), 152–155.

Berliner, D. C. (2002). Educational research: The hardest science of all. *Educational Researcher, 31*(8), 18–20.

Berliner, D. C. (2006). Our impoverished view of educational reform. *Teachers College Record Online, 108*(6), 949–995.

Beverley, J. (2005). Testimonio, subalternity, and narrative authority. In N. Denzin & Y. Lincoln (Eds.), *Handbook of qualitative research* (3rd ed., pp. 547–557). Thousand Oaks, CA: Sage.

Bishop, R. (2005). Freeing ourselves from neocolonial domination in research: A Kaupapa Maori approach to creating knowledge. In N. K. Denzin & Y. S. Lincoln (Eds.), *Handbook of qualitative research* (pp. 109–138). Thousand Oaks, CA: Sage.

Bracey, G. (2003). *On the death of childhood and the destruction of public schools.* Portsmouth, NH: Heinemann.

Cendales, L., Torres, F., & Torres, A. (2005). "One sows the seed, but it has its own dynamics": An interview with Orlando Fals-Borda. *International Journal of Action Research, 1*(1), 9–42.

Chambers, R. (2002). *Participatory workshops: A sourcebook of 21 sets of ideas & activities.* London, UK: Earthscan.

Chenfeld, M. B. (2007, August/September). Handcuffed in the garden of thorns. *Reading Today, 25,* 20.

Cho, J., & Trent, A. (2006). Validity in qualitative research revisited. *Qualitative Research, 6*(3), 319–340.

Christensen, L. . (1998). Writing the word and the world. In W. Ayers, J. A. Hunt & T. Quinn (Eds.), *Teaching for social justice.* New York: Teachers College Press.

Christensen, L. (1999). Critical literacy: teaching reading, writing and outrage. In C. Edelsky (Ed.), *Making justice our project: Teachers working toward critical whole language practice.* Urbana, IL: National Council of Teachers of English.

Christensen, L. (2000). *Reading, writing and rising up: Teaching about social justice and the power of the written word.* Milwaukee, WI: Rethinking Schools Ltd.

Christensen, L. (2009). *Teaching for joy and justice: Reimagining the language arts classroom.* Milwaukee, WI: Rethinking Schools.

Cloues, R. (2008). Reading first, libraries last. *Rethinking Schools, 22*(3), 25–28.

Coles, G. (2003). *Reading the naked truth: Literacy, legislation, and lies.* Portsmouth, NH: Heinemann.

Cummins, J. (2007). Pedagogies for the poor? Realigning reading instruction for low income students with scientifically based reading research. *Educational Researcher, 36*(9), 564–572.

Darling-Hammond, L. (2004). From "separate but equal" to "No Child Left Behind": The collision of new standards and old inequities In D. Meier & G. Wood (Eds.), *Many children left behind: How the No Child Left Behind Act is damaging our children and our schools* (pp. 3–32). Boston, MA: Beacon Press.

Darling-Hammond, L., & Youngs, P. (2002). Defining "highly qualified teachers": What does "scientifically-based research" actually tell us? *Educational Researcher, 31*(9), 13–25.

Davies, B., & Harré, R. (1990). Positioning: The discursive production of selves. *Journal of the Theory of Social Behaviour, 20*, 43–65.

Denzin, N., & Lincoln, Y. (2005). Introduction: The discipline and practice of qualitative research. In N. Denzin & Y. Lincoln (Eds.), *Handbook of qualitative research* (pp. 1–32). Thousand Oaks, CA: Sage.

Donmoyer, R. (2001). Paradigm talk reconsidered In V. Richardson (Ed.), *Handbook of research on teaching* (4th ed.) (pp. 174–197). Washington, DC: American Educational Research Association.

Edelsky, C. (1996). *With literacy and justice for ALL: Rethinking the social in language and education* (2nd ed.). Philadelphia, PA: Taylor & Francis.

Edelsky, C. (Ed.). (1999). *Making justice our project: Teachers working toward critical whole language practice*. Urbana, IL: National Council of Teachers of English.

Eisenhart, M. (2005). Science plus: A response to the responses to scientific research in education. *Teachers College Record 107*(1), 52–58.

Erickson, F. (2005). Arts, humanities and sciences in education research and social engineering in federal education policy. *Teachers College Record, 107*(1), 4–9.

Fals-Borda, O. (1976). *El problema de como investigar la realidad para transformarla* [The problem of how to investigate reality to transform it] . Bogotá, Colombia: Fundación para el Análisis de la Realidad Colombiana— FUNDARCO.

Fals-Borda, O. (1985). *Knowledge and people's power: Lessons with peasants in Nicaragua, Mexico, and Colombia* (B. Maller, Trans.). New Delhi, India: Indian Social Institute.

Fals-Borda, O. (1991). Some basic ingredients. In O. Fals-Borda & M. A. Rahman (Eds.), *Action and Kowledge: Breaking the monopoly with participatory action research* (pp. 3–12). New York, NY: The Apex Press.

Fals-Borda, O. (Ed.). (1998). *People's participation: Challenges ahead*. New York, NY: The Apex Press.

Feuer, M., Towne, Lisa, & Shavelson, R. (2002). Scientific culture and educational research. *Educational Researcher, 31*(8), 4–14.

Flecha, R. (2000). *Sharing words: Theory and practice of dialogic learning*. Lanham, MD: Rowman & Littlefield.

Freire, P. (1992). *Pedagogy of the oppressed*. New York, NY: Continuum.

Freire, P. (1994). *Pedagogy of hope*. New York, NY: Continuum.

Freire, P. (1998). *Pedagogy of freedom: Ethics, democracy, and civic courage*. Lanham, MD: Rowman and Littlefield.

Freire, P. (2005). *Pedagogy of indignation*. Boulder, CO: Paradigm Publishers.

Freire, P. (2007). *Daring to dream: Toward a pedagogy of the unfinished*. Boulder, CO: Paradigm Publisher.

Freire, P., & Macedo, D. (1987). *Literacy: Reading the word and the world*. Westport, CT & London: Bergin & Garvey.

Gaventa, J. (1991). Toward a knowledge democracy: Views of participatory research in North America. In O. Fals-Borda & M. A. Rahman (Eds.), *Action and knowledge: Breaking the monopoly with Participatory Action Research* (pp. 121–134). New York, NY: The Apex Press.

Gee, J. P. (2005). It's theories all the way down: A response to scientific research in education. *Teachers College Record 107*(1), 10–18.

Goodman, K. (2006). Pedagogy of the absurd: There is an agenda behind the 'reading wars' and it harms teachers and students. *Rethinking Schools, 20*(3), 30–32.

Gramsci, A. (Ed.). (1985). *Selections from cultural writings (1910–1920)*. Cambridge, MA: Harvard University Press.

Guba, E. G., & Lincoln, Y. S. (1982). Epistemological and methodological bases for naturalistic inquiry. *Educational Communications and Technology Journal 31*, 233–252.

Guba, E. G., & Lincoln, Y. S. (1989). *Fourth generation evaluation*. Newbury Park, CA: Sage.

Guba, E. G., & Lincoln, Y. S. (2005). Paradigmatic controversies, contradictions, and emergent confluences. In N. K. Denzin & Y. S. Lincoln (Eds.), *Handbook of qualitative research* (pp. 191–215). Thousand Oaks, CA: Sage.

Hacking, I. (1999). *The social construction of what?* Cambridge, MA: Harvard University Press.

Hall, B., Gillete, A., & Tandon, R. (Eds.). (1982). *Creating knowledge: A monopoly? Participatory research in development*. New Delhi: Participatory Research Network.

Harding, S. (2006). *Science and social inequality: Feminist and postcolonial issues*. Urbana & Chicago, IL: University of Illinois Press.

Hess, C., & Ostrom, E. (2007). Introduction: An overview of the knowledge commons. In C. Hess & E. Ostrom (Eds.), *Understanding knowledge as a commons: From theory to practice* (pp. 3–25). Cambridge, MA: MIT Press.

Horton, M., & Freire, P. (1990). *We make the road by walking: Conversations on education and social change*. Philadelphia, PA: Temple University Press.

Hostetler, K. (2005). What is "good" education research? *Educational Researcher 34*(6), 16–21.

Howe, K. R. (2009). Epistemology, methodology, and education sciences. *Educational Researcher, 38*(6), 428–440.

Hursh, D. (2004). No Child Left Behind: The rise of educational markets and the decline of social justice. In J. O'Donnell, M. Pruyn & R. C. Chávez (Eds.), *Social justice in these times* (pp. 173–190). Greenwich, CT: Information Age Publishing.

Hursh, D. (2008). *High-stakes testing and the decline of teaching and learning: The real crisis of education*. Lanham, MD: Rowman & Littlefield.

Kaestke, C. (1993). The awful reputation of education research. *Educational Researcher, 22*(1), 23–31.

Kincheloe, J., & Berry, K. S. (2004). *Rigor and complexity in educational research: Conceptualizing the bricolage.* London, Great Britain: Open University Press.

Kohn, A. (2006, September 6). The truth about homework: Needless assignments persist because of widespread misconceptions about learning. *Education Week.* Retrieved from http://www.alfiekohn.org/ teaching/edweek /homework.

Kohn, A. (2007). *The homework myth: Why our kids get too much of a bad thing.* Philadelphia, PA: Da Capo Lifelong Books.

Krashen, S. (2008). Bogus claims about 'Reading First.' *Rethinking Schools, 22*(3), 32–33.

Krashen, S. D. (2010, January). *Comments on the LEARN Act.* Retrieved from www.sdkrashen.com.

Kuhn, T. (1962). *The structure of scientific revolutions.* Chicago, IL: University of Chicago Press.

Kvale, S. (1989). *Issues of validity in qualitative research.* Lund, Sweden: Studentlitteratur.

Lather, P. (1986). Issues of validity in openly ideological research: Between a rock and a soft place. *Interchange, 17*(4), 63–84.

Lather, P. (1993). Fertile obsession: Validity after poststructuralism. *Sociological Quarterly, 34*(4), 673–693.

Lather, P. (2008). New wave utilization research: (Re)Imagining the research/policy nexus. *Educational Researcher, 37*(6), 361–364.

Lévi-Strauss, C. (1966). *The savage mind.* Chicago, IL: University of Chicago Press.

Levine, A. (2007). *Educating researchers.* Washington, DC. Retrieved from http://www.edschools.org/EducatingResearchers/index.htm

Lincoln, Y. S. (1995). Emerging criteria for quality in qualitative and interpretive research. *Qualitative Inquiry, 1,* 275–289.

Lincoln, Y. S. (1997). What constitutes quality in interepretive research? In C. K. Kinzer, K. A. Hinchman, & D. J. Leu (Eds.), *Inquiries in literacy: Theory and practice.* Chicago, IL: National Reading Conference.

Lincoln, Y. S., & Guba, E. G. (1985). *Naturalistic inquiry.* Beverly Hills, CA: Sage.

Lincoln, Y. S., & Guba, E. G. (2003). Paradigmatic controversies, contradictions, and emergent confluences. In N. K. Denzin & Y. S. Lincoln (Eds.), *The landscape of qualitative research: Theories and issues* (pp. 253–291). Thousand Oaks, CA: Sage.

Lipman, P. (2006). "This is America" 2005: The political economy of education reform against the public interest In G. Ladson-Billings & W. F. Tate (Eds.), *Education research in the public interest* (pp. 98–116). New York, NY: Teachers College Press.

Lynd, R. (1939). *Knowledge for what?* Princeton, NJ: Princeton University Press.

Macedo, D. (2006). *Literacies of power: What Americans are not allowed to know* (Expanded ed.). Boulder, CO: Westview.

Mackenzie, B. D. (1977). *Behaviourism and the limits of scientific method.* Atlantic Highlands, NJ: Humanities Press.

Max-Neef, M. (1991). Human scale development: *Conception, application and further reflections.* New York, NY: The Apex Press.

Max-Neef, M. (1998). Economy, humanism and neoliberalism. In O. Fals-Borda (Ed.), *People's participation: Challenges ahead*. London, UK: The Apex Press: Intermedia Technology Communications.

Maxwell, J. (1996). *Qualitative research design: An interpretive approach*. Thousand Oaks, CA: Sage.

McMahon, K. (2009/2010). Testing kindergarten: Young children produce data—Lots of data. *Rethinking Schools, 24*(2), 42–44.

Meier, D. (2004). NCLB and democracy. In D. Meier & G. Wood (Eds.), *Many children left behind: How the No Child Left Behind Act is damaging our children and our schools* (pp. 66–78). Boston, MA: Beacon Press.

Moss, P. A., Phillips, D. C., Erickson, F. D., Floden, R. E., Lather, P. A., & Schneider, B. L. (2009). Learning from our differences: A dialogue across perspectives on quality in education research]. *Educational Researcher, 38*(7), 501–517.

National Assessment of Educational Progress (NAEP). (2009). National reading scores for 4th and 8th graders *The Nation's Report Card–-Reading*: Retrieved from http://nationsreportcard.gov/reading_2009/nat_g8.asp.

National Research Council. (2002). *Scientific research in education*. Washington, DC: National Academic Press.

Rahman, M. A. (1994). *People's self development: Perspectives on participatory action research; a journey through experience*. Dhaka, Bangladesh: University Press Limited.

Ravitch, D. (2010). *The death and life of the great American school system: How testing and choice are undermining education*. New York, NY: Basic Books.

Ravitch, D., & Flanders, L. (2010, July 20). Diane Ravitch: Race to the top or skim off the top? Retrieved from *GRITtv*.

Reyes, M. L., & Alcón, J. (Eds.). (2001). *The best for our children: Critical perspectives on literacy for Latino students*. New York, NY: Teachers College Press.

Rodriguez-Brandāo, C. (2005). Participatory research and participation in research: A look between times and spaces from Latin America. *International Journal of Action Research, 1*(1), 43–68.

Scheurich, J. J. (1997). *Research method in the postmodern* (vol. 3). Bristol, PA: The Falmer Press, Taylor and Francis.

Schön, D. (1983). *The reflective practitioner: How professionals think in action*: New York, NY: Basic Books.

Smith, J. K., & Hodkinson, P. (2005). Relativism, criteria and politics. In N. K. Denzin & Y. S. Lincoln (Eds.), *Handbook of qualitative research* (pp. 915–932). Thousand Oaks, CA: Sage.

Smith, L. D. (1986). *Behaviorism and logical positivism: A reassessment of the alliance*. Stanford, CA: Stanford University Press.

Smith, L. T. (1999). *Decolonizing methodologies: Research and indigenous peoples*. London, UK: Zed Books.

Sroufe, G. E. (1997). Improving the "awful reputation" of education research. *Educational Researcher, 26*(7), 26–28.

Streck, D. (2006). The scale of participation: From municipal public budget to cities' conference. *International Journal of Action Research, 2*(1), 78–97.

Streck, D. (2007). Research and social transformation: Notes about method and methodology in participatory research. *International Journal of Action Research, 3*(1& 2), 112–130.

Stringer, E. (1996). *Action Research: A handbook for practitioners.* Thousand Oaks, CA: Sage Publications.

Valenzuela, A. (Ed.). (2005). *Leaving children behind: How "Texas-style" accountability fails Latino youth.* New York, NY: SUNY Press.

Wallis, C. (2006, September). The myth about homework. *Time, 168* (10), 57.

Whitehurst, G. J. (2008). *Rigor and relevance redux: Director's biennial report to Congress.* Washington, DC: Institute of Education Sciences.

Willinsky, J. (2002). Democracy and education: The missing link may be ours. *Harvard Educational Review, 72*(3), 367–392.

Willinsky, J. (2005). Scientific research in a democratic culture: Or what's a social science for? *Teachers College Record, 107*(1), 38–51.

Wolcott, H. F. (1990). On seeking—and rejecting validity in qualitative research. In E. W. Eisner & A. Peshkin (Eds.), *Qualitative inquiry in education: The continuing debate* (pp. 121–152). New York, NY: Teachers College Press.

Wood, G. (2004). A view from the field: NCLB's effects on classrooms and schools. In D. Meier & G. Wood (Eds.), *Many children left behind: How the No Child Left Behind Act is damaging our children and our schools* (pp. 33–50). Boston, MA: Beacon Press.

Yatvin, J. (2002). Babes in the woods: The wanderings of the National Reading Panel. *Phi Delta Kappan, 83*(5), 364-369.

Chapter 4

Epistemological Relevance of Action in RAP: Blurring the Line between Research and Activism

Myriam N. Torres

The idea of making social transformation a research purpose (or principle) seems to me a bit *grandiose and naïve*...I wholeheartedly support the goals of social transformation. And it is certainly one of my hopes that my research *would result* in social transformation. But to make social transformation a requirement of the research process seems to me to *unnecessarily blur the line between research and political action* (Anonymous Reviewer C. *Educational Research Journal,* 2009, emphasis added)

The quotation above represents the current revived belief in the separation of research from political action, which is especially prominent in the education research community. This myth is even so enhanced as to naively expect that our research will somehow magically contribute to social transformation. The rationale is that someone sometime will use those ideas and by themselves or integrated with others will trigger some social change. Actually, this expectation is really what is grandiose and naïve. Why cannot social action be part of the research project? Action research has been around for many decades, ever since Kurt Lewin (1946) started his research in the United States in the

1940s and 1950s. Unfortunately the education research establishment is gaining terrain by:

1. promoting market-oriented management and discourse of research institutions (Hanley, 2005; Slaughter & Rhoades, 2004);
2. developing standards for publication of qualitative education research (American Educational Research Association, 2006, 2009) under the guise of rigor and improvement of quality;
3. changing the funding priorities and the practices of peer review, thus leading to the exclusion of types of research such as Research as Praxis, which does not fit into those standards, funding priorities, and discourse of scientism.

The quotation above attests to the application of those exclusionary practices. This new orthodoxy, as Howe (2009) calls it, is a "repositivization" of education research (Lather, 2008).

One of the three major guiding principles of RAP—collective action and transformation for social justice—was elaborated in chapter 2. Action is a distinctive and constitutive characteristic of RAP. Furthermore, collective action is intimately linked with radical participatory democracy. Obviously this idea, though not new, is still not accepted by most researchers, be they positivists or interpretivists. The idea of action as part of the process of research is definitely a blurring of the border between conventionally separated areas of research and social action connected with that research.

The purpose of this chapter is threefold:

1. document the epistemological significance of transformative action in RAP work;
2. examine the beliefs and practices of education research that ignore and/or sanction this significance;
3. describe how lifting the line between "research" and political action is not only necessary but urgent to embrace by education researchers committed to social justice and strengthening democracy.

In the rest of the chapter, first I lay out the urgency for more effective grassroots actions by illustrating a loud unison call by intellectuals/activists coming from different fields, institutions, and organizations. A historical look at the link between grassroots social movements and participatory research, which is central to RAP work, follows. Subsequently, I discuss the inaction by education researchers and the consequences of this self-restriction. Last, I elaborate on the epistemological relevance of action as mobilization for social justice in RAP work.

Urgent Unison Call for Grassroots Action at All Levels, Including Research

By definition, RAP is a border crossing of disciplinary fields and thus is interdisciplinary. Therefore, the discussion of the epistemological relevance of action should be framed in a global perspective to better understand the urgency of grassroots mobilizations and the building of common ground. I want to bring in the voices of scholars, writers, activists, organization officials, politicians, and people's advocates, who have convinced themselves of the need for bottom-up people's organization to put pressure on governments and those in power to consider their demands.

Why do we need to mobilize? Unfortunately, the reality we are living today is not pretty: globalization of poverty, with roughly a third of all human beings living in poverty worldwide (United Nations, 2007), growing day by day; the dangerous rise of global warming; escalation of wars; neo-colonialism; blatant injustices against which people can do little, and governments increasingly controlled by corporations. In fact, as Perkins (Perkins, 2004, 2007) confirms, most countries (certainly the United States) have plutocracies, rather than democracies. The proclaimed democracies merely serve as a façade. As I think of this grim picture at the beginning of this chapter, I hear my inner colonized voice say "don't start with a negative picture." However, as I argue and document in this chapter, one of the causes of scarcity of more effective grassroots organizations nationwide and worldwide is our immersion into the "culture of niceness" that prevents us from paying necessary attention to the depth and extension of the problems we are facing, problems of education obviously included. Too many prefer to live in a permanent denial of such a reality and stay comfortable, thinking very simplistically in dichotomies: good-bad, positive-negative, capitalism-socialism, white-black, and so on). Barbara Ehrenreich (2009) in her book *Bright-Sided: How the Relentless Promotion of Positive Thinking Has Undermined America,* comments that the forced "positive thinking" mantra leads people to blame themselves for problems and illnesses of which they are mostly the victims, not the causal agents. She, like Baker (2009) argues that the opposite of "positive thinking" is not "negative thinking" but a realistic understanding of the crude and cruel realities, especially for those people who are the most vulnerable and marginalized in this society.

Those of us who make the effort to get out of this binary positive-negative thinking and understand the reality from many different perspectives are hearing the resounding unison call for grassroots organization and mobilization. This call is coming from various fields, domains of knowledge, and social organizations. These are not just cries from the "leftist" activists, as some may think. They come from conscientious human beings who, through their work, engagement, and commitment to the improvement of living conditions around the world come to feel a moral obligation to denounce injustices and abuses and call for collective action. The following are only a few recent notable examples: The U.S. professor Elinor Ostrom (Goodman, 2009) received the 2009 Nobel Prize in Economics for her research on community self-organization, independence from government, and external corporations and agencies. She clarifies:

> I'm not denigrating that officials can do something very positive, but what we have ignored is what citizens can do and the importance of real involvement of the people, as opposed to just having somebody in Washington or at a far, far distance make a rule.... So we have to look *ground up* (emphasis added).

This declaration resonates with the notions of self-development and self-reliance at the core of the transformative principle of RAP. For example, Rahman (1994) describes a phenomenon going on since the 1970s in "the Other Africa," the one that we do not hear about or see through the media depiction of the "savage" continent. Actually, the theory of "alternative development" (Max-Neef, 1991, 1998), or development more comprehensive than that described by conventional economic indicators to involve a full-scale human development, is at the core of RAP.

In the same line of thinking about development, Irene Khan (2009), head of Amnesty International, elaborates on the idea of the human dimensions of development, beyond economic investment, in her book *The Unheard Truth: Poverty and Human Rights*. She was asked by *Democracy Now* Co-host Amy Goodman to "talk about the connection between poverty and human rights":

> Well, you know, if you ask the poor people, 'What's your condition?' what you hear from them is about discrimination. They can't get to school because they are women [common in Bangladesh]. They can't get jobs because they're an ethnic minority. They're excluded. You hear deprivation. You hear about discrimination, insecurity. Poor people live in fear, fear of losing their jobs, losing their homes, not knowing where their next meal is coming from, and sometimes living in war situations. War impoverishes people. And so, you can make economic investment, and maybe a farmer can improve his crop yield, but that does not guarantee the security of land tenure that he needs. You can build a school. That's one way of investing in the economy, but that doesn't ensure that girls will get to school as much as boys. So what I'm saying is that if you want to really help poor people get out of poverty, then you have to respect their rights, and you have to empower them, because they will then demand their rights and, through this process of dignity, get out of poverty.

Khan illustrates her claim with what has happened in her native country, Bangladesh, where successive governments were unable to meet the needs of the poor people. Some native activists and organizations inside and outside have facilitated the organization of people, with microcredits and education, especially for women, and the changes were real: infant mortality went down while education and employment for women went up. "And those are very big achievements that have been made because of civil society, because of people organizing themselves and demanding their rights."

Another collective voice—Urvashi Vaid (2009)—contributes to this worldwide chorus. A leader in the Lesbian, Gay, Bisexual, and Transgender (LGBT) communities, she brings up the problem of stagnation in organizations like these when they become institutionalized. She suggests renovation at the grassroots through the new generation of activists:

> I ran the National Gay and Lesbian Task Force, and I have a lot of affection and empathy for what it takes to build an LGBT movement and an infrastructure. I've been part of building that infrastructure from the local, state, national and now international level. And we need those organizations. Without them doing the day-in, day-out work of training, organizing, education, advocacy, you wouldn't have the conditions for progress.... At the same time, what happens in almost every social movement is that organizational development can actually stifle grassroots innovation and activism.

Joining this chorus is also the president of Malvides (Nasheed & Robinson, 2009), a small and, until now, barely known island in the Indian Ocean. This island has an altitude above sea level, and is one of the lowest landmasses in the world. Its government, under the leadership of President Mohamed Nasheed, found a very original way to bring the world's attention to the dangerous consequences of global warming: he conducted a cabinet meeting under water wearing scuba gear. In a speech he delivered to the Society for Ethical Culture on the eve of the 2009 UN General Assembly opening session, and in conversation with Mary Robinson, the former president of Ireland and the former UN High Commissioner for Human Rights, President Nasheed explained that the entire island and many low places like it will be under water if the global temperature rises 1.5 degrees centigrade. His government and those of other small island nations adopted a resolution to change modes of production and consumption:

> We are talking about another industrial revolution where renewable technology and greener technology remain at the heart of the new transformation, the transition of our economies to more [sic] greener methods of producing and consuming things...basically, more investments in re-

newable energy, and more energy-efficient usage, and regulations to that effect..../ But also, very importantly, more trying to understand more of what is happening.

How does President Nasheed plan to achieve these laudable goals? He sees strength in people's participation from the bottom up. In his message to the audience, as required by Robinson, he confesses: "Well, you know, believe me, politicians would never do anything unless it has some link to votes, and therefore—no, I'm one of them.... And, you know, leaders really don't think at all. No, they have their thinking done by the people. And, therefore, grassroots activism is so important to move leaders." So far, every one of these collective voices is looking at radical participatory democracy, whether it is called bottom-up, ground-up, grassroots activism, or simply asking people about their own situations and how to improve them.

Others have been more imaginative in their plea for grassroots mobilization for real feasible change. After many years of advocacy and activism, Ralph Nader (Nader, 2009a) started to wonder about the real possibilities of making major changes with comparatively meager resources compared to trillion-dollar industries. Thus, he imagined what he calls a "practical utopia," meaning something viable but it is still unattained. He actually designed a detailed plan, strategies, and budget including real names of superrich people in various sectors of society who actually are very concerned by the wrong direction in which the country is going. The whole idea is to take the country back from the madness, greed, and selfishness. Nader uses fiction to raise awareness of the limitations of documenting the rampant greed and corruption of the elites who are dismantling social services and rolling back progressive policy at all sectors of society. He even calls for a pause in documentation because it has frozen the imagination:

It's important, I think, for all of us to stop just documenting and documenting and diagnosing and proposing these things, when there's no power behind, there's no juggernaut, there's no pressure to organize the mass of the citizenry in the directions that really reflect their public sentiment, to use Abraham Lincoln's phrase (Nader, 2009b).

I found Nader's proposal a realistic and very persuasive utopia. We often see spectacles such as the health industry spending millions in lobbying and campaign contributions (Goodman, 2009b); Tumulty & Scherer, 2009), media advertising, pundits and commentators, who most of the time add to the manufacture of confusion and misinformation, and so-called grassroots "tea-parties" and rallies, which are just fearful, scared, and desperate people. Chris Hedges (2006) describes these people and documents how they have been used and for whose benefit. Recently, many of these same people have been paid to perform as a make-believe movement of concerned citizens (Potter, 2009). This sequence of events occurs even when the Congress has a democratic majority, and the White House a Democratic president. The problem is bigger than routine partisan politics. Thomas Frank (2008) exposes how the conservative right has built a movement which he calls the "Wrecking Crew" that started four to five decades ago. Demarrais (2006) also describes a good follow-up of this movement. According to Frank, one of the lemmas of this movement is "less government in business and more business in government." Another campaign is called "defunding the left," which actually means to dismantle social services, social programs, common good, regulations in the public interest, anything that sounds to them like "socialism."

Therefore, R. Nader's (2009b) proposal to make an alliance between grassroots organizations and somewhat enlightened, older, superrich, "Meliorists," to work with top-down leadership and resources, in order to make radical change possible, is worth paying attention to, even though it is still utopia. These are the "strategic alliances" that Apple (2006) talks about, to make research serve the public interest.

The Rethinking Schools editorial board (Rethinking Schools Editorial, 2009), a grassroots organization of educators itself, joins the chorus by asking: Where is our community organizer-in-chief? They remember Obama as a community organizer working to close the gap between "The world as it is and the world as it should be." Their point is that progressives must counteract the pressure of the right on him: "But how Obama and his administration respond to PRESSURE for the right will depend, in part, on our ability to do community organizing ourselves" (p. 5). How? They urge that "We need to build strong, multi-constituency coalitions that fight to protect and transform public schools so that they serve all children equitably and make education an integral part of the struggle to create the world as it should be" (p. 7).

Teachers from large cities such as Los Angeles, Chicago, New York, Washington, DC, and Detroit have been holding caucuses with unions and with parents. Teachers are engaged in several struggles: against excessive testing, layoffs, the closing of neighborhood schools, and the explosion of charter schools as non-profit but mostly private. Their problem with the latter is the passing money from public funds to private hands with much less accountability, if any. Teachers want participation. Certainly, teachers' unions are not reacting and leading these initiatives as they should be; they typically do too little, too late. Activist teachers are breaking with the American Federation of Teachers (AFT) and moving to "Teachers Unite," a more active organization for defending public education. Its members are convinced that in order to resist this systematic dismantling of public education, teachers need to organize collectively (Abowd, 2009).

Historical Linkage between Grassroots Social Movements and RAP

The chorus of voices calling for grassroots activism includes the voices of socially conscious individuals committed to counteract dominance, exploitation, greed, and shamelessness of the corporate elite of the world. However, social activism has developed and is mostly perceived as independent from systematic collective reflection and research on those actual and proposed actions. In this regard, research and social action are two separate worlds. In the education research culture, not only action is separated from research, but practice in general is considered apolitical as it is implied in the seminal report of the National Research Council (Feuer et al., 2002; National Research Council, 2002).

As has been indicated in Chapter 2, RAP involves interplay among research, political action and educational practice. Rodriguez-Brandão (2005) reviewed the historical development of participatory research in Latin America and came to the conclusion that it is an important part in advanced grassroots social movements, rather than preceding them. He found that grassroots social movements started to feel that social organization, popular mobilization, and transformation projects needed a new way to produce knowledge and that participatory research is the way to do that. The idea of connecting research and sociopolitical action is definitely a move beyond research as just data collection, to start hearing the voices of the collective as a two-way participation: popular participation in the investigation process, and participation of research in the course of popular action. These participations also have pedagogical value. Educators and researchers in the Third World disseminated some practices of popular participation as ways of contesting the social order. These practices contrast with the mainstream action research of Europe and the United States, which retains for the most part the neo-colonizing vocation. Participatory research, Rodriguez-Brandão argues, should be proposed as a research activity that is not less reliable and strict than academic research yet it is a more collective, participatory, and popular activity. Participatory research should be part of the flow of the collective action. The questions and challenges that arise in the social action component define the need and style of participatory research procedures.

For Freire (1992, 2000), Fals-Borda (1976, 1980, 1985, 1991, 1995, 1998, 2005), Rahman (1991a, 1994) and many other pioneers and followers of the participatory action research (PAR) movement, the bases are radical participatory democracy and transformative action toward social change in the public interest, with a particular emphasis on the most marginalized people. The quote at the beginning of this chapter, from a major journal, shows the gap between research and political action—just because this is the way. It is unquestionably accepted and used as a criterion of publication gate keeping.

Along the same line of thinking, de Souza's (1989) keynote at the third World Encounter on Participatory Research held in Managua, Nicaragua, alludes to the theme of the encounter "Knowledge, Democracy, and Peace," as interdependent and interactive. He points to the importance of a critical reflection on collective actions as sources of knowledge and understanding, not merely the application of knowledge. For him, when the action itself becomes an object of knowledge by the popular sectors of people, they become historical subjects as they gain agency and hence collective power. Their empowerment propels them to engaging in even more impacting and emancipatory actions.

Danilo Streck (2006, 2007, 2009) describes an experience in which civic, community, and political education takes place alongside a social movement and participatory research. This is a large-scale experience involving all sorts of stakeholders in the "participatory city budgets." Over 100 cities in Brazil have engaged in this civic-political experiment. He traces its roots back to the "Movement of Grassroots Communities," which grew in parallel with the military dictatorship beginning in 1964. The vision of this movement was of the people participating on an equal footing in the planning of public interest issues. Such participation was the key to radical democracy. Participating in planning city budgets is critical for many of the public interest programs and services to exist and work under the common-good principle. Popular active participation in this process, assures Streck (2007) is a "school" in which people learn about the role of the government and their responsibilities and rights as citizens, as well as the significance of their participation in efforts to disrupt patterns of exclusion, segregation and injustice. Nuñez-Hurtado (2005) accounts for a similar large-scale civic-political experience, in the State of Michoacán, Mexico, of citizens' participation in government planning and co-management through citizens' consultation workshops. These examples of democratic participation show clearly how research, education, and political action are intermingled in RAP type of work, in which radical participatory democracy enables people to study and act collectively on their own behalf.

Following Rodriguez-Brandão (2005), Streck (2007) argues that the fundamental factor is not so much the popular participation in the research, but the involving of participatory research in the popular movement. Radical democratic participation of people in civic-political activities such as the participatory budget experiment in Brazil is a form of reconstructing the public sphere, which is indispensable for democracy to work for the public interest for all people, not just for the elites.

Standardized minds, using Sacks' (1999) expression, reject RAP type of research because they do not think that the rigor of the research can be maintained, when research interplays with teaching and socio-political action. For Streck (2007), scientific rigor does not come from correct application of instruments and control of variables. Rigor has to do with the ethical-political commitment to effectively help a given community to develop a collective understanding of their problems and to devise strategies of self-organization and struggle toward improving their living together.

The Inaction of Progressive Education Research and Society as a Whole

It is not uncommon that progressives and their organizations fall short in advancing their causes and end up doing too little, too late. In education, the few teachers who are actively defending public education and the teaching profession from privatization and corporate takeover are feeling that frustration (Abowd, 2009). Domination holds sway if there is no longer enough resistance. In this section, I am going to examine some conceptual and political frames that prevent progressives from bridging the gap between research and sociopolitical action.

Progressives are awakening to the open and not-so-open advances of the right wing neoliberalism—faith in the market as the best organizing principle of government and society. There is no alternative (TINA for short), as Margaret Thatcher used to preach (George, 1999; Giroux, 2002, 2004). What is worrisome is that the neoliberal doctrine is advancing faster than the awakening and counteractions of progressives and is becoming entrenched in all sectors of society at national and international levels, to the point of reaching immunity to change of political party in Washington, despite promises and good intentions.

What should be clear by now is that there has emerged a "new alliance" of conservatives and liberals on the basis of free market ideology, known as neoliberalism (Apple, 2004). This doctrine has been embraced and executed by corporations, which in education has led to a corporate takeover. In chapter 1 on "Denunciation," this issue was developed to some extent. In this chapter 4, I describe the connection between the neoliberal corporate takeover of education and how it is reflected in education research. This impact seems to go hand in hand with what Patti Lather (2008) calls "repositivization" of education research, and Howe (2009) refers to it as neo-positivism, not post-positivism as his critics (e.g., R. B. Johnson, 2009) allege. It is clear that the "repositivization" of educational research, largely influenced by funding opportunities and diffusion through publications, has tremendous implications for diversity of research approaches and especially for radically different research paradigms such as RAP (Torres, Coppola, Huerta-Charles, & Reyes, 2006). As this repositivization of research with all its implications takes hold, progressive researchers, with few exceptions, seem to buy into the rhetoric of standards and rigor of "Education Sciences." I honestly think that progressives lack the will to engage in counteracting activities that are visible and coordinated enough to stop this regression in education research. Those progressive and critical researchers who are engaged in activism do not cover all the fronts, for instance, the media-echo-chamber that the right-wing neoliberal agenda has monopolized for decades (Demarrais, 2006). R. Johnson (2009) names quite accurately the type of system we are now living under: a "structurally dysfunctional money politics system." I will add that it may be dysfunctional for progressive individuals, but it functions perfectly for the "Wrecking Crew" (Frank, 2008) of elites and corporations. Johnson was referring specifically to the financial industry, the key player in the economic and social crisis we are living now worldwide. Chomsky (2009), very appropriately, characterizes this state of affairs as a "democratic deficit."

The repositivization of education research is, therefore, not an isolated phenomenon. It is part and parcel of the Neoliberal globalized capitalist forces. O'Connor (2007) argues that the alleged scientific neutrality of the expert is actually a smokescreen for advancing the conservative agenda at all levels. The focus on method and the crunching of numbers for producing indexes, scores, and stats, which are submitted to heavy manipulation with the help of the corporate media, is just a distraction. O'Connor also documents that the self-proclaimed education research scientists actually do not care for empirical data; these are only used as a cover-up.

Lather (2008) in reviewing Hess (2008) edited book, claims that the highly publicized Institute of Education Sciences, which is part of the repositivization process of education research, has just produced "policy entrepreneurs" and not the convergent replicable and cumulative findings about education theory and practice they promised to justify the creation of such an institute in the first place. The discourse on rigor, which is a characteristic of this "new orthodoxy" (using Howe's term) of education research sciences did not prevent the "Reading First" debacle. Lather asks: What do the standards and evidence look like where exclusion and fixities of what is scientific and not are precisely the debate? Challenging the results is at the very core of scientific activity, she remarks.

The epistemological and methodological principles at the root of this new orthodoxy are at the core of the positivist paradigm of research. Based on the 2002 National Research Council Report (2002). Howe (2009) synthesizes those principles:

1. pose questions to study empirically;
2. link research to related theory;
3. use methods to investigate questions directly;
4. provide explicit chain of reasoning;
5. replicate and generalize;
6. disclose data and methods for professional peer review.

Even though these principles are presented as sufficiently open so that no research approach is constrained by them, the truth is that any research project that does not concord with those principles is not considered scientific, or cognitively significant. In particular, a RAP type of investigation, which in principle is guided by radical democracy and transformative action, does not match or is even compatible with the above principles, which are supposedly universal. Therefore, RAP-type reports does not fit into those standards, obviously. I will elaborate on this incompatibility later.

The repositivization of education research brings to the forefront traditional categories of research (basic-applied, scientific-non-scientific), and hierarchies of knowledge (basic-applied or theoretical-practical). This narrow way of thinking compresses an entire spectrum of approaches into conceptual binaries, of which one side is inherently weaker, hence reinforcing hegemonic thinking about research principles (above) and criteria of validity (objectivity, rationality, empiricism, reliability, and generalizability) (American Educational Research Association, 2006, 2009). This closed system determines the standard response to what and whose reality counts? Whose knowledge counts? Knowledge for what purpose? Whose interests are served given certain research results?

Knowledge for What?

This new orthodoxy of research as fundamentally positivist constrains the relevance of research results to merely empirical tests; worse than that, it excuses education researchers from the ethical duty of the social responsiveness of their research. This relevance of research to policy, to practice, to society is considered the task of others such as policy makers (who often are not educators and are even anti-educators) or the problem of the practitioners. In truth, most research results are irrelevant to practitioners, which is not surprising, given the different worlds in which researchers and practitioners have been living throughout history. Lynd (1939) describes this abyss in the social sciences as a division between scholars and technicians. The scholar "simply works ahead within a studio with walls relatively sound-proofed against the clamorous urgency of the world outside" (p. 2). For the scholars, immediate relevance is not deemed important because any contribution, whether relevant or not to social problems, is *new knowledge* that contributes to the "master system of progress" (p. 2) of science and society. Relevance is condoned by "the self-justifying goodness of 'new knowledge' about anything, big or little" (p. 2). Meanwhile practitioners' work is driven by the immediate urgency. Both sides work without feeling an urgent need to synchronize their worlds.

Hegemonic thinking about utilization of research results considers relevance as a threat to rigor, and therefore the knowledge generated by research projects that look for social relevance is by definition less scientifically valid. Henig (2008) conveys this concept by wondering: "how far down the path of relevance researchers want to go" (p. 62). It implies that making research useful is not a priority goal. The rigor-or-relevance antinomy is part of the positivist research orthodoxy, hence excluding other considerations. Departing from the orthodoxy of education research, Lather (2008) proclaims that the use of research results (relevance) is more a philosophical than an instrumental/empirical problem. For RAP researchers, use of research is an ethical and political commitment. In reviewing Hess's (2008) edited book on relevance of research for policy), Lather points out that, although the contributors to the book have moved beyond research rigor as the guarantee for school improvement, their sense of utility of research has no moral commitment. In Jameson's (1981) terms, research relevance merely meaning application in practice without moral commitment reflects a "political unconsciousness." Even when the application of research results is meant to improve specific educational practices, further action is often suggested or recommended in very nebulous ways to anyone interested in applying them.

As we know, the gap between education theory and practice, rather than narrowing, is getting wider. The reasons for that have been discussed in the previous sections and can be summarized here as follows:

1. Division of labor between researchers and practitioners, with no urgent reason for collaboration;
2. Lower status accorded to practical knowledge or practitioner-initiated research;
3. Separation between research and action, and especially between research and political action for social transformation.

When I refer to action, I am thinking of several dimensions: from individual to collective action, from primarily language actions to social movements, from local to global scope. Alongside these dimensions, there can be several levels of action. Here are some examples:

1. Unveiling, denouncing, documenting injustices, biases, etc: These types of actions are definitely more than just producing new knowledge (Lynd, 1939; Harding, 2003; Freire, 2005);
2. Speech acts: e.g., writing a letter, signing a document, performing theater, singing, writing self-narratives, writing poetry, etc.;
3. Facilitating others to become aware and educated by reaching out to people and having them understand the issues as they have been documented;
4. Getting organized and planning collective actions;
5. Building a social movement.

So far I have discussed how conventions in research, especially the new orthodoxy, result not only in separating theory from practice, and practitioners from researchers but also in dismissing socio-political action as part of the research process and of academia. These ideas are justified by the long-held but also very worn-out premise of scientific "neutrality" (Harding, 2006; Howe, 2009).

However, not only the positivists excuse researchers for the lack of social responsiveness of their research. As Greenwood and Levin (2003) remark that "hard-line interpretivists" consider

commitment to action as naïve and outside the realm of the research activity. Delgado-Gaitán (1993) illustrates the conflict of an
ethnographic researcher considering personal and professional
activism as requested and expected by the research participants.

Another hindrance in bringing transformative action alongside
research emerges from mainstream postmodernist researchers,
which has been examined in Chapter 1. What is important to
mention here is the paralyzing phenomenon that results when
postmodernists become obsessive in their critique of anything that
seems merely modernist (foundational and universal claims,
consensus, rationality, stability, clarity, certainty, liberation,
transformation and so on). They end up falling into what Cole
(1994) refers to as "the poverty of contingency theory," which leads
them to a state of paralysis. This prevents even temporary consensus, and hence the building of common ground for planning and
carrying out collective actions. Postmodernists of this type reject
any liberation project and transformative collective action, claiming they are not possible either in theory or practice. In addition,
following the dictum of Lyotard (1984) that there is nothing
outside language, they rely on language and self-narrative as the
only ways to carry out actions.

Like neoliberalism, paralyzing postmodernism cultivates fatalism. Freire (2003) argues that the main threat to our projects for
making the world better is fatalism. In the same vein, Darder et
al. (2009) point also to the postmodernists' paralyzing impact on
critical pedagogy and progressive movements. The intense attention to the politics of difference, which many took to the extreme of
absolute contingency, resulted in fragmenting organizations and
dismantling the political vision of liberation and emancipation,
rendering them impossible and illusive. The postmodernist overemphasis on difference promotes the segmentation of what could
be considered unique situations, but in fact are common experiences of oppression and exploitation.

The expected result from both the neoliberal takeover and the
paralyzing postmodernism, is fatalism. Herbert (2009) describes a
worrisome passivity in American society:

Americans have tended to watch with a remarkable (I think frightening) degree of passivity as crises of all sorts have gripped the country and sent millions of lives into tailspins. Where people once might have deluged their elected representatives with complaints, joined unions, resisted mass firings, confronted their employers with serious demands, marched for social justice and created brand new civic organizations to fight for the things they believed in, the tendency now is to assume that there is little or nothing ordinary individuals can do about the conditions that plague them. He attributes this fatalism to lack of personal responsibility. This passivity and sense of helplessness most likely stems from the refusal of so many Americans over the past few decades to acknowledge any sense of personal responsibility for the policies and choices that have led the country into such a dismal state of affairs and to turn their backs on any real obligation to help others who were struggling.

Many will agree with Herbert's perception. Although we cannot excuse individuals from their responsibility for others, such a perception should include the socioeconomic and political forces that generate these crises, and indicate who are the most responsible.

The Epistemological Significance of Collective Action and Mobilization toward Social Transformation

So far it is clear that there is a concerted loud call from all the progressive sectors for grassroots mobilization, that there is a historical link between the RAP type of research and grassroots social movements, and that inaction by social and educational researchers has no justifiable excuses. In RAP, action for social transformation is a constitutive dimension of the research process. Certainly, action is not only the "application" of research results but also can be a source of knowledge and understanding. De Souza (1990) refers to it as an "epistemological pertinence of action." In RAP type of work, researchers and the community meet to explain past actions and those yet to be realized actions in a critical and self-critical mode. Mariño (1990) considers that participatory research can precede action, accompany action and follow action. Likewise Vio-Grossi (1983) maintains that it is widely understood that in order to fully understand a given social reality, we should attempt to change it. Tensions, contradictions, interests, and agendas will surface. For him, "There does not exist valid knowledge that is not originated and proven in the action" (p. 31). Therefore, action in RAP type of work is not just the "application" of research results, nor is it mere activism. De Souza argues that by making collective action the object of knowledge by the actors themselves, we have a way to strengthen community building and agency enhancement. All these facilitate consensus for future collective actions on their own behalf while overcoming dichotomies such as theory-practice, subject-object, popular knowledge-formal academic knowledge.

Fals-Borda's (1970, 1976, 1980) pioneering work on "how to study reality in order to transform it" points to participatory action research (PAR) as a possibility for common people to create knowledge and science during the process of organized collective action. PAR is an ideological and intellectual movement that prepares people to assume their role as subjects of history. Fals-Borda became convinced that for academic research to have social and political relevance, it is necessary to involve popular knowledge and common sense. For Fals-Borda (1991a, 1991b) popular science is a challenge to the often "prophylactic and arrogant" hard-line scientific knowledge. Both Fals-Borda (1970) and Rodriguez-Brandão (2005) contend that conventional practices of social and educational research are forms of colonization and oppression which ignore and devaluate ordinary people's knowledge, and the one coming from the so-called "Third World" countries, while imposing theories, frameworks, paradigms, and practices from "advanced" countries. Awakening to this exclusion and colonization and seizing the opportunity to share the products of collective research are important moment of popular action itself.

The problem with conventional social and educational research is not only the colonizing aspect but also their exclusionary practices, as documented by postcolonial and feminist researchers such as Sandra Harding (2006). She examines the scientific principles of "objectivity," "neutrality," "rationality," and "good method," which, she argues, are driven by militarism, profits, self-serving mythologies, and lack of self-criticism. Nonetheless, these are used as smokescreens to prevent researchers from taking social responsibility up-front in their research projects. Harding demonstrates how political values of the researcher are infused in each and every step of research, despite his or her alleged neutrality and objectivity. Denying and hiding those political values makes the research even more biased and less objective. Similarly, Gaventa (1991) points out the exclusionary and elitist knowledge system in North America, and how research has become corporate driven by vested interests. For him, participatory research implies the democratization of knowledge while communities engage in transformative actions. The knowledge system is hence bottom-up and democratic. This concept has promoted policy such as the "right to know" and the historical recuperation of knowledge and experience. The truth is, as de Souza (1990) points out, that in order for a social change to benefit the common people and the public interest, it needs to engage them from the bottom-up. Streck (2006, 2007) has illustrated this with the large-scale experience of participatory research in Brazil called the "participatory budge."

Research for What?

As indicated in the previous section, *Knowledge for What?* can be answered in many different ways. In education research, *knowledge for what* often implies the application of theoretical and instrumental knowledge to the improvement of learning, teaching, schooling, and to informing education reform and public policy. This type of application has been called "applied research." However, these applications for improvement address for the most part the instrumental dimension of educational practices and environment. Issues such as democratic education, well-being, and human fulfillment of students, teachers, and administrators as well as fostering an environment for joy and creative imagination, receive less attention, if any. "Why isn't a kindergartner's Happiness Index taken as seriously as his [her] phonemic awareness score? Why don't we ask high school students what you want? Ask that—and shut up and listen to the answers. These questions are neither frivolous nor rhetorical" assert educators Emery and Ohanian (2004). These authors point to the issue of moral commitment that Lather (2008) contemplates in connecting education research and practice—the social usefulness of research is more philosophical (values driven) than instrumental. Lynd (1939) expresses beautifully the philosophical foundations of social and educational research. "The values of humans living together in the pursuit of their deeper and more persistent purposes constitute the frame of reference that identifies significance for social science" (p. 189). The instrumental emphasis in applied research addresses issues that ultimately do not count for people as we can see in the questions raised by Emery and Ohanian. In addition, there are many questions that nobody asks about some empiricist principles and procedures. Lynd digs into them: "No informed person questions nowadays the indispensability of objective data-gathering and of the exhaustive statistical analysis of those data for all they are worth. The only question that is being raised here concerns the need to ask 'what are they worth for what?' Objective empiricism can become as much of a blind alley as can logical speculation." (p. 129)

For Lynd, this pure empiricist knowledge is not helping people but helping to support the belief that "more knowledge is better." Hence, courses, batteries of courses, dissertations are done without raising the question what to do other than giving more lectures, teaching more courses, and writing more dissertations and publications. He describes, 70 years in advance, what the theme of the 2009 American Educational Research Association (AERA) Annual Conference: "Disciplinary Inquiry: Education Research in the Circle of Knowledge" really means.

Pioneers of RAP such as Orlando Fals-Borda, Anisur Rahman, Francisco Vio-Grossi, Rajesh Tandon, Camilo Torres, Paulo Freire, Carlos Rodriguez-Brandão have been educated according to conventional paradigms of research. Then, as their careers progressed, they found disjunction between the academic work and the need for addressing social and educational problems. Fals-Borda (Cendales, Torres, & Torres, 2005) recounts his journey in conceptualizing research as praxis. The central questions were: Research for what? To transform what? And why? Fals-Borda insists that theory and practice should go hand in hand and not become separate stages or moments. There must be an action-reflection rhythm: knowledge for what? Knowledge for whom? Whose knowledge counts? These questions were not asked by academia, at least his preparation as a researcher and his experience as an academic over many years. Many have had this quite common experience, including the author.

RAP work overcomes the pseudo-neutrality of science because both inside and outside researchers have an ethical-political commitment to work with the poor and marginalized communities and groups toward transforming their lives and work conditions, from local to global (de Souza, 1990). This dynamic contrasts with the conventional research practices and beliefs about the primary values of research and the de facto hierarchy of knowledge/research by which the closer to applied knowledge, the less scientific value is given, at least in the social sciences and humanities. Today, as academic capitalism expands (Hanley, 2005; Slaughter & Rhoades, 2004) there has been developed a new configuration of hierarchies of knowledge which has tremendous implications in equality and equity in academia. Today, the status of knowledge depends on how many millions of dollars it brings in grants to the university or research center. Engineering and physical sciences have risen to the top with juicy grants, so their faculty members receive higher salaries. The knowledge generated in Colleges of Education does not attract millions in grants; therefore their faculty members are at the bottom of the pay scale. To add insult to injury, this unequal and unjust salary differential is called "equity pay adjustment."

Lynd (1939) critiques the social science relevance of his times, which is not much different from today, when achievement of human well-being is considered an automatic by-product of money-making, and progress in science and society is located in the future, thus justifying the value of *new* knowledge. The assumption is that *new* and *more* knowledge is always better and constitutes the main reason for research, even in the case of applied research. According to this way of thinking, he argues, extreme differences in power and extreme inequality are assumed to be temporary; hence we should not be worried. Those problems will be solved with ever more *new* knowledge.

Given that RAP type of work is openly ideological, its pioneers and practitioners do not hide this stance. Rahman (1991a) clarifies this point: "The basic ideology of participatory action research is that self-conscious people, those who are currently poor and oppressed, will progressively transform their environment by their own praxis. In this process others may play a catalytic and supportive role but will not dominate" (p. 13). Fals-Borda (Cendales et al., 2005) gives Anisur Rahman the credit for being the main contributor (theoretically and practically) to the radical participatory dimension of research, at a time when Action Research was being stripped of its democratic and liberating dimensions and reduced to an instrumental problem-solving type of activity.

When Rahman (1991b, 1994) refers to oppressing structures, he is also referring to the realm of knowledge production. Based on his vast experience in Asia and Africa, he knows firsthand how by supporting the creation and/or strengthening of grassroots autonomous organizations, and engaging their members in dialogical inquiries of their own history and socioeconomic conditions, ordinary people are able to generate the knowledge basis of their own self-development. He has found that this self-development and self-reliance have better chances to occur when the external agents are non-governmental self-reliance promoting organizations. In "Glimpses of the 'other Africa'" (Rahman, 1991b, 1994), Rahman builds a very comprehensive understanding of the notions of self-development and self-reliance based on a vast number of grassroots projects in various African countries. Self-development comes from people's own felt needs, their resources and organizational efforts. Self-development is opposed to pseudo-development as promoted by international or other types of external organizations with a colonizing mentality.

Along the same line of thinking, Max-Neef (1991, 1998), the director of an international institution called "Alternative Development Center," developed and tested in 21 countries a "theory of development on a human scale." Its researchers identified nine basic human needs: sustenance, protection, love or affection, participation, understanding, creation, leisure, identity, and freedom. By redefining poverty in terms of meeting these needs, they found that the richest countries have poorly met many of these needs; in contrast, economically poor countries were rich in ability to meet several of these basic human needs. In addition to the inaccurate picture of development based mostly on economic indicators, they came up with what they called a "threshold hypothesis." This hypothesis challenges the very basis of development as merely based on economic indicators. Economic growth, as conventionally defined, improves people's lives up to a certain point. Beyond that point, more economic growth begins to deteriorate the quality of life, because new problems are created by that very growth. Beyond the threshold point, the way to eradicate poverty is by introducing a better income distribution. This is a new model of social life based on human needs, not just material goods. All in all, as Rahman and Fals-Borda (1991) assure, PAR is both a philosophy and a methodology of research since it is oriented to life as self-development and human fulfillment. Collective action is necessary in order to achieve these objectives.

Specifically in the area of education, Jean Anyon (2005) provides very important information concerning radical possibilities for a "new social movement," which she considers should be led by educators. Where most people see problem zones—e.g., concentration of poor people in the so-called "inner cities"—she sees these places as "fertile soil" for community organization and mobilization. Anyon demonstrates that social movements have created paths for social changes, which have benefited the poor, minorities and the middle class. According to her, there are millions (7.56) of grassroots groups working for progressive causes; however, what is missing is the coordination of these groups across neighborhoods in the cities and at the regional and national levels. She illustrates how, in American history, social movements are catalysts for the enactment of social justice legislation, progressive court decisions, and other equity policies. In the same light, when educators work with community residents as equals for improving education, a social movement can emerge. Anyon believes that educators have relatively accessible opportunities to become agents of change. Even though Anyon does not talk about action in research, she compiles much relevant information with which she challenges all of us as educators, to engage in this "new social movement." She does that with conviction and commitment.

Fatalist, paralyzing ideology is everywhere in society and in the academia as well. Either it comes from the new orthodoxy of research fed by the neoliberal ideology, or it comes from the paralyzing postmodern conceptual framework. In the first case, people's inaction is a political strategy; in the second case—paralyzing postmodernism—people's inaction is a conceptual trap. Critics coming from either of these two alleys see RAP inquiries as naïve, idealist, or simply impossible. We have never claimed that this type of work is easy. As Freire (2003, 2005) assures us, working against the grain toward a better world is difficult but not impossible. What we need to do is to fight together with solidarity and commitment. For him, the main obstacle is not the extreme power of the ruling classes and its corporate allies but the fatalist ideology of the people who happen to be their victims. Freire challenges us to reinvent the ways of our struggles and actions and constantly give testimonio of coherence between talk and action. In his later work, he stresses our right and duty to change the world for the better, which for him mean: more peaceful, just, sustainable, and democratic. This work requires us to have a dream, that is, a lucid perception of changes needed to make the world better for more people. For Freire, working toward this dream requires that we understand our historical conditions and actions, including how dominant classes and cultures work against the public interest and the well-being of the majorities.

Action Knowledge, Self-Development, and Social Ethics

The ethical and moral dimension of RAP goes beyond the "informed consent" (institutional compliance), and professional ethics of honest and responsible behavior to include social and civic responsibility, first of all for research participant-communities and society in general. Christians (2003) calls the former "external" ethics and considers it as based on the premise of value neutrality. In contrast, "social" ethics has to do with the specific needs of human daily life. For him, institutional review boards (IRBs) are the legacy of John Stuart Mill, August Comte, and Max Weber. "Value-neutral science is accountable to ethical standards through rational procedures controlled by value-free academic institutions in the service of impartial government" (p. 220). Actually, IRBs protect the subjects, only according to their own protocols; rather, IRBs are designed to protect the institutional liability and not the public interest in society at large. He argues that social science research cannot be reduced to "external" ethics. "Social" ethics as understood in the "feminist communitarian" model (Denzin, 1997) generates social criticism and resistance while empowering the self and others toward taking action. Exclusive focus on external or individual ethics allows us to acknowledge only partial responsibility, while researchers abdicate their social responsibilities. For Christians, social ethics, rather than resting on neutrality, "rests on a complex view of moral judgments as integrating into an organic whole, everyday experience, beliefs about the good, and feelings of approval and shame of human relations and social structures" (p. 223). In this philosophy of ethics, the moral domain is situated for the purpose of human life.

Making a similar argument pro social ethics but in the realm of action research, Greenwood and Levin (2003) ask: "Why is it proper for us to hold academic social researchers accountable to higher standards of social responsibility?" They maintain that with some exceptions, university-based research is anti-praxis and mostly oriented to self-service within the structure of academia. Generations of researchers believe that their work in research is by itself valuable to society. Therefore, there is little sense of urgency despite efforts of more praxis-oriented researchers. The problem is that small changes are not sufficient to achieve necessary transformations, given that research is driven by vested private interests rather than public interests. Greenwood and Levin come to the conclusion that a systematic and strong collective effort is necessary to make any change in the culture of research in academia and in the public. They are convinced that action research can be a viable vehicle to promote that change.

Higher standards of social responsibility are not only important but urgent. Many praxis-oriented feminist researchers are working on this pursuit. Socially useful research is the utilization of research within a frame of moral commitment, not just for instrumental reasons, Lather (2008) explains. Fine (1994) and Fine, Weis, Weseen, and Wong (2003) deal with a dilemma of qualitative researchers concerning the representation of multiple voices and especially what Fine calls the qualitative colonizing discourse of the 'other." This interrogation took place while she was also moving into a paradigm of participatory research and embracing the role of activist working with the community while doing research.

Lack of social responsibility and dilemmas concerning which voices to include or represent should not be central problems in RAP work if the experience is guided by the principles of radically participatory democracy and transformative collective action. It is expected that research participants are fully engaged in the decision making in each step of the research process including any action and of course the use of the results. This is the ideal situation; obviously there will be conflicts and people who attempt to take advantage of others. As indicated in Chapter 2, in the section on commitment, one of the roles of the external researcher is to devise the conditions for participatory democracy to take place.

Action Research Expansion: Co-optations and Variations

It is common that researchers from the so-called "First World" ignore the multiple origins of RAP research in any of its forms: participatory research, militant research, participatory action research in various countries of the so-called "Third World." Kemmis and McTaggart (2005) describe the expansion of participatory action research, starting in the First World and moving to the third world in the fourth wave. Rodriguez-Brandão (2005) noted that participatory research authors from the third world also ignore their counterpart from the First World.

In the literature, the origins of action research are usually traced back to Kurt Lewin's (1946) studies, which he termed quasi-experiments in democratic management in factories. He was concerned with the theory-practice divide, and wanted to study an alternative to Taylor's (1911) "scientific management" and its direct connections to behaviorism. Action research, for Lewin and his fellow students, was a way to achieve greater effectiveness through democratic participation in the process of production. This is why Adelman (1997) considers Lewin a "scientist of action."

There is no doubt that Lewin's notion of action research consti-tuted by far a strong alternative to the mechanical and dehuma-nizing character of "scientific management." Action research represented not only a challenge to conventional behaviorist research but a democratic alternative. The nexus between theory and practice is inherent to its nature: "No action without research, no research without action" (Lewin, 1946). However, his under-standing of action research was not grounded on the ideal of liberation and transformation of the social conditions beyond their workplace toward social change, starting with the participants. Action researchers in the Third World (e.g., Fals-Borda, 1976, 1985, 1991a; Mariño, 1990; Rahman, 1994; Rodriguez-Brandão, 2005) were aware of the lack of Lewin's action research approach of the transformative liberating goal. They started using varia-tions of the name to include this component in the title. They added 'participatory" to action research. For many, the liberating approach became participatory action research—PAR, or simply participatory research. The work of many pioneers on this strand of action research is spread out around the world: Freire (1992), Horton and Freire (1990), Hall and collaborators (1982), Rahman (1994), Fals-Borda (1976), Carr and Kemmis (1986), McTaggart (1997), Stringer (1996), among others. These are intellectuals who have reached the understanding that traditional knowledge production and social-educational research practices and assump-tions are instruments of colonization and domination and do not bring the proclaimed benefit that most First World researchers assume. Functionally similar conditions of oppression and exploitation create this climate for understanding and building alternatives to the dominant paradigms of research.

Altrichter and Gstettner (1997) examine the history of action research in Germany and question the Lewinean origins of action research. They found historical references to J. L. Moreno, a charismatic Swiss physician, social philosopher and poet, who was known for inventing new terms. By 1913, he was already thinking of participants as "co-researchers." He used terms such as "interaction research," or "action research," which he characterized as: field-based research, participation of ordinary people interested in the research subject, and improvement of the social situation as the aim of research. Altrichter and Gstettner consider that the German renaissance of action research has stronger roots in Moreno's ideas than to Lewin's. However, in the literature Lewin is cited more frequently.

Unfortunately, as various strands of action research spread around the world and become institutionalized, they also have been assimilated into more conventional paradigms. Using Habermas's (1972) categories of human interests and knowledge, Grundy (1988) traced the history of action research and could identify three major approaches that correspond to three distinctive philosophies and research methodologies:

1. the scientific technical view of problem solving;
2. the practical deliberative; and
3. the critical emancipatory.

Action research as problem solving, its most common practice, is basically an assimilation into the positivist paradigm, in which the action can refer to treatments or intervention/changes to be tested empirically in order to solve the problem at hand. The second approach—the practical deliberative action research approach—has been nested into the phenomenological interpretivist paradigm, hermeneutics and insiders' meaning-making methodology. It has taken the modes and shapes of the mainstream qualitative approaches. The third approach to action research is grounded more on Marx, Gramsci, and Habermas, and less on Kurt Lewin and Karl Rogers (Rodriguez-Brandão, 2005). Participatory action research, emancipatory action research, research as praxis, and many others with a similar basic focus are devoted to making research a liberating and transformative human experience.

Greenwood and Levin's (2003) approach to action research may be an illustration of the third trend of this movement—emancipatory action research. They consider that action research can play an important role in critiquing conventional academic research in social and educational realms and serve as a good vehicle to change the purposes of research inside academia as well as the relationships of the university with the communities, which often are used as objects of research but do not benefit from such research. They assert that many social groups that are marginalized in society often hope that research would help solve their everyday problems such as discrimination, unemployment, poverty, and illnesses. They do not care if the university has x number of grants or about its rank with respect to other universities, or how many publications, research resumes or awards their researchers have received. This is a commonsense understanding of relevance and social responsibility of research by people, but it is not considered urgent in academic terms. Application is the problem of practitioners, academics argue. Greenwood and Levin maintain that all social research should be action research; that is, social researchers must be held accountable to higher standards of social responsibility than they are today. Why action research? They ask: "For action researchers, social inquiry aims to generate knowledge and action in support of liberating social change" (p. 146). They argue that action research is not a retreat from science as many positivists and "hard-line interpretivists" believe. Once they hear of action research, they call it activism and hence a departure from "real" research: "For hard line interpretivists, we will be seen as so naïve as not to understand that it is impossible to commit ourselves to any kind of action on the basis of any kind of social research" (p. 147). The quote at the beginning of this chapter reflects this belief precisely.

Concluding Remarks

1. The time is ripe to become engaged in a social movement led by educators as Jean Anyon (2005) calls for. Research in all its forms needs to be intimately linked to this movement. Some teachers in large cities have started mobilizing and making alliances with parents and other community leaders (Abowd, 2009). The latest news has to do with an outrageous attack on public education in California, specifically the University of California system, where budget cuts are devastating while students' tuition increased 32%. The movement is growing rapidly given that they made a "Solidarity Alliance" among students, faculty and workers of the UC system (Nader, Roy, Misse, & Cohen, 2009).

2. Research as praxis type of work, in which research, education, and communitarian action are intertwined, can help strengthen this type of social action. Action can be a rich source of knowledge and understanding as well as social renewal. Public education is at peril and requires determination on our part to rescue it. Here it is important to remember the 1964 speech of Mario Savio's speech (leader in the free speech movement) concerning our moral obligation to act when we face extreme acts of injustice and power abuse: "There's a time when the operation of the machine becomes so odious, makes you so sick at heart, that you can't take part, you can't even passively take part, and you've got to put your bodies upon the gears and upon the wheels, upon the levers, upon all the apparatus, and you've got to make it stop" (Democracy University Series, 2004).

References

Abowd, P. (2009, November). Teacher reformers: Battle over public education. *Z Magazine*, 9–11.

Adelman, C. (1997). Action Research: The problem of participation. In R. McTaggart (Ed.), *Participatory Action Research: International contexts and consequences* (pp. 79–106). New York, NY: SUNY Press.

Altrichter, H., & Gstettner, P. (1997). Action research: A closed chapter in the history of German social ccience? In R. McTaggart (Ed.), *Participatory action research: International contexts and consequences* (pp. 45–78). New York: SUNY Press.

American Educational Research Association. (2006). Standards for reporting empirical social science research in AERA Publications. *Educational Researcher, 35*(6), 33–40.

American Educational Research Association. (2009). Standards for reporting in humanities-oriented research in AERA publications. *Educational Researcher, 38*(6), 481–486.

Anyon, J. (Ed.). (2005). *Radical possibilities* New York, NY: Routledge.

Apple, M. (2004). *Ideology and curriculum* (3rd ed.). New York: Routledge Falmer.

Apple, M. (2006). Interrupting the right: On doing critical educational work in conservative times. In G. Ladson-Billings & W. F. Tate (Eds.), *Education research in the public interest* (pp. 27–45). New York, NY: Teachers College Press.

Baker, C. (2009, June-July). When facing reality is not "negative thinking." *Free Press, 7,* 4.

Carr, W., & Kemmis, S. (1986). *Becoming critical: Education, knowledge and action research*. Barcombe, UK: Falmer.

Cendales, L., Torres, F., & Torres, A. (2005). "One sows the seed, but it has its own dynamics": An interview with Orlando Fals-Borda. *International Journal of Action Resear1*(1), 9–42.

Chomsky, N. (2009, October). Coups, UNASUR, and the US. *Z Magazine, 22,* 21–26.

Christians, C. G. (2003). Ethics and politics in qualitative research In N. Denzin & Y. S. Lincoln (Eds.), *The landscape of qualitative research: Theories and issues* (2nd ed.) (pp. 208–243). Thousand Oaks, CA: Sage.

Cole, S. E. (1994). Evading the subject: The poverty of contingency theory. In H. W. Simons & M. Billig (Eds.), *After postmodernism: Reconstructing ideology critique* (pp. 38–57). Thousand Oaks, CA: Sage.

Darder, A., Baltodano, M., & Torres, R. (2009). Critical pedagogy: An introduction In A. Darder, M. P. Baltodano & R. D. Torres (Eds.), *The critical pedagogy reader* (2nd ed.) (pp. 1–20). New York, NY: Routledge/ Taylor & Francis.

Delgado-Gaitán, C. (1993). Researching change and changing the researcher. *Harvard Educational Review, 63*(3), 38–411.

Demarrais, K. (2006). "The haves and the have mores": Fueling a conservative ideological war on public education *Educational Studies, 39*(3), 201–240.

Democracy University Series. 2004). The 2004 Mario Savio memorial [DVD]. In R. Cole (Producer), *Free Speech Movement 40th Reunion. Vol. 71.1,*: Los Angeles, CA: Justice Vision.

Denzin, N. (1997). *Interpretive ethnography: Ethnographic practices for the 21st century:* Thousand Oaks, CA: Sage.

Ehrenreich, B. (Writer) & Goodman, A. (Director), (2009). Author Barbara Ehrenreich on "Bright-sided: How the relentless promotion of positive thinking has undermined America". In S. A. Kouddous (Producer), *Democracy*

Now. Retrieved from: http://www.democracynow.org/2009/10/13/uthor barbara_ehrenreich_on_bright_sided.

Emery, K., & Ohanian, S. (2004). *Why is corporate America bashing our public schools?* Portsmouth, NH: Heinemann.

Fals-Borda, O. (1970). *Ciencia propia y colonialismo intelectual [Endogenous science and intellectual colonialism]*. Mexico, D. F.: Editorial Nuestro Tiempo.

Fals-Borda, O. (1976). El problema de como investigar la realidad para transformarla [The problem of how to investigate the reality to transform it] (38 pages). Bogotá, Colombia: Fundación para el Análisis de la Realidad Colombiana—FUNDARCO

Fals-Borda, O. (1980, April). *La ciencia y el pueblo [Science and people]*. Paper presented at the International Forum on Participatory Research, Ljubljana, Yugoslavia.

Fals-Borda, O. (1985). *Knowledge and people's power: Lessons with peasants in Nicaragua, Mexico, and Colombia* (B. Maller, Trans.). New Delhi, India: Indian Social Institute.

Fals-Borda, O. (1991a). Some basic ingredients. In O. Fals-Borda & M. A. Rahman (Eds.), *Action and knowledge: Breaking the monopoly with participatory action research* (pp. 3–12). New York, NY: The Apex Press.

Fals-Borda, O. (1991b). Remaking knowledge. In O. Fals-Borda & M. A. Rahman (Eds.), *Action and knowledge: Breaking the monopoly with Participatory Action Research* (pp. 146–164). New York, NY: The Apex Press.

Fals-Borda, O. (1995, April 8). *Research for social justice: Some north-south convergences*. Paper presented at the Plenary Address at the Southern Sociological Society Meeting, Atlanta, GA.

Fals-Borda, O. (1998). Part III: Theoretical and practical experiences In O. Fals-Borda (Ed.), *People's participation: Challenges ahead* (pp. 155–220). New York, NY: The Apex Press.

Fals-Borda, O. (2005). Participatory (action) research in social theory: Origins and challenges. In P. Reason & H. Bradbury (Eds.), *Handbook of action research* (Concise paperback ed.). London, England: Sage Publications.

Feuer, M., Towne, L., & Shavelson, R. (2002). Scientific culture and educational research. *Educational Researcher, 31*(8), 4–14.

Fine, M. (1994). Working the hyphens: Reinventing self and other in qualitative research. In N. Denzin & Y. Lincoln (Eds.), *The Sage handbook of qualitative research* (pp. 70–82). Thousand Oaks, CA: Sage.

Fine, M., Weis, L., Weseen, S., & Wong, L. (2003). For whom? Qualitative research, representations and social responsibilities. In N. Denzin & Y. S. Lincoln (Eds.), *The landscape of qualitative research: Theories and issues* (2nd ed.) (pp. 167–207). Thousand Oaks, CA: Sage Publications.

Frank, T. (2008). *The wrecking crew: How conservatives rule*. New York, NY: Macmillan Audio.

Freire, P. (1992). *Pedagogy of the oppressed*. New York, NY: Continuum.

Freire, P. (2000). Cultural action for freedom (rev. ed.). *Harvard Educational Review*.

Freire, P. (2003). *El grito manso [The gentle shout]*. Buenos Aires, Argentina: Siglo XXI Editores.

Freire, P. (2005). *Pedagogy of indignation*. Boulder, CO: Paradigm Publishers.

Gaventa, J. (1991). Toward a knowledge democracy: Views of participatory research in North America. In O. Fals-Borda & M. A. Rahman (Eds.), *Action and knowledge: Breaking the monopoly with participatory action research* (pp. 121–134). New York, NY: The Apex Press.

George, S. (1999, March 24–26). *A short history of neoliberalism.* Paper presented at the Conference on Economic Sovereignty in a Globalising World.

Giroux, H. (2002). Neoliberalism, corporate culture, and the promise of higher education. The university as a democratic public sphere. *Harvard Educational Review, 74*(2), 425–463.

Giroux, H. (2004). Neoliberalism and the demise of democracy: Resurrecting hope in dark times. *Dissident Voice.* Retrieved from idewww.dissntvoice.org / /Giroux0807.htm

Goodman, A. (Writer) & Goodman, A. (Director), (2009, October 13). US professor is first woman to receive Nobel in economics [Democracy Now]. In S. A. Kouddous (Producer). Retrieved from http://www.democracynow.org /2009/ 10/13 /headlines#8.

Goodman, A. (Writer) & Goodman, A. (Director), (2009, October 23). Report: 2.3 Drug Lobbyists for Every Lawmaker [Democracy Now]. In S. A. Kouddous (Producer), Retrieved from http://www.democracynow.org2009/10/23/.

Greenwood, D. J., & Levin, M. (2003). Reconstructing the relationship between universities and society through action research In N. Denzin & Y. S. Lincoln (Eds.), *The landscape of qualitative research: Theories and issues* (2nd ed.) (pp. 131–166). Thousand Oaks, CA: Sage Publications.

Grundy, S. (1988). Three models of action research. In S. Kemmis & R. McTaggart (Eds.), *The action research reader.* Geelong, AU: Deakin University Press.

Habermas, J. (1972). *Knowledge and human interests* (J. J. Shapiro, Trans.). London, England: Heinemann.

Hall, B., Gillete, A., & Tandon, R. (Eds.). (1982). *Creating knowledge: A monopoly? Participatory research in development.* New Delhi: Participatory Research Network.

Hanley, L. (2005). Academic capitalism in the new university. *Radical Teacher Journal.* Retrieved from http://findarticles.com/p/articles/mi_m0JVP.

Harding, S. (2006). *Science and social inequality: Feminist and postcolonial issues.* Urbana & Chicago, IL: University of Illinois Press.

Hedges, C. (2006). *American fascists: The Christian Right and the war on America.* New York, NY: Free Press.

Henig, J. (2008). The evolving relationship between researchers and public policy. In F. M. Hess (Ed.), *When research matters: How scholarship influences education policy* (pp. 41–62). Cambridge, MA: Harvard Education Press.

Herbert, B. (2009, October 27). Changing the world. *New York Times.* Retrieved from http://www.commondreams.org/view/2009/10/27-1

Hess, C., & Ostrom, E. (Eds.). (2006). *Understanding knowledge as a commons: From theory to practice.* Cambridge, MA: MIT Press.

Hess, F. M. (Ed.). (2008). *When research matters: How scholarship influences education policy.* Cambridge, MA: Harvard Education Press.

Horton, M., & Freire, P. (1990). *We make the road by walking: Conversations on education and social change.* Philadelphia, PA: Temple University Press.

Howe, K. R. (2009). Epistemology, methodology, and education sciences. *Educational Researcher, 38*(6), 428–440.

Jameson, F. (1981). *The political unconscious: Narrative as a socially symbolic act.* Ithaca, NY: Cornell University Press.

Johnson, R. (Writer) & Goodman, A. (2009, November 2). How Wall Street and its backers on Capitol Hill silenced a critic calling for greater regulation of derivatives [*Democracy Now*]. In S. A. Kouddous (Producer). Retrieved from www.democracynow.org/2009/11/2/how_wall_street.

Johnson, R. B. (2009). Toward a more inclusive "scientific research in education." *Educational Researcher, 38*(6), 449–457.

Kemmis, S., & McTaggart, R. (2005). Participatory Action Research: Communicative action and the public sphere. In N. K. Denzin & Y. S. Lincoln (Eds.), *Handbook of qualitative research* (3rd ed.) (pp. 559–603). Thousand Oaks, CA: Sage.

Khan, I. (Writer), Goodman, A. Gonzalez, J. (Directors), (2009). Amnesty International Head Irene Khan on "The unheard truth: Poverty and human rights" [*Democracy Now*]. In S. A. Kouddous (Producer). Retrieved from http://www. democracynow.org/2009/10/16/amnesty_international_head_.

Lather, P. (2008). New wave utilization research: (Re)imagining the research /policy nexus. *Educational Researcher, 37*(6), 361–364.

Lewin, K. (1946). Action research and minority problems. *Journal of Social Issues, 2*, 34–36.

Lynd, R. (1939). *Knowledge for what?* Princeton, NJ: Princeton University Press.

Lyotard, J. F. (1984). *The postmodern condition: A report on knowledge* (G. Bennington & B. Massumi, Trans.). Minneapolis, MN: University of Minnesota Press.

Mariño, G. (1990). La investigacion participativa pa' semianafalbetas y positivistas arrepentidos [Participatory research for semiliterates and repentent positivists]. *Dimension-Educativa, Aportes 20*, 35–57.

Max-Neef, M. (1991). *Human scale development: Conception, application and further reflections.* New York, NY: The Apex Press.

Max-Neef, M. (1998). Economy, humanism and neoliberalism. In O. Fals-Borda (Ed.), *People's participation: Challenges ahead.* London, England: The Apex Press: Intermedia Technology Communications.

McTaggart, R. (1997). Reading the collection. In R. McTaggart (Ed.), *Participatory action research: International contexts and consequences* (pp. 1–23). New York, NY: State University of New York Press.

Nader, L., Roy, A., Misse, B., & Cohen, M. (Writer) & Goodman, A. (Director), (2009, November, 17). Why are we destroying public education? University of California students and staff prepare for system-wide strike to protest cuts [Democracy Now]. In S. A. Kouddous (Producer). Retrieved from http:// www.democracynow.org/2009/11/17/why_are_we_destroying_public.

Nader, R. (2009a). *Only the superich can save us!* New York, NY: Seven Stories Press.

Nader, R. (Writer) & Goodman, A. (Director), (2009b). Ralph Nader on the G-20, healthcare reform, Mideast talks and his first work of fiction, "Only the *super-rich can save us!" [Democracy Now]. In S. A. Kouddous (Producer),* Retrieved from http://www.democracynow.org/2009/9/21/ralph_nader_on.

Nasheed, M., & Robinson, T. (Writers) & Goodman, A. (Director), (2009). Island Nation of Maldives Holds Cabinet Meeting Underwater to Highlight Danger of Global Warming [Democracy Now]. In S. A. Kouddous (Producer), Retrieved from http://www.democracynow.org/2009/10/19/island_nation

National Research Council. (2002). *Scientific research in education*. Washington, DC : National Academic Press.

Nuñez-Hurtado, C. (2005). A participatory citizen consultation: The case of the State of Michoacán. *Internationa Journal of Action Research, 1*(1), 121–151.

O'Connor, A. (2007). *Social science for what? Philanthropy and the social question in a world turned rightside up*. New York, NY: Russell Sage Foundations.

Perkins, J. (2004). *Confessions of an economic hit man*. San Francisco, CA: Berrett Koehler.

Perkins, J. (2007). *The secret history of the American empire*. New York, NY: Dutton.

Potter, W. (Writer). & Goodman, A. (Director), (2009, July 16). "They dump the sick to satisfy investors": Insurance exec turned whistleblower Wendell Potter speaks out against healthcare industry [*Democracy Now*]. In S. A. Kouddous (Producer). Retrieved from http://www.democracynow.org /2009 /7/16/

Rahman, M. A. (1991a). The theoretical standpoint of PAR. In O. Fals-Borda & M. A. Rahman (Eds.), *Action and knowledge: Breaking the monopoly with participatory action research*. New York, NY: The Apex Press.

Rahman, M. A. (1991b). Glimpses of the "other Africa." In O. Fals-Borda & M. A. Rahman (Eds.), *Action and knowledge: Breaking the monopoly with participatory action research* (pp. 84–108). New York, NY: The Apex Press.

Rahman, M. A. (1994). *People's self development: Perspectives on participatory action researc: A journey through experience*. Dhaka, Bangladesh: University Press Limited.

Rahman, M. A., & Fals-Borda, O. (1991). A self-review of PAR. In O. Fals-Borda & M. A. Rahman (Eds.), *Action and knowledge: Breaking the monopoly with Participatory Action Research* (pp. 24–34). New York, NY: The Apex Press.

Rethinking Schools Editorial. (2009). Where is our community organizer-in-chief? *Rethinking Schools, 24*(1), 5–7.

Rodriguez-Brandão, C. (2005). Participatory research and participation in research: A look between times and spaces from Latin America. *International Journal of Action Research, 1*(1), 43–68.

Sacks, P. (1999). *Standardized minds: The high price of America's testing culture and what we can do to change it*. Cambridge, MA: Perseus Books.

Slaughter, S., & Rhoades, G. (2004). *Academic capitalism and the new economy: Market, state, and higher education*. Baltimore, MD: Johns Hopkins University Press.

Souza, J. F., de. (1989). Ponencia de apertura del III Encuentro Mundial de Investigación Participativa [Keynote at the opening of the III Worldwide Encounter on Participatory Research], *Investigación Acción Participativa* (Aportes, 20) (pp. 79–91). Bogotá Colombia: Dimensión Educativa.

Streck, D. (2006). The scale of participation: From municipal public budget to cities' conference. *International Journal of Action Research, 2*(1), 78–97.

Streck, D. (2007). Research and social transformation: Notes about method and methodology in participatory research. *International Journal of Action Research, 3*(1 & 2), 112–130.

Streck, D. (2009). Popular education and participatory reserch: Facing inequalities in Latin America. *Internationa Journal of Action Research, 5*(1), 13–32.

Stringer, E. (1996). *Action research: A handbook for practitioners.* Thousand Oaks, CA: Sage Publications.

Taylor, F. W. (1911). *The principles of scientific management.* New York, NY: Harper Bros.

Torres, M. N., Coppola, B., Huerta-Charles, L., & Reyes, L. V. (2006, April). *Why is a "research-as-praxis" type of investigation excluded as an option in the AERA proposal submission menu?* Paper presented at the American Educational Research Association Annual Meeting. San Francisco, CA.

Tumulty, K., & Scherer, M. (2009, October 22). How drug-industry lobbyists won on health-care. *Time Magazine.* Retrieved from http://www.time.com/time/politics/article/0,8599,1931595,1931500.html#ixzz1931510MvE1931599GZH.

United Nations. (2007). *2007 Human development report—United Nations development program.* New York, NY: Author.

Vaid, U. (Writer) & Goodman, A. (Director), (2009, October, 13)). The fight for equality: A look at the state of the gay rights movement [*Democracy Now*]. In S. A. Kouddous (Producer), Retrieved from http://www.democracynow.org /2009/10/13/the_fight_for_equality_a_look.

Vio-Grossi, F. (1983). *La investigación participativa y la educacion de adultos en America Latina: Algunos problemas relevantes* [Participatory research and adult education in Latin America: Some relevant problems] (Vol. 10). Mexico. CREFAL.

Chapter 5

Decolonizing Family Literacy in a Culture Circle: Reinventing the Family Literacy Educator's Role

Loui V. Reyes & Myriam N. Torres

Family literacy is not a new concept. Family literacy programs have been part of social work and community health programs for many years. With the advent of the No Child Left Behind Act (NCLB), family literacy has become a part of school activities; first, it was a background activity and now it is in the foreground.

A literature review of family literacy programs reveals various focuses. There are programs that focus more on how to 'fix' the child's family and communities (e.g., Bird, 2005; Snow et al., 1991; Taylor, 2005). Other programs focus more on how to 'fix' the child (e. g., Anglum et al., 1990).

Other types of family literacy programs are rooted in the liberal compassionate *'pobrecito'* (pity) type of attitude, discourse, and practices (e.g.,Purcell-Gates, 1995). Those who follow this approach accept differences among families but naively work to 'help' them become literate as if the families had no literacy practices and were living in a vacuum. They take on a caring, supporting role for these 'poor people' who are unable to care 'appropriately' for their children. For example, consider a European American middle-class family literacy educator who genuinely believes that the schools are not serving the families of poor and immigrant children, and she is angry at this reality. She expresses her care for those families by showing them the 'right track'—how to become literate within the frame of her own culture. What is problematic with this scenario is that she is not aware of the various and equally valid popular family literacy practices. She does not acknowledge the power unbalance between schools and those non-mainstream families, which is actually the very thing she is fighting against. Early childhood family literacy is situated in the intersection between the areas of family literacy and early childhood literacy. Traditionally the early childhood domain has been rooted in the psychological theories of child development, which is considered endogenous to the individual and enacted by environmental conditions. Consequently, the success of a given early childhood family literacy program relies heavily on the performance of individual children. Thus, it becomes easy to blame the child or his/her family when a given literacy program fails, rather than examining the relevance of the program to the culture and life experiences of the children and their families. The deficit thinking model Valencia, 1997) is embedded in the rationale and evaluation of these types of programs (Hanon, 2003).

There are other perspectives of early childhood family literacy programs that are rooted in the sociocultural perspectives. Razfar and Gutiérrez (2003) demonstrate how the sociocultural view of early literacy helps educators understand the culturally mediated character of learning and the situatedness of cognitive functioning in cultural and social contexts. In the same vein, but with critical lenses, we situate our early childhood family literacy approach, described later, as participatory, democratic, liberating, and dialogical, hence based on the work by Freire (1992), Fals-Borda (1985), and Lankshear (1993), among others. We cannot agree more with Hall et al. (2003) as well as with all the authors of the *Handbook of Early Childhood Literacy* in their purpose to focus on children's and their families' strengths and potentialities and not on their weaknesses.

Traditionally non-mainstream families have been 'colonized' by measuring them against the European American middle-class family literacy practices (Ada and Zubizarreta, 2001; Panofsky,

2000; Valdés, 1996). Most family literacy programs implemented at schools and other organizations, despite having good intentions, are actually motivated by the idea of 'fixing' those non-maintream families, rather than collaboratively identifying and solving the problems that alienate both the families and their children and obstruct their progress toward full literacy.

The majority of family literacy projects are conceived and implemented within an instrumentalist and utilitarian view of education and are imposed arbitrarily having the greatest impact on non-mainstream families. The model followed is often referred to as 'functional literacy' (similar to the United Nations Educational, Scientific and Cultural Organization [UNESCO] worldwide programs) and is driven by the 'efficiency' paradigm. Andrade et al. (2000) call it 'competence-based-skills banking education'. According to this model, the needs assessment, design, implementation and evaluation of a family literacy program are determined and controlled by experts either in the school system or at other institutions. Families become fair targets to be changed or trained to improve their 'parenting skills' with the ultimate goal of supporting the school work of their children (Panofsky, 2000; Valdés, 1996). These programs are of doubtful success due to the colonizing mentality that underlies the understanding of family literacy problems and solutions. The end result is actually more marginalization from school for those families, given the fact that such special programs actually turn into tracking systems (De Carvalho, 2001). In brief, these family literacy programs fall short because they take those practices that are different from the 'norm' (Eurocentric middle-class practices) as 'deficient' without understanding literacy practices and possibilities in the context of participants' cultures and languages. Our critical family literacy approach, even though it is still in the margins, not only opposes the problems of the deficit thinking model but creates venues for the empowerment of families and/or child caretakers as demonstrated in this chapter.

The purpose of this chapter is twofold: (1) Describe and document the colonization and decolonization process of a family literacy program as evidenced by the participants' engagement in a 'culture circle'; and (2) Describe and critique the role of the 'decolonizing family literacy educator' in navigating the complex dynamics of a culture circle inherent in a Freirean-based family literacy project. In order to do this, the authors have co-reconstructed a reflective narrative of the lived experience of the first author, who was a consultant and family literacy educator in the project.

About the Relative-Care Family Literacy Program

The state in which this program was carried out had established education policies on family literacy that are rooted in the deficit thinking model of 'fixing' families. To comply with these education policies the state made funding available for new programs. The program referred to here began as a response to the state's public Request for Proposals. The first author participated in writing the proposal based on the possibility of building a more socially and culturally responsive family literacy program, one distinct from the mainstream programs already in operation in the state. However, as with all state initiatives, the 'statement of work' outlined the specific outcomes expected in alignment with state competence standards applying to early care and education. The development of the relative-care curriculum was as follows: first, there were created seven three-member teams composed of experts in the field of early childhood and family-daycare providers. The developers of the family literacy curriculum, who were called 'consultants,' had to have experience with adult training and at least three years of working with young children; at a minimum, they had an associate of arts degree in early childhood or a related field. Consultants were recruited from the communities in which the family literacy project would be implemented. The role of the consultants was to plan and actually provide the training of the participants in the Relative-Care Curriculum project. Each consultant was responsible for developing a module by starting with a literature review on the topic of the assigned module, guided by 'best practices' and 'competencies', as defined by the state's early childhood professional development system (Turner, 2002). Second, each team was assigned a module with the set of competence standards to be used to guide its development. Third, the teams met in a large group and presented their modules to receive feedback from the other teams for revising the modules. Fourth, upon revision of the modules, the seven three-member teams received training in adult learning principles and the delivery of the Relative-Care Curriculum. Fifth, two teams were selected to carry out an 18-hour pilot program of the Relative-Care Curriculum training, one in a rural community and the other in an urban community.

Pilot Study

The family literacy project had the overall purpose of providing formal training to caregivers who care for children of their relatives. Caregivers included grandparents, uncles, aunts, cousins, and in-laws. The pilot project was implemented during a four-month time span, during which nine modules were presented as follows: (1) child growth and development, (2) guidance, (3) learning environments, (4) social and emotional development, (5) business practices, (6) literacy and numeracy, (7) language, (8) family and community, and (9) health and safety. Each module was assigned two hours for its implementation. The total Relative-Care Curriculum training project lasted 18 hours and was offered every other week for two hours on agreed days.

Participants

Participants in this pilot study were recruited by a local early-childhood training agency from a rural and an urban setting. The participants were mothers and grandmothers, fathers and grandfathers, cousins, aunts, and uncles, who provided care to children of their relatives. Participants included in the report, which constitutes the basis for this chapter, were all Latinos from a rural setting.

Twenty participants were involved in the project: 2 males (1 grandfather, and 1 uncle) and 18 women (of whom 9 were grand-mothers, and the others were aunts and cousins). They provided care for the children of their relatives (sons, daughters, sisters, brothers, cousins).The majority of the families of the children under relative care would be considered as dual parent (mother and father); the single ones were headed by the mother. The average number of children in a family was three. The community in which the families live has almost no employment opportuni-ties, making it necessary to commute to a large border city and to a middle-size city for employment in low-paying service labor. In the dual families both parents were employed. Because the com-munity where the families live lacked center-based childcare, these families relied heavily on family members for care of their young children. That was the main reason for choosing this rural community to carry out this pilot project. Participants involved in the Relative-Care Curriculum project were between 20–70 years old. The participants care for relatives' children ranging from birth to 13 years old. The first language of all participants was Spanish; 15 of them were first-generation Latino immigrants, and the other 5 were recent immigrants themselves.

Setting

The family literacy pilot study took place in a 'colonia' located in a rural community in southern New Mexico and in a middle-size city. In this article we report on the project in the rural communi-ty. The community is considered a 'colonia,' according to the federal and state governmental categories. It is defined as: '. . . unincorporated border communities that often lack adequate water and sewer systems, paved roads, and safe, sanitary housing.' (http://maps.oag.state.tx.us/colgeog/ colonias.htm). However, this geographic category is different from the Spanish use of the term 'colonia,' which refers to a neighborhood that is an officially recog-nized segment of a city. As we can see, the term has been embed-ded with a negative connotation, which applies also to its inhabitants. This borderland 'colonia' had a population of 6,117 (2000 Census). The median resident age is 28.6 years. The median household income is US$22,692/year. Races in this community include: Hispanic (64.5%); White Non-Hispanic (31.9%); Native American (2.2%); Black (1.3%).

Relative-Care Curriculum Facilitators in a Rural Community

There were three facilitators: The first author (Latino with a doctoral degree in Early Childhood Education) was the leader of the team with two other women (Latinas, completing their masters' degrees in Early Childhood Education). Their average experience in the field of early care and education was 20 years. Their experience included: center-based childcare, home childcare, resource and referral, training, and out-of-school time. All three members of the team are very committed to working with low-income, marginalized Latino communities.

Inquiry Approach of the Pilot Study

The pilot study was set up as an evaluative research. The process was as follows:

1. Identification of parameters and indicators for evaluation: participants' satisfaction index; participants' input concerning the organization of the Relative-Care Curriculum modules (units); participants' and trainers' input about the usefulness of the content as well as comments on the appropriateness of the scheduled times and days for the training sessions.
2. Construction and/or definitions of the instruments for data collection. The sources of data included participants' pre-self-assessment, evaluation of each module by participants and providers of the training, field notes by trainers, final evaluation, videotapes of a session, and collegial dialogues among trainers.

3. Design of the plan for collecting information.
4. Gathering of data based on the parameters and indicators.
5. Review by trainers and project coordinators of the data collected.
6. Passing of the data to an external evaluator to analyze and recommend improvements for the training program. At this point it entered into the bureaucratic process in which the authors are not involved.

Alternative Study of the Family Literacy Experience

Actually, this report is a reflective narrative co-constructed through a sustained collegial dialogue between the authors based on their lived experiences in the field of family literacy, especially the experience of the first author in the pilot study described. We understand reflective narrative as the examination of the whole situation toward understanding colonizing mainstream family literacy practices as well as exploring ways for decolonization. We conducted a careful examination of the data collected in the pilot study using Paulo Freire's approach to family literacy. We used this approach as a theoretical framework to analyze the data and organize the emergent themes that included the voices of participants in the culture circle. Succinctly, literacy means that participants learn to read and write the word and the world, starting from their own reality (Freire, 2005). This approach to literacy includes democratic participation in building the curriculum to make it relevant and socially responsive, engagement in a relational and liberating pedagogy, promotion of 'conscientization,' collective and trans-formative action aimed first of all toward benefiting the participants and their communities.

We share a mutual interest in the Freirean approach to family literacy as a way of working toward social justice. We have been involved with several community projects targeting family literacy for Latinos. Our work specifically includes the deconstruction of the metanarratives in early childhood literacy and critical media literacy of children's literature and media entertainment. We are very engaged in building culture circles in these Latino communities as a means to promote critical understanding of the unbalance between their own family literacy practices and those imposed on them by the governmental and social agencies as well as to build their collective conscientization and countervailing power. We believe that this is a good path toward decolonization of family literacy.

Theoretical Framework for Decolonizing Family Literacy Practices

Decolonizing discourse, as celebrated by postmodernists and postcolonialists, works toward rethinking the Eurocentric systems of thought, reasoning, and ways of knowing and teaching and making them no longer tenable. Although not completely in the same postmodernist decolonizing frame, we built upon this postmodernist tone using Paulo Freire's (1970/1992) liberating literacy practices. For him education is not neutral. It serves to domesticate or to liberate from oppression. This notion holds true in the area of family literacy. Liberating family literacy, as conceived and practiced by Freire and his collaborators, acknowledges, values, and promotes diverse literacy practices and understandings through democratic participation, both in building and implementing those programs through inquiry and in creatively transforming relations with schools.

Working to overcome the prevalent instrumentalist and ethnocentric focus of family literacy programs, educators may embrace the Freirean perspective (e.g., Lankshear, 1993). From this perspective, the overarching goal of family literacy programs should be to create an environment for the growth of critical consciousness of participants by devising opportunities for them to confront and overcome those institutions, ideologies, and situations that keep them from naming and shaping their worlds. In other words, families—parents and children—should be prepared to read the word on the basis of their own reading of their world (Freire and Macedo, 1987). Freire has developed a dialogical-relational pedagogy to achieve that critical consciousness and to move toward

collective liberation of those who have been constantly marginalized from the school's white middle-class culture. We believe that
a Freirean-based family literacy project holds promise for the
decolonization of those subordinated groups.

In a Freirean-based family literacy project there exists a role
for a person to spearhead the project. Freire calls that person a
'tutor' or 'leader coordinator' (Freire, 1970/1992) or a 'cultural
worker' (Freire, 1998), while Lankshear (1993) names him or her a
'co-coordinator.' One of the terms more commonly used for those
educators who want to distance themselves from the 'banking
model' of education and embrace a 'liberating' model is that of
'facilitator' (Freire, 1970/1992; Horton and Freire, 1990; Shor and
Freire, 1987). Freire and Macedo (1987) problematize the real
implications of the 'facilitator' role. They fear that it may imply a
hidden controller, or a laissez faire teacher, or a messianic redee-
mer of the poor, weak and ignorant. The role of the 'co-coordinator'
is not just 'banking' content in participants, according to Lankshear (1993) but helping participants explore contradictions in
their own perceptions, to ask questions that create cognitive dise-
quilibrium, and to emphasize the process of co-creation of knowledge based on the reflection of their own daily experiences. We
call this 'co-coordinator' a *decolonizing family literacy education.'*
What we have learned from our family literacy praxis is that
'culture circles' are in continual re-creation and that this requires
a continual reinventing of the role of the 'decolonizing family
literacy educator.'

One of Freire's key pedagogical features is that of 'culture circles'. A culture circle is a distinctive learning environment in
which 'participants' (not pupils) meet to dialogue in the presence of
a 'co-coordinator' in order to understand critically their worlds and
define the ways they can participate in shaping those worlds and
improving their life conditions. The culture circle is rooted in the
philosophy of dialogism, which Freire (1970/1992) embraced and
further developed. From this philosophical viewpoint, being
human means 'being-in-relation' with other people and with
nature as co-creators of culture and participants in its transformation through dialogue. In a culture circle people meet to dialogue

on issues endogenous to their own lived experiences and concerns. Freire (n.d.) always started with the discussion and critical understanding of the notion of 'culture,' hence the name of 'culture' circle. He used it as way to demonstrate how culture is created and sustained by participants' own ways of living and knowing, which facilitate their recognition of the possibilities for building the power to create culture. Embracing this role sets the path for the participants in the culture circle to see the power of becoming literate as a tool for enhancing communication and democratization of their sociocultural practices.

The dialogues that take place in the culture circle enact the democratic idea of symmetrical relations of power, which are based on the assumption of 'equal rights for simultaneously existing, experiencing persons' (Bakhtin, 1984), which Bakhtin coins as 'polyphony.' In the Bakhtinian sense, 'polyphony' means multiple voices, interaction of diverse voices, and struggle of ideological views. Even though this is an important step in the process of transformation of culture and power relations, it is not sufficient for changing and reshaping the participants' worlds. These dialogues should be aimed at building solidarity based on their shared concerns and problems in order to embrace collective actions toward improving their life conditions, in their own terms of equality, equity, democracy, and peace. Actually, collective action is a significant component of Freire's family literacy practices. It implies creating a space in which participants in a given family literacy culture circle gain power to reshape or recreate family literacy curricula and practices that are relevant to the participants' and their communities' interests, needs, culture, and possibilities. This does not imply that family childcare practices that are harmful to their children should not be questioned and changed. Of course they should. However, the change should come from the collective dialogues in a culture circle rather than from top-down colonizing practices.

The idea of families participating in the study of their own childcare practices, as well as in the critique and transformation of those practices, is central to the notion of *decolonization* as referred to here. First of all, we are going to situate decolonization within and beyond post-colonial theory. For Dirlik (1997) post-colonial theory includes the confrontation of the legacy of colonialism in terms of institutional authority, discourses, knowledge, power, and social relations. Nonetheless, San Juan (1998) argues that although this confrontation helps to denounce and unveil the embedding nature of colonial dominance after independence revolutions, it has had unexpected consequences. Post-colonialism brought the diaspora of free play, multiple perspectives, polyphony, and language games, which have been promoted to some extent by the fall of communism as an alternative to capitalism. It also generated a large number of restrictions that hold back progressive and emancipatory discourses and projects. Invoking universal humanistic values and truths, achieving consensus to engage in collective transformative actions toward possible dreams and a hopeful future for all, which are central to emancipatory perspectives, became restrictive under the post-colonial 'regime.' Within this framework we consider 'decolonization' of social practices as a *re-vision* of post-colonialism, based on Freire's philosophy of life and education using dialogue in culture circles, in order to recuperate the possibilities for discourse and collective actions for liberation from oppressing conditions. People participating in these dialogical encounters can work to enhance their critical consciousness and collective self-empowerment. Thus, we will move from merely polyphony to collective action, which should be planned and carried out with full participation of the families themselves, to avoid the perpetuation of colonization at levels that may be deemed invisible to most people, including the colonized.

The Lived Experience of the Decolonization Process and the Reinvention of the 'Decolonizing Family Literacy Educator' in a Culture Circle

As mentioned earlier, the first author, co-proponent and consultant of the family literacy project, accepted his involvement even though he knew it was based on a top-down perspective of family literacy. He had already seen this as a launching pad for moving the program away from family literacy colonizing practices. Under the top-down curricular perspective under which this family literacy program was framed, participants are treated as passive recipients of new information delivered by consultants. Hence participants were perceived in this case as ignorant of this basic knowledge and having no valuable experience in the care of children of their relatives. In the family literacy culture circle reported here, participants were given a pre-self-assessment before the actual training, with the intention to provide the consultants with useful information concerning the degree of familiarity participants had with the various topics of the modules. The general character of the questions and the artificiality of a paper-and-pencil type of pre-self-assessment did not produce the expected useful information—participants marked the highest score on each of the topics they were going to be taught, supposedly indicating a strong familiarity with the curriculum content and practices.

Upon the completion of the pre-self-assessment, the trainers analyzed the participants' responses, and realized that the instrument did not serve its purpose, which was to reveal what the participants really knew or needed to know about the specificities of the modules' content. The data showed that all 20 participants rated their knowledge in the pre-self-assessment questionnaire as level 4, which in terms of the state early childhood competency standards implies 'having a clear idea about the topic and can explain it.'

After implementing the first module on 'Child Growth and Development,' it was quite obvious that participants actually did know a great deal about the module's content. As a result, the trainers were afraid that participants were going to be disappointed with the training and the modules already designed and started to dialogue about what would be the best strategy to address the dilemma they were in: that is, to continue the training as prescribed or to take a new direction, that of *co-opting* the curriculum. They chose the latter. Co-opting the curriculum implied for the family literacy educators use of the modules to spearhead the examining and the sharing of participants' know-

ledge and experiences about the subject matter and to expand
them in accordance with their needs and interests.

Engaging in co-opting the curriculum was a painful and somewhat risky decision for the trainers because, among other things,
it required them to re-examine their role as trainers and to develop a new one. The word 'trainers' in-itself conveys the notion of
top-down instruction. They rather wanted to see themselves as
'facilitators' of participants' liberation. In this respect Sidorkian
(1999) theorizes that for change to happen in educational leaders,
an incident must occur that energizes the actors toward new ways
of doing things, toward reinventing their roles.

Standardization of the Family Literacy Curriculum Using Child Development Stages

Through postmodern lenses, Canella (1997) refers to child development stages as a western Eurocentric construction, a result of
positivist research: 'A language of normality and pathology is
generated with the larger universalistic discourse.' (Canella, 1997:
41). Thus, 'judgmental surveillance of these populations is
justified.' (Canella, 1997: 41) For her, this is no less than a means
of domination: 'The construction of universal child truth or reality
creates a power position for adults and especially psychologists,
educators, and other experts who sanction judgment, control,
manipulation, correction, and regulation of those who are
identified as children' (Canella, 1997: 41), and by extension their
caregivers in the family literacy project reported here. This compa-
tibility between universal child growth and developmental theory
and a top-down curriculum manifests itself as a 'one size fits all'
approach, which facilitates the pathologization and colonization of
non-standard family literacy practices. This applies also *within* the
Latino culture. Zentella (2005) problematizes the often monolithic
perception of the Latino cultures concerning child rearing including language socialization:

> The choices Latinos make about how to raise their children in the United
> States depend on the information and opportunities they are given and

their ability to counteract the damaging language ideologies shaped by the market value of English, English-only campaigns, and a legacy of linguistic purism and linguistic insecurity that is erasing Spanish. (Zentella, 2005: 10)

Thus, we need to recognize that within the Latino cultures there may exist some child-rearing practices that are compatible with these universal stages of child development.

Participants in a Culture Circle Resist the Top-Down Curriculum

The process of conscientization cultivated in the 'culture circle,' on which this article is based, animated participants in it to resist the top-down curriculum. They presented some of the resistance behaviors some authors (Giroux, 2001; hooks, 1994; McLaren, 1995) have considered as passive resistance (indifference, a sabotaging attitude, disengagement) and active resistance (protesting, arguing with the trainers, sabotaging behavior). For example, in the *business practices* module, participants rejected the notion of 'business' as a component of family affairs. In some cultures in Latin America, family affairs cannot be mixed with business affairs; to do so is to downgrade familial relationships. This insensitivity engendered a sense of profanity for these participants. Collegial dialogue helped facilitators understand that the most probable reason for this rejection was that the meaning of 'business' in some Latino cultures (coming from Latin America) does not apply in the same contexts as it does for English-speaking people. This was seen in the reaction of one of the participants:

Para mí, la razón que cuido a los niños de mi hermano es porque los quiero. Yo no se los cuido por ganancia, sino para ayudarle. Estoy muy molesta con este 'training.' Lo hago porque amo a estos niños, no porque estoy en un negocio.
[For me, the reason that I take care of my brother's children is because I love them. I don't take care of them to get paid. I am uncomfortable with this training. I take care of these children because I love them, not because it's a business.]

When the participant concluded her statement, the entire group of participants, in unison, said: 'We agree! We take care of the children because we love them, not to make money.'

The dialogue between the two facilitators, after facing the participants' rejection of the business module, started as follows:

> Loui: Boy! This group has really made a problem of this module. Maybe they [participants] are right. What they understand about child care is totally different from that framed in the business practices module.
> Cathy (pseudonym): Yeah, I agree. Maybe we should rethink this [business] module in terms of care instead of a business. I didn't have any idea how their culture tells them what care of relatives' children is. Culture plays a real role in this module.

It was quite obvious to the facilitators that the module was framed in terms of business practices without taking into account the participants' culture. It is clear from these statements that facilitators understood the reason for participants' refusal of the training. The content of the 'business' module was against their familial values, which in this Latino cultural group are not compatible.

Another instance of resistance to the top-down curriculum can be seen in the implementation of the 'Literacy' and 'Numeracy' modules. The module activities for supporting young children's literacy and numeracy development were irrelevant to the participants' literacy practices. Suggested activities included ideas for purchasing books, CDs, and other materials for children without considering that the participants have their own materials and resources. Also, what was missing in the activities was their cultural relevance to diverse populations. The activities required caregivers to participate with the children in these activities; however, the problem was that the caregivers were not familiar with the contextual meaning of the activities, making it impossible for them to participate as the modules suggested. Participants were never asked what areas or ideas they wanted to learn as part of the curriculum; here again what was taught/delivered was not what the participants wanted. When the facilitators made the statement that every parent should read to their children and that a good time to do that is right before bedtime, one of the participants resisted that notion by pointing out the differences that existed between their own literacy practices and those implied in the training:

> Es muy importante saber que todos nosotros tenemos diferentes modos de enseñar a escribir, leer, y contar. Todos lo podemos hacer diferente. [It is very important to know that we all have different modes of reading, writing, and numeracy. We all have our own ways.]

This response challenged the facilitators once again because they should have balanced the top-down curriculum by co-opting it, instead of being patronizing as seen in the reaction of this participant. The worst thing was that the facilitators were so shocked by this participant's reaction that they did not take advantage of this opening by participants and failed to engage in this precious learning opportunity. Now we can say that this failure was perhaps because of the facilitators' inexperience in reinventing themselves and dealing with the emergent issues of the cooptation process.

One of the major problems that a top-down curriculum engenders is that of ignoring the topics that participants really want to learn. For example, participants brought up their concern about 'Spanglish' as observed in the children they care for:

> Lo que sabemos es que nuestros niños no están conscientes de que están hablando en dos idiomas. Creen ellos que así es como se habla. Lo que necesitamos es mas estudio que nos pueda ayudar a corregir este problema.
> [What we know is that our children are not aware that they are speaking in two languages. They really believe that the way they are speaking is correct. What we need is to study more about how to correct this problem.]

Why Were the Participants Resisting the Curriculum?

The course participants were finding the family literacy curriculum on childcare and development somehow inappropriate to their own views and values. The facilitators realized this through their collegial dialogues after each 'training' session. This was not something new for them, given their long careers in organizing and conducting childcare training events. However, the participants' resistance to the top-down curriculum was the catalyst for facilitators to come to understand that reinventing their role as 'decolonizing family literacy educators' constituted another dimension in the work. The top-down curriculum creates a fertile ground for participants to resist. This was observed when one of the participants candidly asked the facilitator how many children he had. In retrospect the intent of her question was to set the stage for the game of 'catching the teacher' since she had 14 children of her own and cares for her great grandchildren. She really meant that she had vast experience in caring for children, something that the curriculum did not take into account. We may say that this was actually an eloquent way of resisting a top-down undemocratic curriculum.

Reinventing the Role of the Family Literacy Educator Through a Relational Pedagogy in a Culture Circle

Through collegial dialogue, the facilitators took seriously the tasks of rethinking the course curriculum, the pedagogy, and consequently their own roles. Their participation in the culture circle, through a relational pedagogy, started to change. They had understood that the curriculum was written to bring participants up to the awareness level about early childhood care and development as opposed to the competency level. What they learned was that the participants actually demonstrated understanding at the competency level. The difference between these two levels is that the former is just empirical knowledge about early childcare and development, whereas the latter is demonstrated when the caregiver is also able to explain and carry out the 'appropriate' childcare and development practices. For instance, the grandmother with 14 children of her own who now takes care of 4 great-grandchildren demonstrated that she was at the competence level. She shared with the circle her knowledge about the need to 'burp' infants after their bottle. She proceeded to demonstrate to the group several ways of burping infants.

The realization that most participants were at the competence level led the trainers to 'co-opt' the technocratic instrumental pedagogy tied to the top-down curriculum and to opt for a *relational pedagogy*. This implied a leveling of power, which created an atmosphere in the culture circle that supported each participant's voice and acknowledged participants' experiences and knowledge. The co-optation included changing the role implied by being trainers, or even facilitators, to that of 'decolonizing family literacy educator.' Implicit in this new role within a relational pedagogy was to become vulnerable. Being vulnerable means accepting and exposing oneself to criticism and refutation from the participants, who now feel free and safe to disagree. His/her vulnerability positions the liberating educator to approach symmetry in power and knowledge relationships, which is at the core of a dialogical and relational pedagogy. Thus, the implementation of the curriculum was negotiated by having the participants name what they knew as a baseline for building the curriculum together. The decolonizing family literacy educators then intentionally created a space to reflect on their work immediately after each session. During the hour's drive back to their work sites, they used the time to formally debrief and document their reflection on the session. The analysis started by filling out the session's evaluation form, which prompted them to examine the reactions of the participants, the training process, the course content, and their own new role.

These reflective dialogues led these family literacy educators to realize that they themselves had strong emotions about family literacy, and they became angry and embarrassed that the curriculum was planned without involving the participants. Once the facilitators named the origin of their anger and embarrassment, they intentionally *co-opted* the curriculum by negotiating it with the participants. They agreed to cover the topics of the top-down curriculum but from the *bottom-up*, using a *relational pedagogy* through a culture circle, from a Freirean approach to family literacy. Continuing the process of reinventing their role as 'decolonizing family literacy educators,' they arrived at the conclusion that it was more important in this project to involve participants in building the curriculum than to face the contractual consequences of not following the 'top-down curriculum.' However, they contemplated the possibility that, if they were dismissed, someone else might come in to implement the colonizing curriculum that they refused to implement. They felt as if they were walking through a minefield. The consequence of taking this position put more demands on their energy for working on the project, since it included additional planning time with the specific purpose of strategizing ways to answer the question: What if the project administrators or the funding agency came to supervise the facilitators' job? The situation undoubtedly was very demanding because, besides the planning, there was a need to deal with high levels of uncertainty. This, in fact, is inherent in the planning process of participatory curriculum development and implementation.

The decolonizing family literacy educators and participants worked in the culture circle with the idea of polyphony, which means that every member of the circle had a voice. They wanted to validate participants' experiences and popular knowledge about early childcare and development. However, early in the process they realized that if no member of the circle would be challenged about their child rearing practices, many children would continue suffering from bad practices such as spanking. The question of who has the power and knowledge about the best practices for guiding children led them to rethink polyphony as simply a *liberal* sharing of practices and values. Although it is important to create a polyphonic environment in which participants feel comfortable in sharing their perspectives about the topic, this is not sufficient because polyphony by itself does not allow for the transformation of practices that participants have with children and other adults.

This is where postmodernists (e.g., Lather, 1991, 1994) fall short. Lather (1994), for example, brings up various tales for the same data-event concerning students' reactions to her liberating curriculum on women studies. We argue that this polyphony in interpreting data is problematic because it not only creates a sense of diversity and multiplicity, but it is also insufficient for changing practices to become more liberating. Inherent in polyphony is the impossibility of reaching any consensus, which leads us to immobility and absolute relativism (everything is contingent to the situation)—what Cole (1994) refers to as the 'poverty of contingency theory'.

A relational pedagogy requires improvement in early childcare and development as a collective work, which implies at least an attempt to negotiate a temporal consensus. This means that there is a dialogue in which polyvoicedness is examined in the light of what is best for young children in order to promote a transformation of childcare practices. This is not an easygoing process. It is tense and conflicting and produces a great deal of anxiety. In a certain way, the decolonizing family literacy educators were facing participants' anger and frustration as they worked toward temporal consensus. At the same time, these educators started to doubt whether co-opting the curriculum was a good idea and thought that perhaps the 'expert' role was less complicated.

To illustrate the complexity of implementing a relational pedagogy, the first author remembers a time in which he literally challenged one of the participants by approaching him in a 'macho' man-to-man style. The context of this disagreement was in the area of 'child guidance.' The participant believed that spanking a child was appropriate and that he had a given right as a father. On the other hand, the educator's position was that spanking was not acceptable. He viewed it as violence, whereas the participant viewed it as appropriate for the child's best interest. Both reached the point that their words were full of fury. 'Que macho eres pegándole a los niños? Por que no me pegas a mi?' [Hitting children makes you macho? Why don't you hit me instead?]. What we can see in this illustration is that relational pedagogy is not necessarily a romantic sweet dialogue. On the contrary, there can be strong positions that may clash, and the family literacy educator cannot mediate them because in a relational pedagogy s/he becomes part of the conflict. This is undoubtedly an indication of shared power, which is at the core of a relational pedagogy. In this situation, as a result of cultivation of dialogue, the other group participants became the mediators and were confident in doing so.

Undoubtedly, in a relational pedagogy there is a requirement that the role and power of the decolonizing family literacy educator be shared. In this case he was part of the group, and it was the group that mediated the disagreement between him and the group member. This mediation moved the group toward a temporal consensus about studying in depth the issue of spanking young children. Actually, the energy of the disagreement fueled collective work to consider alternatives to spanking. By assuming the risks of co-opting the curriculum and embracing liberating family literacy practices, we need to accept that responsibility by facing our mistakes and trying to amend them publicly with humility. This also makes us vulnerable. We learned the lesson that Freire (1998) refers to, when the teacher becomes the student of his/her students.

As we consider alternative practices rooted in a relational pedagogy, there emerges the question: who liberates whom? Following Freire's ideas of liberation (1970/1992; Shor and Freire, 1987), it is the people who liberate themselves through dialogical understanding of their 'limit situations' and through solidarity, through collective action. The motivation for liberation lies in the hope for a better world; it is not hope for the sake of hope. For Freire (2003, 2005) the main threat of falling into despair and hopelessness is the fatalism and immobility that comes from the neo-liberal ideology and some postmodernists. Hope implies 'transformation and indignation,' he argues. Liberation in the Freirean sense is not what a messianic person does for others but an ongoing struggle of collective conscientization and action mediated by dialogical encounters. In the same vein, for Erich Fromm (1970) change for the well-being of humankind cannot happen without hope. For him, hope is neither passive nor violent but rather being ready for action that transcends the status quo in the search for life alternatives in contrast to death or dehumanizing alternatives. Based on Freire's and Fromm's works, we believe that the transformation of family literacy practices rests on hope. But we cannot ignore the power relationships that exist in families and communities and which are deeply rooted in gender, class, and race inequities. For example, in several Latino cultures there strongly persists the concept and practice of *machismo*, by which young boys are forbidden to cry and encouraged to play aggressively. This may constitute an issue for discussion, study, and action in the culture circle's future encounters.

What we report in this chapter is a lived experience of a certain moment of the project's life. Our motivation to continue working in this borderland community rests on our hope for collective action toward more humanistic, socially and culturally responsive family literacy practices of childcare and development.

Concluding Remarks

In reinventing the family literacy educator as a co-optor of family literacy colonizing curricula, there are many issues to consider. First, the liberating educator must problematize the top-down curriculum of universal early childcare and development. Based on Canella's (1997) critique of universal stages in child development, we can say that the curriculum as first envisioned was an instrument of colonization of participants. The fact that they were considered ignorant and that their experiential knowledge was not worth taking into account constitutes an irrefutable instance of colonization.

Second, in order to create a bottom-up curriculum the decolonizing family literacy educator needs to involve the community in that creative process by using a relational pedagogy that is based on a dialogical philosophy and participatory democracy. The liberating educator cultivates 'polyphony,' which eventually must evolve into a dialogue conducive to transformation of participants and educators in a dynamic manner. This evolution ensures that participants and liberating educators understand their realities and work toward temporal consensus for collective action that improves their life conditions. Otherwise, polyphony merely generates different perspectives and does not conduce to transformation.

Third, the decolonizing family literacy educator's role is very demanding and requires exorbitant amounts of energy both physical and emotional. It is important to understand that educators who want to be co-optors in this manner are not always going to be successful. In addition, not being able to follow up on the community developments confronts them on ethical grounds.

Fourth, the decolonizing family literacy educators should understand that transformation occurs at different levels. Their role is transformed from sole expert to that of a participant in the project at hand, which requires these educators to reinvent their role continuously. Continual reinvention is the result of the dynamics of the culture circle: polyphonic dialogue, temporal consensus of a shared hope that motivates us to collective transformative action.

Fifth, the limitations of this work are twofold. On one hand, the tremendous demands of the family literacy course implementation caused the decolonizing family literacy educators to lose sight of the utopia of better practices of childcare: responsive to children's well-being, respectful and loving, and thus free from violence and suffering. These demands include project obligations, the challenges associated with the co-opting of the top-down curriculum, and the involvement with participants. On the other hand, the timeline of the funding agency worked against this liberating effort. What the decolonizing family literacy educators learned was that there is a conflict between the duration/time of the funded project and the timescale of the community. Thus, as the funded project ended, so did the liberating educators' work. This abrupt ending is an ethical issue from the perspective of relational pedagogy. At this point we are back in the community and are making this report accessible to participants, to get their feedback and thus reconnect with them as a culture circle.

Sixth, in the context of participatory democracy, the decolonizing family literacy educator is an equal participant in the culture circle. As such, he/she may be involved in conflicts. What is important to know is that if dialogue is cultivated in that culture circle, the mediation of these conflicts is a matter of negotiation among the members in conflict with the participation of the other group members. The resolution of the conflict moves the culture circle to a temporal consensus that allows them to engage in transformative action.

To conclude, we ask the question: So, why do family literacy educators want to reinvent themselves as decolonizing educators— co-optors—in order to de-colonize top-down literacy curricula in early childcare and development? We do not engage in this work with a messianic spirit, or want to save the poor from their unfortunate conditions, or desire to appease our necessity of feeling good. We do it because we know that it is a social responsibility to work as educators *with* people in order to understand and shape a world that is more just, democratic, sustainable, and peaceful.

References

Ada, A.F. and Zubizarreta, R. (2001) 'Parent Narratives: The Cultural Bridge between Latino Parents and Their Children,' in M. d l. L. Reyes and J. Halcón (eds) *The Best for Our Children: Critical Perspectives on Literacy for Latino Students*, pp. 229–44. New York: Teachers College Press.

Andrade, R., Denmat, H.G.L. and Moll, L.C. (2000) 'El Grupo de las Señoras: Creating Consciousness within a Literature Club,' in M.A. Gallego and S. Hollingsworth (eds) *What Counts as Literacy: Challenging the School Standard*. New York: Teachers College Press.

Anglum, B.S., Bell, M.L. and Roubinek, D.L. (1990) 'Prediction of Elementary Student Reading Achievement from Specific Home Environment Variables,' *Reading Improvement* 27: 173–84.

Bakhtin, M. M. (1984) *Problems of Dostoevsky's poetics*. Minneapolis, MN: University of Minnesota Press.

Bird, V. (2005) 'The Literacy and Social Inclusion Project: A New Model for Building Parental Skills,' *Literacy* 39(2): 59–63.

Canella, G.S. (1997) *Deconstructing Early Childhood Education: Social Justice and Revolution*. New York: Peter Lang.

Cole, S.E. (1994) 'Evading the Subject: The Poverty of Contingency Theory,' in H.W. Simons and M. Billig (eds) *After Postmodernism: Reconstructing Ideology Critique*, pp. 38–57. Thousand Oaks, CA: Sage.

De Carvalho, M.E.P. (2001) *Rethinking Family-School Relations: A Critique of Parental Involvement in Schooling*. NewYork: Teachers College Press.

Dirlik, A. (1997) *The Postcolonial Aura*. Boulder, CO: Westview Press.

Fals-Borda, O. (1985) *Knowledge and People's Power: Lessons with Peasants in Nicaragua, Mexico, and Colombia*, trans. B. Maller. New Delhi: Indian Social Institute.

Freire, P. (1970/1992) *Pedagogy of the Oppressed*. New York: Continuum.

Freire, P. (1998) *Teachers as Cultural Workers: Letters to those Who Dare Teach*. Boulder, CO: Westview.

Freire, P. (2003) *El Grito Manso* [The Gentle Shout]. Buenos Aires, Argentina: Siglo XXI Editores.

Freire, P. (2005) *Pedagogy of Indignation*. Boulder, CO: Paradigm Publishers.

Freire, P. (n.d.) *Educación Como Práctica de la Libertad*. Bogotá, Colombia: Lerner.

Freire, P. and Macedo, D. (1987) *Literacy: Reading the Word and the World*. Westport, CT and London: Bergin and Garvey.

Freire, P. and Macedo, D. (1996) 'A Dialogue: Culture, Language, and Race,' in P. Leystina, A. Woodrum and S.A. Sherblom (eds) *Breaking Free: The Transformative Power of Critical Pedagogy*, pp. 199–228. Cambridge, MA: *Harvard Educational Review*, Reprint Series # 27.

Fromm, E. (1970) *La Revolución de la Esperanza: Hacia una Tecnología Humanizada*, trans. D. Jiménez C. Bogotá, Colombia: Fondo de Cultura Económica.

Giroux, H. (2001) *Theory and Resistance in Education: Toward a Pedagogy for the Oppressed*. Westport, CT: Bergin and Garvey.

Hall, N., Larson, J. and Marsh, J. (eds) (2003) *Handbook of Early Childhood Literacy*. Thousand Oaks, CA: Sage.

Hanon,P.(2003) 'Family Literacy Programmes', in N. Hall, J. Larson and J. Marsh (eds) *Handbook of Early Childhood Literacy*. Thousand Oaks, CA: Sage.

hooks, b. (1994) *Teaching to Transgress: Education as the Practice of Freedom*. New York: Routledge.

Horton, M. and Freire, P. (1990) *We Make the Road by Walking: Conversations on Education and Social Change*. Philadelphia, PA: Temple University Press.

Lankshear, C. (1993) 'Functional Literacy from a Freirean Point of View,' in P. McLaren and P. Leonard (eds) *Paulo Freire: A Critical Encounter*. New York: Routledge.

Lather, P. (1991) *Getting Smart: Feminist Research and Pedagogy with/in the Postmodern*. New York and London: Routledge.

Lather, P. (1994) 'Staying Dumb?: Feminist Research and Pedagogy within/in the Post-modern,' in H.W. Simons and M. Billig (eds). *After Postmodernism: Reconstructing Ideology Critique*, pp. 101–32.Thousand Oaks, CA: Sage.

McLaren, P. (1995). *Critical Pedagogy and Predatory Culture: Oppositional Politics in a Postmodern Era*. New York: Routledge.

Panofsky, C.P. (2000) 'Examining the Research Narrative in Early Literacy: The Case of Parent-Child Book Reading Activity', in M.A. Gallego and S. Hollingsworth (eds) *What Counts as Literacy: Challenging the School Standard*, pp. 190–212. New York: Teachers College Press.

Purcell-Gates, V. (1995) *Other People's Words*. Cambridge, MA: Harvard University Press.

Razfar, A. and Gutiérrez, K. (2003) 'Reconceptualizing Early Childhood Literacy: The Sociocultural Influence,' in N. Hall, J. Larson and J. Marsh (eds) *Handbook of Early Childhood Literacy*. Thousand Oaks, CA: Sage.

San Juan, E., Jr (1998) *Beyond Postcolonial Theory*. New York: St Martin's Press.

Shor, I. and Freire, P. (1987) *A Pedagogy for Liberation: Dialogues on Transforming Education*. South Hadley, MA: Bergin and Garvey Publishers.

Sidorkian, A.M. (1999) *Education, the Self, and Dialogue*. New York: State University of New York Press.

Snow, C.E., Barnes,W .S., Chandler, J., Goodman, J.F. and Hemphill, L. (1991) *Unfulfilled Home and School Influences on Literacy*. Cambridge: Cambridge University Press.

Taylor, C. (2005) 'It's in the Water Here: The Development of a Community Focused Literacy Strategy,' *Literacy* 39(2): 64–7.

Turner, P. (2002) *Essential Elements of Quality: Best Practices*. Albuquerque, NM: University of New Mexico Press.

Valdés, G. (1996) *Con Respeto: Bridging the Distances between Culturally Diverse Families and Schools*. New York: Teachers College Press.

Valencia, R.R. (1997) *Conceptualizing the Notion of Deficit Thinking*. London: Falmer Press.

Walker, G.H.,Jr and Kuerbitz, I.E.(1979) 'Reading to Preschoolers as an Aid to Successful Beginning Reading,' *Reading Improvement* 16: 149–54.

Zentella, A.C. (2005) 'Introduction: Perspectives on Language and Literacy in Latino Families and Communities,' in A.C. Zentella (ed.) *Building on Strength: Language and Literacy in Latino Families and Communities*. New York: Teachers College Press and CABE-California Association for Bilingual Education.

Index

critical qualitative research

Shirley R. Steinberg, *General Editor*

The Critical Qualitative Research series examines societal structures that oppress and exclude so that transformative actions can be generated. This transformed research is activist in orientation. Because the perspective accepts the notion that nothing is apolitical, research projects themselves are critically examined for power orientations, even as they are used to address curricular, educational, or societal issues.

This methodological work challenges modernist orientations and universalist impositions, asking critical questions like: Who/what is heard? Who/what is silenced? Who is privileged? Who is disqualified? How are forms of inclusion and exclusion being created? How are power relations constructed and managed? How do different forms of privilege and oppression intersect to affect educational, societal, and life possibilities for various individuals and groups?

We are particularly interested in manuscripts that offer critical examinations of curriculum, policy, public communities, and the ways in which language, discourse practices, and power relations prevent more just transformations.

For additional information about this series or for the submission of manuscripts, please contact:
Shirley R. Steinberg | msgramsci@gmail.com

To order other books in this series, please contact our Customer Service Department:
(800) 770-LANG (within the U.S.)
(212) 647-7706 (outside the U.S.)
(212) 647-7707 FAX

Or browse online by series:
www.peterlang.com